Existence and the Good

Existence and the Good

Metaphysical Necessity in Morals and Politics

Franklin I. Gamwell

Published by State University of New York Press, Albany

© 2011 State University of New York

All rights reserved

Printed in the United States of America

No part of this book may be used or reproduced in any manner whatsoever without written permission. No part of this book may be stored in a retrieval system or transmitted in any form or by any means including electronic, electrostatic, magnetic tape, mechanical, photocopying, recording, or otherwise without the prior permission in writing of the publisher.

For information, contact State University of New York Press, Albany, NY
www.sunypress.edu

Production by Eileen Meehan
Marketing by Anne M. Valentine

Library of Congress Cataloging-in-Publication Data

Gamwell, Franklin I.
  Existence and the good : metaphysical necessity in morals and politics / Franklin I. Gamwell.
      p. cm.
  Includes bibliographical references (p.) and index.
  ISBN 978-1-4384-3593-0 (hardcover : alk. paper)
  1. Ethics. 2. Theism. 3. Metaphysics. 4. Religion and ethics.
5. Democracy—Philosophy. 6. Democracy—Religious aspects. I. Title.

BJ47.G29 2011
171'.2—dc22   2010032054

10 9 8 7 6 5 4 3 2 1

To David Tracy

Contents

Preface	ix
Introduction	1
Chapter 1	
The Metaphysics of Existence	17
The Western Background	19
The Necessity of Existence	22
The Task of Metaphysics	30
Chapter 2	
The Metaphysics of Subjectivity	39
Totality and Meaning	39
Totality Is Prior to Meaning	49
Chapter 3	
The Metaphysics of God and the World	59
Final Real Things	59
The Divine Individual	71
God and the World	85
Chapter 4	
The Metaphysics of Human Purpose	93
Decision for a Self-Understanding	93
The Comprehensive Good	101
Human Purposes	107
The Good of Human Rights	115
Chapter 5	
The Metaphysics of Democracy, Part 1	127
Introduction	127
Democracy without Metaphysics	130
Democracy without Metaphysics: A Critique	135

Chapter 6
The Metaphysics of Democracy, Part 2 — 147
    The Principle of Communicative Respect — 147
    Constitutional Principles of Justice — 156
    Democracy and Substantive Justice — 164
    Democracy and the Comprehensive Good — 171

Notes — 179

Works Cited — 199

Index — 203

Preface

The title of this book, *Existence and the Good*, intends to signal two related interests that have, in one way or another, occupied my attention for some time. One is the importance of metaphysical necessity—and, specifically, a theistic metaphysics—to a critical understanding of human life within the surrounding entirety of things in which we find ourselves. The second is the importance of teleology—or, more precisely, a comprehensive good—to moral and political theory. The argument here relates the two by defining the good to which morals and politics are properly directed through the theistic metaphysics and thus a divine purpose. In its own way, then, the book appropriates the words of Thomas Jefferson, marking both our private and public responsibilities through "the Laws of Nature and of Nature's God."

The attempt to redeem a comprehensive purpose for morals and politics requires discussion of metaphysics in two senses. On the one hand, metaphysics in what I call the strict sense explicates the necessary character of all existence or reality as such; on the other hand, metaphysics in what I call the broad sense explicates the necessary character of subjective existence as such and, thereby, of specifically human life. Metaphysics in the broad sense concerns life with conscious purpose, our existence by way of deciding how we will understand ourselves, and this book seeks to clarify authentic self-understanding in relation to the ultimate nature of things, explicated by metaphysics in the strict sense. This twofold understanding of metaphysics, then, provides the backing for the supreme moral principle and, through it, for democratic principles of justice. Accordingly, the argument here also reflects my abiding concern to show how specifically religious convictions about the human condition in relation to the whole of reality are important to the promise of democratic politics.

Three academic colleagues and friends have carefully read the manuscript at some stage in its development and have offered proposals for revision: Philip E. Devenish, Schubert M. Ogden, and Alexander F. Vishio. I am most grateful for their generous help, encouragement, and friendship. In addition, I express my gratitude for the discussion and critique of some ideas herein by participants in a conference at the Center for Process Studies in Claremont, California, and for the critical readings of the anonymous readers for publication. Naturally, none of these people is responsible for deficiencies in the book, but all of them have served the reader by improving the work.

I take the liberty of dedicating the book, as an expression of my abiding gratitude and admiration, to David Tracy, my teacher, colleague, and friend.

I also express my thanks for permission to reprint in revised form substantial portions of my essay, "The Purpose of Human Rights," *Process Studies* 29/2 (2000): 322–46, subsequently republished in *Mississippi College Law Review* 22, no. 2 (2003): 239–61. Further, I express special thanks to Matthew R. Petrusek for his careful and thoughtful preparation of the index.

Introduction

The good life and the common good, this work argues, require a metaphysical backing. In contrast, moral and political theories today widely deny the credibility of metaphysics and assume that conceptions of good action and justice can be redeemed without thought about the ultimate nature of things. Thereby, these theories deny the source of their own validity, casting moral and political good adrift. This introduction summarizes how succeeding chapters seek to discredit the assumption and to establish principles for human life and community that depend on metaphysical necessity.

Naturally, a summary introduction cannot sufficiently defend its assertions. Typically, therefore, I will here only mention the arguments in question, asking patience until later discussion can pursue the greater clarity they need and respond to criticisms they may evoke. On the whole, this summary follows the course pursued within the subsequent chapters, although a few occasions counsel some relatively minor reordering of the relevant points.

Without a metaphysical backing, morals and politics are also separated from religion. At least, this occurs insofar as religious beliefs include understandings of human life in relation to all things, and thus a religion cannot be fully clarified without explicating its metaphysical affirmations. To be sure, some moral thinkers agree that religions include beliefs about how adherents should orient their lives, even while these thinkers deny that valid moral principles require any conception of a comprehensive order. Similarly, some political philosophers concede that citizens might rely on religious convictions as they participate in politics, even while these theorists deny that principles of justice depend on metaphysical conditions. At least to first appearances, however, such views are inconsistent with many or most religions, for which moral and political good can never be separated from their ground in ultimate reality. This book is not focused on a discussion of religion, but I will argue that metaphysical necessity in morals and politics includes a theistic backing.

Beginning with chapter 4, the book explicates directly an idea of moral responsibility marked by a metaphysical telos for all things. We are morally bound by a comprehensive purpose and thus a comprehensive good to which all of our activities ought to be directed. In human life, this good is the maximal unity-in-diversity or richness of everyone's experience. That same good, I argue, authorizes certain principles of human rights and, through them, more specific norms of human interaction. The latter include democratic politics, that is, government where "we the people" are sovereign and, through full and free discussion and debate, should pursue justice as the general empowerment of all. At least in this respect, Thomas Jefferson had it right: our common life is accountable to "the Laws of Nature and of Nature's God."

The final two chapters, then, pursue the metaphysical authorization of democracy. Virtually all recent democratic theories endorse religious freedom as a political principle, even while they require principles of justice, at least constitutional principles, without metaphysical implications. In contrast, I will argue, democracy itself can be vindicated only on theistic grounds. At the same time, democracy so prescribed is politics by the way of reason, and thus a democratic constitution cannot properly announce or stipulate the grounds for its own vindication. To the contrary, the way of reason requires the sovereignty of every citizen over her or his belief about the ultimate terms of political assessment. Hence, democracy on theistic grounds also endorses—indeed, provides the only consistent endorsement of—religious freedom.

But if morals and politics depend on ultimate reality, the indispensable beginning toward making this point is a defense of metaphysics. This is needed because contemporary theories of human practice, in seeking their autonomy from metaphysics, exemplify a dominant consensus marking Western philosophy as a whole during the past two centuries. On this majority view, all study of ourselves and the world around us must be independent of beliefs about reality or existence as such. Perhaps this view betrays how the immense success of modern empirical science seemed to render metaphysics irrelevant, if not an obstacle, to understanding ourselves and the world. More recently, I expect, greater familiarity with cultures and societies other than one's own has evoked, somewhat paradoxically, a heightened sense of how understanding is conditioned by cultural and social context and, thereby, a profound suspicion of claims to universal truth. In any event, the dominant consensus rejects a philosophical tradition beginning in classical Greece and stretching through medieval thought into early modernity. At least since the achievement of Immanuel Kant, the question of "being qua being," as Aristotle defined it, has increasingly been discredited because the inquiry addressing it is said to be meaningless or futile or a matter of mere speculation.

In due course, I will commend a neoclassical metaphysics first given systematic formulation by Alfred North Whitehead. Whitehead's most comprehensive work, *Process and Reality: An Essay in Cosmology*, is notably—perhaps notoriously—characterized by idiosyncratic terminology. Although I credit his reasons for introducing unfamiliar terms, a contemporary appropriation of his achievement can and should, I believe, avoid the neologisms some have found uninviting, and I will seek to propose a metaphysical account without recourse to them. But simply moving through how neoclassical metaphysics might now be restated would not take full measure of the dominant consensus. Indeed, the dismissal of metaphysics is, I venture, even more entrenched in our contemporary intellectual context than was the case when Whitehead wrote—to the point where a commitment to philosophy without metaphysics is now, in the minds of most, beyond the need for further critical attention. This contemporary circumstance, I suspect, results in part from significant failure to understand the alternative metaphysics Whitehead offers. Whatever other conditions are involved, however, it remains that important arguments against the metaphysical project lie behind its marginal status in Western philosophy today. Any contemporary pursuit of this project, therefore, must first defend its viability against the reasons given to reject it. Summarily stated, this requires attention to both Kantian and post-Kantian critiques, and this task will occupy the first two chapters.

Chapter 1 begins with a brief review of the Western background, in order to show the legacy of Immanuel Kant within the postmetaphysical or nonmetaphysical consensus we now inherit. Whatever differing assessments have been given of Kant's own project, his deconstruction of traditional metaphysics has been massively influential in subsequent philosophy. For all that, however, both Kant and the metaphysics he rejected share a central conviction: they both affirm that we can name something solely by negation. In one way or another, traditional metaphysics asserts an eternal being or realm of beings on which everything else depends, and this eternality can be described only by negating in all respects the changeable, temporal nature of all other things. For Kant, things-in-themselves are unknowable, and thus the metaphysical quest to know their nature is futile. Nonetheless, he did not doubt the presence—or, at least, the possibility—of things-in-themselves, which can be named only by negating all the features of whatever appears in our experience.

Supposed thoughts of something described solely in negative terms are logically equivalent to the statement "nothing exists." On first reading, this statement seems to assert only the complete absence of existence. Logically, however, it also asserts the existence or possible existence of something named only by negation because, in either case, the grammatical subject of "exists" is completely negative. And "nothing exists," the first chapter argues, is a nonsensical statement; it is merely a supposed statement because it is logically impossible and thus meaningless. Against both traditional metaphysics and Kant's unknowable things-in-themselves, this recognition opens a revised metaphysical project. Because "nothing exists" is logically impossible, "something exists"—where every "something" can be described in positive terms—is a logically necessary statement. Moreover, any other statement about existence implied by "something exists" is also logically necessary, and we may seek a system of logically necessary understandings of existence. It then follows that strictly all things, from the lowliest bit of matter or energy to the divine reality, if there is one, must be properly described in the same metaphysical terms—whatever differences may also be on display. In other words, no logical possibility can be named by seeking completely to negate the terms applicable to everything else.

Accordingly, chapter 1 arrives at the following definition of metaphysics: the critical study of what must be the case because the complete absence of existence is impossible—or, what comes to the same thing, the critical study of what must be the case because something must exist. The phrase "what must be the case" should be emphasized. On this accounting, metaphysics is concerned with logically necessary understandings of existence and thus with necessary features or characteristics of all actual and possible things—characteristics common to and thus definitive of anything that is so much as possible. Hence, the object of metaphysical thought can be called reality as such or existence as such or the possible as such—and I use these three descriptions interchangeably. Correspondingly, "metaphysical" may be used to designate the character or characteristics of things metaphysics as a critical study seeks to explicate. Because all such metaphysical features are necessary, it follows that no one of them can be present unless all others are present, and this is why logically necessary statements about existence form a metaphysical system. Such a system is the ideal for neoclassical metaphysics.

The first chapter concludes with a commentary on Whitehead's definition of the metaphysical endeavor—namely, "to frame a coherent, logical, necessary system of general ideas in terms of which every element of our experience can be interpreted" (1978, 3). At least on one reading, this states precisely the quest to characterize existence or the possible as such. "Every element of our experience" means every conceivable thing, whereby the system of ideas is, as Whitehead also says, "adequate." "Coherent" is used in an emphatic sense to mean that all the implications of any valid metaphysical idea also imply it. An adequate and coherent system of ideas is, I argue, necessary; that is, it designates what must be the case because the complete absence of existence is impossible.

But if chapter 1 opens an alternative to both traditional metaphysics and its Kantian denial, neoclassical metaphysics cannot be sustained without attention to the post-Kantian critique of universal reason. Notwithstanding the limits Kant placed on our understanding, he never doubted universal principles of theoretical and practical reason, insisting only that these give us no knowledge of things-in-themselves. In contrast, many subsequent thinkers have deconstructed both the traditional metaphysical project and its Kantian successor because both affirm principles of thought independent of a subject's historicity or historical context, its specific location within the human adventure. Neoclassical metaphysics is also included within this indictment, and no thinker, I judge, has given more influential expression to the critique of universal reason than did Martin Heidegger. Accordingly, chapter 2 takes up Heidegger's challenge.

Heidegger is an especially appropriate conversation partner because he agrees that "nothing exists" is logical nonsense, even while he implicitly critiques the metaphysical conclusions for which chapter 1 argued. The complete absence of beings—"the Nothing," as Heidegger calls it—cannot be consistently thought as an object; it is, nonetheless, encountered by Dasein in the "mode of attunement." Thereby, the abyss of Being is the source of all cognitive affirmation and negation. Only because one is "held out into the nothing," in other words, are beings brought to the light of understanding, "that they are beings—and not nothing" (1993, 103). Thus, the meaning of beings is inseparable from the totality opened within the temporality of a finite understanding, its engagement within a "clearing" or historically dependent disclosure. Thereby, Heidegger reaches in effect an indictment of universal reason, and chapter 2 seeks a more extended clarification of how Heidegger's thought issues this critique.

Attending especially to that consequence, the chapter then argues for the following summary statement of his account: *totality presupposes meaning*. In other words, beings as a whole and thus the similarities and differences among them presuppose a historically situated or inherited lifeworld and thus prestructure of understanding. In this sense, there is no correct or incorrect understanding except as circumscribed by some "clearing" within the human adventure.

"Totality presupposes meaning" is, I argue, a pragmatically self-contradictory assertion because its truth cannot itself be circumscribed by the specific historicity of someone who asserts it. If "all meaning and truth about beings is located" were itself true, its truth could not depend on some location within the human adventure, and thus this understanding of beings is inconsistent with the claim to truth made for it. Accordingly, Heidegger's discussion of "the Nothing" as something encountered in the mode of attunement is similarly suspect. In exploring this problem, the chapter seeks to answer possible replies on Heidegger's behalf and finds the same pragmatic inconsistency within the critique of universal reason generally. To the contrary, I conclude, *totality is prior to meaning*; that is, totality is given prior to understanding, where "prior" here means prior in the experience of a subject. "Consciousness presupposes experience, and not experience consciousness," Whitehead writes (1978, 53), so that understanding is derivative from nonconscious experiencing. The latter relates us to the metaphysical structure of actualities and possibilities that is independent of historically situated contexts of meaning, and our awareness always includes an implicit understanding of it. Moreover, the neoclassical account of this structure, I argue in a later chapter, does justice to Heidegger's best reasons for renouncing the Western metaphysical tradition, especially its failure adequately to think the temporality of understanding.

The engagement with Heidegger also introduces another sense of "metaphysics," namely, the critical study of subjectivity as such, the features or characteristics necessary to every possible occurrence of subjectivity. Correspondingly, "metaphysical" may be used to designate the character or characteristics of subjectivity that metaphysics in the second sense studies. I call this metaphysics in the broad sense—in distinction from metaphysics in the strict sense, the critical study of "being qua being" or existence as such, on which the first chapter is focused. The two are systematically related because the features necessary to subjectivity in general include but reach beyond the features necessary to existence in general. If, for instance, temporality is a feature defining all conceivable existence, then every occurrence of subjectivity is temporal; but subjectivity is also self-conscious, a feature not necessary to all existence. Subjective existence, in other words, is a specific kind of existence. Having discussed these systematically related meanings, I subsequently use "neoclassical metaphysics" to name both. One might also speak of "transcendental metaphysics," with the same two related meanings. Every valid statement about subjective existence in general is transcendental because every denial of the statement is pragmatically self-contradictory, the act of denial implying what is denied. Every valid statement about existence as such is transcendental because every denial of the statement is logically self-contradictory; that is, the statement is logically necessary.

The features defining subjectivity in general, I argue, include certain inescapable understandings, for instance, an awareness of the totality as given prior to meaning. I call these "original beliefs" and show their implicit presence even if we are not explicitly aware of them. Among our original beliefs, the book later contends, is an affirmation of the comprehensive purpose, a pursuit directed by the comprehensive or metaphysical good that defines a telos for all things. Belief in this purpose, even if only implicit in our awareness, makes every occurrence of subjectivity a moral act. Because we understand the moral telos, we can choose against it, and the comprehensive purpose defines the decision we ought to take. Hence, articulating the two meanings of "metaphysical" or "transcendental" is important because the book will argue for moral responsibility in relation to a telos in the ultimate nature of things. Moral decision is characteristic of all subjects but only subjects and, therefore, is a transcendental feature in the broad but not the strict sense. In contrast, the comprehensive good is a metaphysical feature in the strict sense.

Before turning directly to the metaphysics of human purpose, however, the defense of neoclassical metaphysics against both Kantian and post-Kantian dismissals must be complemented by a metaphysical account of existence. Chapter 3 pursues a detailed outline of neoclassical metaphysics in the strict sense, seeking in all essentials to argue for the necessity of its conclusions. The outline is required for two reasons: first, to sustain through a substantive proposal the credibility of metaphysical necessity in the strict sense, and second, to provide terms in which to explicate the comprehensive good and, thereby, how this metaphysical necessity is present in morals and politics. I am sensible of the dense character some of this chapter may seem to have, and I do my best to achieve clarity. If a reader is principally interested in the moral and political consequences and is willing, for purposes of discussion, to grant this metaphysical account when it is later summarized in relevant aspects, she or he can, in my judgment, turn directly from the discussion with Heidegger to chapter 4.

Metaphysical necessity, chapter 3 begins, entails a single kind of metaphysically fundamental thing. All true metaphysical statements imply each other, and thus all metaphysical features are somehow exemplified wherever any one is exemplified. Following Whitehead and Charles Hartshorne, I take the final real things to be microunits of process, each unifying its internal relations to others already unified and, thereby, becoming something to which still others (in its future) will internally relate. Each final real thing, then, becomes an actuality or fully concrete unity-in-diversity. The chapter develops this conception and shows how all other real things or entities, including the macrothings of everyday experience and whatever order there may be in the universe as a whole, can be interpreted in terms of such actualities. For instance, a human individual, meaning thereby the extended self-conscious experiencing made possible by its presence within a human body, is understood as a series of discrete units of process, each sufficiently brief that our fragmentary powers of introspection cannot clearly distinguish among them.

Chapter 3 is especially concerned to show why neoclassical metaphysics implies a divine individual and to clarify God's character. Summarily stated, God is necessary because the idea of actualities implies the difference between those that relate to some of the past, are fragmentary in what they include, and those that relate to strictly all others in all of their detail, are all-inclusive, and the latter are divine actualities. God is the individual who always includes all that has happened or become actual and thus will include whatever else happens when it happens. Accordingly, the divine reality is the series of all-inclusive actualities, each of which includes more than its predecessor because additional fragmentary actualities are received. So conceived, moreover, God differs from the completely changeless and eternal reality so often affirmed in the Western metaphysical and Christian theological traditions. Instead of a supreme being named only by negation, the divine is here the eminently temporal individual, who from everlasting to everlasting has existed and will exist as the ever-changing because ever-increasing unification of whatever has occurred in the world—the individual to whom strictly everything else makes a difference and is thereby given its own everlasting significance.

In this context, the discussion considers some recent critiques of theistic arguments, especially of the so-called ontological argument. Whatever force those refutations have, I argue, depends on the traditional or classical, rather than neoclassical, concept of God.

Still, the latter concept has also been controversial, even among those who have pursued the metaphysics initiated by Whitehead—a debate largely prompted by an apparent difference between Whitehead and Hartshorne themselves on how God should be conceived. At stake especially is how relations between God and the world can be understood with precision, and this question needs a clear answer because its absence threatens the coherence of neoclassical metaphysics. Chapter 3 concludes with this issue. Hartshorne's alternative to Whitehead's apparent view of God is, I contend, more convincing. At the same time, I argue for a refinement of Hartshorne's accounting, namely, for a distinct set of relations implied by the metaphysical necessity marking God's difference from all others. On this proposal, things in the world localize a divine omnipresence, to which they make a difference immediately upon their completion.

Against the background of this neoclassical metaphysics in the strict sense, Chapter 4 returns to the metaphysics of subjectivity because it turns directly to the question of moral responsibility. As mentioned above, all subjects include, at least implicitly, an original belief in the comprehensive purpose and, therefore, choose for or against it. One cannot be a subject without this decision, which I will call the decision to be authentic or inauthentic. The chapter seeks to explicate both the nature of understanding and the seemingly paradoxical character of self-understanding. The self can be both subject and object of the same understanding, I argue, because decision for a self-understanding is the choice with understanding of one's purpose. What we understand when we understand ourselves is the difference for the future we decide to make. Choosing one's purpose consciously, moreover, requires an evaluation of the differing ends open within one's present situation, those that are possible alternatives. Hence, self-understanding involves an implied claim for some view of the good in terms of which alternative possible purposes are assessed. But subjectivity includes an original belief in the comprehensive good as the basis on which all open purposes should be evaluated. Thus, the decision for a self-understanding includes a decision for or against the comprehensive good, a decision for or against one's authenticity.

I call the decision for a self-understanding one's "original decision," and the original decision is, then, complex, embracing both a decision about the metaphysical good and a decision for some specific purpose that is possible in one's given time and place. The first informs the second, and the second implicates the first—or, if we wish, the original decision includes the deepest motivation for our specific choices. In the primary sense of "moral" and "immoral," these terms designate this original decision. A subjective activity is morally good without qualification only if its specific decision expresses a decision to be authentic. But activity may also be moral in a secondary or qualified sense, namely, when its decision for a specific purpose is what would have been chosen had the activity decided for the comprehensive good, even while the motivation for that specific decision may be, in fact, inauthentic. For instance, one may keep a promise and, thereby, obey the moral norm that promises should (barring some overriding moral consideration) be kept; but one may do so because one calculates how a good reputation will serve one's personal advantage in the long run, and the latter is chosen as the supreme good in terms of which specific ends are evaluated. Whether one's activity is authentic can never be, I contend, the object of clear or focused self-consciousness. In that sense we cannot be explicitly aware of our deepest motivation, and the discussion explores at some length the relation between our deepest decisions and those of which we are explicitly aware.

In a word, then, the metaphysics of human purpose and thus of morality is teleological. We ought so to take our decisions as to maximize realization of the metaphysical good. In saying this, one simply reasserts neoclassical metaphysics in contrast to the Kantian tradition, and I argue for metaphysical teleology by showing how nonteleological moral theories are internally problematic. These theories agree with Kant's separation of the moral law from any comprehensive purpose because, for them, actions are right when they exemplify principles or norms that constrain purposes but are not derived from an inclusive evaluation of ends. In recent moral philosophy, the achievements of Jürgen Habermas, Karl-Otto Apel, and Alan Gewirth are notable illustrations of nonteleology. Such theories assert that our chosen purposes are moral or immoral only in some partial respect, namely, whether or not they observe the constraints nonteleological theories place upon them. Thereby, these theories imply that our possible purposes in other respects are morally indifferent.

For Gewirth, as one example, actions are morally pertinent insofar as they affect the generic freedom and well-being of other agents. By implication, then, alternatives for choice are otherwise morally indifferent. But an assertion of moral indifference between or among possible purposes itself implies a moral comparison. Hence, nonteleological theories commit the "partialist fallacy" because they presuppose what they also deny, namely, the evaluation of purposes in all respects. We might make the point by analogy: Let us suppose that someone finds one painting more beautiful than another solely because the first has more vivid colors. By implication, the differing designs of the two paintings are said to make no difference in the aesthetic evaluation. To assert the aesthetic indifference of their designs, however, is itself an aesthetic judgment. Hence, one cannot confine evaluation to whether the colors are more or less vivid without a basis for comparing the paintings—design integrated with color—in their entirety. Similarly, a nonteleological assertion that alternatives for choice are morally indifferent in certain respects presupposes an evaluation of possible purposes in their entirety, and this is why the partialism of nonteleological moral theories is a fallacy.

Given a neoclassical metaphysics, the comprehensive telos must be defined by the features of final real things. Whitehead uses "creativity" as "the category of the ultimate," meaning that it names most explicitly the character of actualities—and he defines creativity: "The many become one, and are increased by one" (1978, 21). An actuality unifies relations to already completed others for the sake of its future. Hence, the good can be only the concrete realization of unity-in-diversity, and I call this the realization of creativity. It follows that all actualities have value, although they may be in themselves greater or lesser realizations of good, depending on the unity-in-diversity or creativity they achieve. When actualization is by way of self-understanding, so that moral decision occurs, we may decide for lesser rather than greater creativity and, thereby, choose immorally.

As noted above, however, what we choose is our purpose. Thus, our own realization of value depends on what we pursue, and we maximize the good we ourselves embody in the present by choosing a purpose that will maximize creativity in the future. This simply repeats that our moral responsibility is defined teleologically, and the comprehensive purpose may be captured in the following moral law: so decide as to pursue maximal creativity in the future as such. This maximal good may also be called the divine good; future creativity wherever realized becomes God's unity-in-diversity because God again and again unifies strictly everything that occurs in the world. Moreover, inclusion within God's becoming is implied by the moral law because, absent the divine good, there would be no meaning to "maximization." Realization in some future multiplicity of individuals cannot be summarily greater or less than it might have been without some single unification of them all.

Because "the many become one, and are increased by one," the achievement of unity-in-diversity possible in the present depends on the situation (the many) in which experience or activity occurs. We should, therefore, speak of human freedom in two senses: On the one hand, freedom can mean emancipation or empowerment, the chance to be creative that is given by the past we inherit. In this sense, freedom varies from human individual to human individual, depending on context. Typically, the most important context is the human past to which one has access, the opportunities provided by one's own past experiences and by the human communities in which one participates. On the other hand, there is moral freedom, with which any given person in any given moment takes her or his original decision and, thereby, decides what it will do with the opportunity presented—whether the greater unity-in-diversity possible will be realized by pursuing maximal creativity in the future or some lesser possibility will be chosen. Achieving the good is, in other words, a common enterprise, in which the empowerment of any given person depends on her or his communities and thus on the good others make available to her or him.

Teleological ethics have been widely criticized as inconsistent with any inviolable human rights. If our supreme obligation is to maximize future good, then, so the indictment holds, even an innocent individual's right to life can be overridden when the greater good is thereby served. Perhaps, for instance, a given person might be sacrificed to a medical experiment because the probabilities of achieving thereby a major medical breakthrough are very high. But this criticism misfires against teleological ethics in general because it misfires specifically against the teleology of neoclassical metaphysics. Chapter 4 shows how a comprehensive telos authorizes what I call social practices, that is, patterns of interaction defined by reciprocal roles and responsibilities that should be observed whatever the consequences. Our pursuit of the good may be indirectly specified to particular actions through such practices, whereby the actions belonging to those practices should not be morally evaluated as if they were independent of these cooperative patterns. All institutions and many other kinds of human association are such forms of interaction.

Among the prescribed practices, the chapter argues, is a universal practice defined by a principle of respect for the communicative rights of all subjects. Like the comprehensive purpose itself, this principle is transcendental or belongs to the metaphysics of morals because the prescribed respect is implied simply by the claim every subject makes for her or his decision. To decide with understanding is to claim moral validity for one's action, and thereby one affirms the right of every other subject to contest its validity. In other words, one's action commits one to communicative respect whatever one's moral beliefs and for that reason, the principle is *explicitly* neutral to all moral differences. At the same time, this universal practice makes no sense unless it *implicitly* serves some moral purpose. Hence, the principle of communicative respect is inseparable from the comprehensive purpose. Moreover, indirect application of that purpose through the principle of communicative respect occurs precisely because realization of the telos is a common enterprise, requiring appropriate forms of community. The chapter then explains how this principle defines human rights and why the obligations they give to us require moral learning.

Democratic politics is a social practice based on principles of human rights, and the final two chapters seek to explicate the metaphysics of democracy. They do so through a conversation with Jeffrey Stout's recent volume, *Democracy and Tradition*. If the nonteleological ethics of Apel or Gewirth is moral theory similar to Kant's, Stout's democratic thought expresses the post-Kantian critique of universal reason. Democracy itself is, on Stout's proposal, a specific tradition with its own form of public reason, and his political thought is, if I understand him correctly, circumscribed by this tradition. Accordingly, Stout's moral theory affirms, as one chapter title in his book asserts, "ethics without metaphysics." His account of democracy is not, he tells us, wedded to this view of ethics, but I argue that his attempt to separate the two is unsuccessful.

Stout's discussion is especially concerned with the place of religious beliefs—and thus "religious conceptions of the good" (Stout 2004a, 2)—within the political process, and he includes them in public discourse even while he finds metaphysics in the sense I defend unconvincing. On his account, the "discourse of most modern democracies is *secularized*" but does not embody a "commitment to *secularism* [or, we may add, to theism]" (2004a, 93). This formulation makes him an especially challenging conversation partner because, in my own way, I endorse a similar neutrality of democratic discourse. For Stout, his account expresses a third alternative between two other positions, each of which gains strength principally from the problems suffered by the other. Rawlsian or contractarian liberals, he says, separate principles of justice (at least, principles for the basic structure of society) from all "comprehensive doctrines" and, thereby, exclude religious views from public reason. The contrary position, which Stout calls "the new traditionalism," circumscribes proper moral and political evaluation within the special revelation authoritative for Christian faith. Both agree that avowedly secularistic discourse and discourse defined within some given religious tradition are the only alternatives, with the liberals affirming the first and the new traditionalists the second, and Stout's criticism of both is, I believe, fundamentally sound. Against both, democratic discourse is secularized and, thereby, neutral or hospitable to both religious and secularistic convictions.

In explicating secularized discourse, however, Stout calls upon the democratic tradition in a way that makes it independent of either secularism or theism. In other words, the constitutional norms of democratic participation are said to be free of any secularistic or religious implications, and this, I argue, makes the ethics of democratic citizenship "ethics without metaphysics." If he rejects the Rawlsian view, namely, that principles of justice to which the basic structure of society should conform are independent of any comprehensive doctrines, Stout is committed nonetheless to *constitutional* principles of justice whose separation from metaphysics defines the democratic exchange of reasons. Accordingly, all citizens should explicitly affirm that separation. As a consequence, chapter 5 contends, Stout's account of secularized discourse is internally problematic: the democratic tradition its citizens should recognize is, in truth, a competitive commitment of the same order as the religious and secularistic views to which it intends to be relevantly neutral. His discussion, critical of two positions to which he proposes his third alternative, has not, I argue, considered all of the options.

The final chapter, therefore, articulates a fourth position, on which democracy itself is authorized only by the comprehensive purpose and thus by metaphysical theism, even while explicit recognition of that backing can never be a condition of democratic citizenship. This accounting keeps distinct the *explicit* provisions of a democratic constitution, on the one hand, and, on the other, the ultimate terms of political assessment the constitution *implies*. Democracy is constituted explicitly by stipulating the conditions of politics through full and free discourse. In other words, a democratic constitution specifies to politics the transcendental principle of communicative respect. Thereby, politics occurs by the way of reason. To respect the right of any subject to contest one's claim to validity is to pledge that, if contested, the claim can be redeemed by argument. I call the constitutional provisions "formative" in character, whereby they do no more (and no less) than constitute a political discourse in which each citizen is sovereign over her or his assessment of every political claim, and "we the people," together as equals, are the final ruling power. Accordingly, the constitution should stipulate the rights by which each member of "we the people" is defined and the decision-making institutions through which the discourse informs governmental activities.

Naturally, politics by the way of reason cannot simply discuss and debate its own constitutional conditions. The democratic discourse is also about the state's activities, about statutory law and public policy, and thus about substantive principles and norms of political order. Because sovereign over her or his assessment of every political claim, each citizen must have the right to affirm any fundamental belief about political community she or he finds convincing. This is, I argue, the political meaning of religious freedom, and thus "religious" in this constitutional principle designates any explicit conviction about the ultimate terms of political assessment. So defined, "religious" is given an extended meaning, inclusive of both religious convictions in a more strict sense of the term and secularistic ones. Any explicit conviction about the grounds for political good is a legitimate contribution to the discourse, where each may be argumentatively validated or invalidated. Indeed, democracy *is* a discourse about religious conceptions of purpose in their relevance to activities of the state. Some will object that all religions are not thereby legitimated because certain religious beliefs are said to be suprarational or beyond argumentative validation. But the way of reason, I argue, simply states a commitment any religious believer already accepts if and when she or he claims validity for a religious belief. In making that claim, whatever the religion in question and even if it purports to be suprarational, one issues the pledge that one's belief can be redeemed by argument.

Neoclassical theism, then, claims to make explicit the comprehensive purpose in which all people originally believe and by which alone democracy itself is authorized. Because it prescribes democracy, however, theism so understood properly guides political decisions only through the force of argument. The pursuit of maximal creativity in the future as such provides, on this account, the ultimate terms of political assessment that ought to be convincing in the full and free political discourse and thus ought to be embodied in political decisions. Chapter 6 proceeds to develop on this basis a substantive principle of justice specifying these ultimate terms to the political order. Because the chance to be creative depends on the context to which a person has access, especially the context of human communities, I argue for justice as general emancipation: the task of politics is to maximize the measure in which general sources of empowerment are equally available to all. The chapter attempts to clarify what this substantive principle means, why it follows from neoclassical theism, and why it is inseparable from the formative principles of a democratic constitution. Democracy, we can say, is democracy on purpose, and that in two senses: in one sense, government by "we the people" is itself authorized only by the comprehensive purpose, and in another, this form of government consists in a full and free discourse about what this comprehensive purpose is and how it should inform activities of the state. In arriving at this conclusion, I hope to complete the case for metaphysical necessity as the required backing for morals and politics.

Chapter 1

The Metaphysics of Existence

We humans live with understanding, conscious of both ourselves and other things. While we also live within limits determined by the past we inherit or the environment in which we are set, we nonetheless are aware of alternative ends at which we might aim and thus are able in some measure consciously to decide what we will be or become. Thereby, human life is a moral enterprise because understanding alternatives for purpose entails decision among them by way of an evaluation. In the history of Western moral and political theory, something similar to this view has often been advanced. Seeking a contribution to this tradition, the present work intends to clarify the most general basis for evaluating alternatives for purpose and to specify such evaluation to politics.

For many eminent Western thinkers, the question of whether human life and community have a most general evaluative basis and, if so, what it is has been central. Moreover, some who have formulated a supreme or comprehensive principle of human purpose have related life by way of evaluation to another aspect of human consciousness, namely, our capacity to be aware of the entirety and to ask about human life within the totality of all things. On many accounts, one expression of this capacity is given by religions in the human adventure, at least some of which explicitly represent in symbols and practices an understanding of the totality or of something said to be its ground and intend to mark the difference this awareness makes or should make to human life.

Another supposed expression of our relation to all things has occurred in the kind of thought and discourse typically called metaphysics, which purports to be theoretical thought about existence with understanding in relation to maximally general characteristics of the entirety. For some thinkers, moreover, the principal importance of metaphysics consists in its service to religious representations. The former seeks critically to understand what must be affirmed in religious symbols and practices in order that awareness of the totality can make the greatest possible difference to human life. This work also seeks to clarify the importance of metaphysics for a critical understanding of morality and politics and, at least in that measure, for religion.

Metaphysics has been central to theoretical thought throughout most of Western history, even if how this kind of thought and discourse should be distinguished from other kinds of theory has been controversial. Within the modern era, however, doubt about metaphysics as a proper part of the philosophical task has become increasingly widespread, and contemporary philosophy, on the whole, continues to be profoundly suspicious of the metaphysical project, at least in what I will call its strict sense. Summarily speaking, metaphysics in this sense is critical thought about maximally general characteristics of existence or about existence as such. So understood, the enterprise is continuous with Aristotle's *Metaphysics*, a treatise given this name when those who collected his works placed it subsequent to his *Physics*. Aristotle famously called the object of metaphysical thought "being qua being," and I intend "existence as such" as an alternative designation of the same object. In using these terms to distinguish the metaphysical task, however, I mean both formulations in a minimal sense similar to Aristotle's first use of "happiness" in his *Nicomachean Ethics*: "Verbally there is very general agreement; for both the general run of men and people of superior refinement say that it [the highest of all goods] is happiness . . . ; but with regard to what happiness is they differ" (1095a16–20).[1] As defining the science of ethics, in other words, "happiness" is a name, the meaning or content of which is precisely what the inquiry must explicate. Similarly, then, to call metaphysics critical thought about being qua being is not itself to endorse Aristotle's or any other particular account of how existence as such is properly explicated.

Still, continuity with Aristotle does pursue a kind of inquiry different from another sense of "metaphysics." I have in mind specifically Immanuel Kant's intention. Kant could title one of his works *Prolegomena to Any Future Metaphysics* because, for him, humans cannot know anything about reality itself or things-in-themselves. On his account, "metaphysics" in the strict sense is impossible, and the term properly designates thought about the necessary conditions of human subjectivity, that is, of theoretical and practical reason, understood to be independent of any characteristics of existence as such. Something like Kant's alternative has been pursued by important subsequent philosophers. But many thinkers, especially in more recent decades, find attempts to explicate subjectivity as such no less problematic than critical thought about being qua being and thus use "metaphysics" to designate both projects, both of which they reject.

There is, then, another possibility, namely, use of the term in both senses in order to credit explication of both subjectivity as such and existence as such. On this third alternative, metaphysics is critical thought about existence as such and, as a specification thereof, about existence with understanding or subjectivity as such. Although very few during the past century have pursued this possibility, the present work seeks to reassert and redeem metaphysics in this twofold sense and, thereby, to clarify moral and political purpose in relation to the entirety. That doing so is decidedly uncommon reveals, on my accounting, how profoundly influential Kant's critique of metaphysics in the strict sense has been. By way of background for the present purpose, then, it will be useful to review briefly the traditional metaphysics Kant discredited and some of the reasons why he denied any such claim to knowledge.

The Western Background

Aristotle's *Metaphysics* treats, among other things, the nature of "first philosophy" as a theoretical science. Telling us that "being" in its primary sense designates "the 'what,' which indicates the substance of the thing" (1028a15), he asks, specifically, "whether first philosophy is universal, or deals with one genus, i.e., some one kind of being" or substance (1026a23–25). If the former, then first philosophy asks about the common character of all substances and thus about "being" as common to every genus. "But if there is something which is eternal and immovable," Aristotle says, "the science of this [one kind of being] must be prior and must be first philosophy, and universal in this way, because it is first" (1026a10, 30–31). Here, we may note, movement is not simply locomotion but, rather, any change. A first substance is completely unchangeable and, therefore, is eternal and, in that sense, is first as "being qua being" (1026a32). Aristotle calls the study of it "theology" (1026a19). We are given, in other words, two possible meanings of first philosophy: on the one hand, study of conditions common to all substances and, on the other, study of the first substance.

In the course of his treatise, Aristotle pursues the inquiry in both senses, and many hold that he cannot be speaking consistently of a single science. If it studies what is universal because common to every genus, metaphysics cannot include study of an immovable substance. The reason is this: On Aristotle's account, movable substances are movable in all respects, that is, subject not only to accidental change but also to generation and corruption or substantial change. As completely unchangeable, the immovable substance is defined by negating movable substances in all respects, and hence the former has nothing in common with the latter. Aristotle seems to concede the point in calling theology the study of one kind of being. As the study of what is common to every genus, then, metaphysics is equivalent to physics, which studies all movable substances, and Aristotle also seems to concede the point when he says: "if there is no substance other than those which are formed by nature, natural science will be the first science" (1026a27–29).

But other readers, often within the Thomistic tradition, hold that both designations of "metaphysics" belong together systematically, at least in the sense that "physics" requires "theology." For Aristotle, as for Aquinas after him, "there are many senses in which a thing may be said to 'be,' but all that 'is' is related to one central point, one definite kind of thing, and is not said to 'be' by a mere ambiguity" (1003a33–34). Thus, for instance, substances and accidents are both said to be, but in differing senses, because the latter, unlike the former, are not "self-subsistent" or cannot "exist independently" but, rather, must qualify a substance (see 1028a14–30). Still, the difference is not mere equivocation, precisely because the being of an accident "is related to one central point," namely, to the being of a substance. But if "being" is equivocal in this way, the reading goes, so, too, is "substance," and the two designations of "metaphysics" belong together. All movable substances are said to be because they are "related to one central point," namely, to the first being or immovable substance. For Aquinas, as is well known, this articulates the world's dependence on a First Cause, "the beginning of things and their last end" (S.T. 1.2.introduction),[2] whose essence is its existence and whose being is completely eternal.

To be sure, one may still ask how movable and immovable substances can have anything in common and, therefore, how there can be a single inquiry called metaphysics. Aquinas not only concedes but also insists that we cannot speak literally (that is, univocally) of something worldly things and their First Cause have in common, and for this reason, metaphysics cannot demonstrate anything about the character or nature of God. To the contrary, first philosophy can show only *that* there is such a being, in distinction from *what* it is, and in this sense, can demonstrate only the *existence* and not the *essence* of God. Nonetheless, this demonstration is sufficient to show the dependence of all worldly substances on a substance in another sense, the divine substance, and, in this respect, the subject matter of metaphysics includes both what is universal to worldly beings and the existence of the first being. Moreover, Aquinas can say that first philosophy also speaks of what is common to both, although such speaking is not literal but, rather, analogical, in the same way that "substance" designates in related senses both beings of the world and their First Cause. Worldly beings have in common with God "the perfections which flow from Him to creatures; which perfections are in God in a more eminent way than in creatures" (S.T. 1.13.3), and accordingly, our names for these perfections cannot predicate literally of God because "they fall short of representing Him" (S.T. 1.13.2).

Aquinas's account of theistic analogies is the focus of a long controversy central to subsequent Western philosophical theology.[3] At present, the relevant point is this: both his proposal and, insofar as it is similar, that of Aristotle relate the two meanings of metaphysics only by asserting that literal designation of completely eternal and thus immovable substance must be by negation. "We reach a proper knowledge of a thing not only through affirmations but also through negations. . . . : through affirmations . . . we know *what* the thing is, and how it is separated from others; but through negations . . . we know *that* it is distinct from other things, yet what it is remains unknown. Now, such is the proper knowledge that we have of God through demonstrations" (S.C.G. 3.39.1).[4] As mentioned above, so much seems to follow from the fact that "immovable" is simply the negation of "movable." This point is important because it helps to clarify Kant's denial that metaphysical knowledge in the strict sense is possible.

For Kant, we cannot have any knowledge of God because, to use Aquinas's formulation, we cannot through demonstration have such knowledge through affirmations. More generally, our possible knowledge of what exists is limited to what in literal terms we can designate positively. To assert, with Aquinas, the possibility of knowing God's existence without knowing God's essence is simply to posit the possibility of knowing what cannot be known. On Kant's reading, metaphysics in its strict sense—Platonic, Aristotelian, Thomistic, Cartesian, or Leibnizian—invariably asserts that changeable existents presuppose or imply some existent or existents completely unchangeable (that is, completely eternal or absolute or unconditional), and, because such an existent or existents cannot be designated in positive terms, the entire enterprise as an inquiry seeking critical knowledge is futile.

To be sure, this leaves available the idea of "first philosophy" in the other Aristotelian sense, namely, the study of what is common to all things in the world. As noted earlier, metaphysics in this sense alone would be, for Aristotle, equivalent to what he called physics; "if there is no substance other than those which are formed by nature, natural science will be the first science" (1026a27–29). But a science of things formed by nature cannot, for Kant, be the study of being qua being. Without relation to a necessary substance, he reasons, what can be studied by natural science depends on what just happens to be given in human experience, and nothing given in this sense could provide knowledge of features common to all possible existents. On Kant's assessment, therefore, the tradition was correct at least in this: unless possible in both Aristotelian senses, metaphysics in the strict sense is not possible at all.

Whether or not that conclusion is correct, it may seem the more compelling given the view that sense impressions are the primary data in human experience of external objects. Kant accepts that view and, on its basis, finds Hume's accounting decisive: natural scientific assumptions about universal features of its subject matter—for instance, the assumption of causal connection—are not present in or implied by sense impressions and, therefore, cannot themselves be known by way of empirical science. For Kant, then, an explication of nature's universal features can only be a critique of theoretical reason, whose conclusions are in truth only about those necessary forms of sensibility and transcendental principles of human understanding by which "object as such," the character of any object as it appears in human experience, is subjectively constituted—and in that critique, Kant effects his "Copernican revolution" and writes the "prolegomena to any future metaphysics."

The Necessity of Existence

Kant's alternative metaphysics has been highly controversial. For some who pursue the so-called linguistic and hermeneutical turns, necessary features of subjectivity are no more accessible than are conditions of existence as such. But this further conclusion emerged, I judge, because Kant first forcefully articulated a subjective turn that released subjectivity from a larger metaphysical context. In any event, Kant's argument against metaphysics in the strict sense has been massively influential. No other single thinker, I venture, is so responsible for the profound suspicion with which contemporary Western philosophy views that pre-Kantian enterprise. Critical thought about being qua being or existence as such seeks finally to know what can be conceived only in negative terms, and thereby the entire project is discredited. So far as I can see, moreover, this conclusion is now widely taken to be so secure that it no longer needs critical assessment.

Nonetheless, this conclusion is, I believe, invalid, and metaphysics in the strict sense should be reaffirmed. We can approach an argument to this effect by noting that Kant's critical turn required his distinction between phenomena or things-as-they-appear and noumena or things-in-themselves. Given that universal features of experienced objects are known only because "object as such" is constituted by human subjectivity, things-in-themselves cannot be known. Kant does not deny their existence; he apparently holds that things-in-themselves are, in some unknowable way, the causes of our sense impressions. In addition, the existence of noumena is, for him, an inescapable postulate of practical reason; affirmation of our own freedom and, further, of God's existence are consequent on our experience of moral obligation. If we leave Kant's moral theory aside, however, his critique of theoretical reason itself at least implies that things-in-themselves *may be* different from appearances because, absent this possibility, the necessary features of phenomena would be metaphysical in the strict sense.

But this required distinction can be expressed only by speaking of things-in-themselves as not-phenomena. Since they cannot be experienced, we cannot describe their possibility in positive terms. Thus, if Kant deconstructed the metaphysical tradition he inherited, he still agreed with Aquinas in this: understandings or conceptions that designate by complete negation are meaningful or possibly true. To be sure, traditional metaphysics is impossible because we cannot *know* something whose designation is solely by negation (for instance, God or a thing-in-itself); but we can nonetheless *think* such a thing. Hence, whether one claims, with Aquinas, to know the existence of something whose essence is unknowable or affirms, with Kant, only that such things are possible, a thought having no positive content is said to make sense. This common ground, I now wish to argue, provides reason to reject both proposals and, at the same time, to reaffirm metaphysics in the strict sense.

So far as I can see, a putative thought whose content is completely negative is, in truth, meaningless. Here and subsequently, I speak of a thought as meaningless in a strong sense. Clearly, we might credit a thought with meaning whenever its supposed content is in fact entertained and somehow related to other thoughts, at least if this occurs within a community of people. In this weaker sense, thoughts can be meaningful even if, on analysis, they turn out to be self-contradictory. Many have argued, for instance, that the very idea of God is, when all implications are considered, self-contradictory; but even if this conclusion is sound, one may still attribute a kind of meaning among believers to thought and speech about God. On my usage here, however, a thought whose supposed content is, in truth, self-contradictory is meaningless, and I will also speak of thoughts in this way when their supposed content is hopelessly vague. In sum, I use "meaningless" to designate a merely putative thought that, in truth, has no content, and in this sense, I will also call such a thought nonsensical. Any putative thought whose supposed content is completely negative is, I will argue, also meaningless because, in the end, such a thought cannot be distinguished from merely putative thoughts that, in truth, have no content.

Consider, for instance, the supposed thought of a colorless yellow thing. Although one may utter the words, the supposed thought is merely putative or meaningless. One may think of something colorless, and one may think of something yellow, but one cannot think of something as simultaneously colorless and yellow. The supposed thought has no content. Moreover, the supposed content is completely negative. Purporting to think of something colorless, one designates something as not yellow; purporting to think of something yellow, one designates the same thing as nothing other than something yellow; and "something not yellow and nothing other than something yellow" is a complete negation. Hence, if some other complete negation—for instance, "God" as Aquinas intends this term, or "noumena" as Kant intends that term—is to make sense, it must somehow be different from putative thoughts that have no content. In truth, however, there can be no such difference because the supposed content of each is completely negative, and a difference in supposed content must be positive. A supposed difference in content that is in no way positive is no different from no difference at all. Hence, a putative thought whose supposed content is completely negative is no different from a putative thought that is meaningless because it has no content.

Any putative existential thought whose content is completely negative implies that "nothing exists" is meaningful or possibly true. To first appearances, perhaps, this formulation seems foreign to both Aquinas and Kant. The former does not say that God is nothing, nor does the latter say this of noumena. Neither intends to assert the complete absence of existence but, rather, purports to think of some necessary or possible existence that cannot be conceived in positive terms and thus must be designated as "that to which thought cannot attribute any positive features." But whether one intends the sheer absence of existence or the possible existence of "that to which thought cannot attribute any positive features," one asserts the following: a statement with the predicate "exists" and a grammatical subject having no positive content is possibly true.[5] In this sense, "nothing exists" is asserted, the supposedly differing uses notwithstanding.

Moreover, the same assertion is implied by every denial of metaphysics in the strict sense, given the following account of such metaphysics: true understandings of existence as such are necessarily true in the strict or logical sense; that is, the propositional content of their denials is self-contradictory or meaningless and, thereby, not possibly true. Throughout, I will use "necessarily true" only in this strict sense and "not possibly true" correspondingly. If one denies that any understanding of existence can be necessarily true and insofar agrees with Kant, one asserts, by implication, that "nothing exists" is possibly true. I wish now to repeat the argument against putative thoughts whose contents are completely negative by showing why "nothing exists" is meaningless. Summarily expressed, the argument is this: given that "something exists" is possibly true, where "something" means a grammatical subject whose content is at least partially positive, "nothing exists" cannot be possibly true because the two statements have no common content.

In pursuit of the point, we might begin with two other statements: "something lives" and "nothing lives." Both are possibly true, but as such, "nothing lives" is not typically used to assert "there are no existents at all, and a fortiori nothing is alive." Typically used, the statement asserts the absence of life under certain specified or specifiable existential conditions. For instance, one might say that nothing lives under the conditions present on Pluto. Given this usage, both "something lives" and "nothing lives" also assert "something exists"; that is, both statements are about existents—the first asserting that at least some among the existing things in question are alive and the second asserting that none of these things is alive. In this sense, we can say that both have "something exists" as a common content, with which each of the two, in its own way, combines further content. Typically understood, in other words, the predicate "lives" implies that any possibly true statement of the form "x lives" (including "nothing lives") is an assertion about existents.

Now, it is apparent that a possibly true statement of the form "x lives" cannot have just any grammatical subject we please. For instance, "this stone lives" is nonsensical, if we posit that "stone" designates a kind of nonliving existent. On that designation, the statement is not possibly true. Moreover, we can, assuming the typical usage of "*x* lives," formulate this conclusion as follows: any possibly true statement of the form "*x* lives" has the content "something exists," but "this stone lives" has no such content because the existence it asserts, namely, that of a certain living thing, is denied by designating the thing as a stone. On typical usage, then, a statement of the form "*x* lives" is meaningless when, by virtue of its grammatical subject, it contradicts the common content implied by the predicate "lives," namely, "something exists."

But some hold that "nothing lives" does not necessarily share with "something lives" this common content because the former may also deny "something exists." In other words, "nothing lives" may have no positive implications because its meaning is solely negative, namely, "nothing exists, and a fortiori nothing is alive," which, on this account, is also possibly true. We may now ask whether the predicate "exists" implies that "something exists" and "nothing exists" have some common content, and, if so, what it is.[6] Since the two differ because "something exists" is at least partially positive and "nothing exists" is not, such common content seems absent. Naturally, the position we are reviewing may deny that any common content is, in this case, required. Nonetheless, one cannot deny that, given some grammatical subjects, "*x* exists" is not possibly true. For instance, "A colorless yellow thing exists" is meaningless, as is any instance of "*x* exists" in which the grammatical subject contradicts itself. Accordingly, any possibly true statement of the form "*x* exists" must have the common content required to distinguish it from a statement of this form that is, by virtue of its grammatical subject, meaningless. But, again, "something exists" is at least partially positive, and "nothing exists" is not, and thus the position in question seems to preclude all candidates for common content in the two statements. To say that "nothing exists" is possibly true appears to imply what it also precludes.

Still, the position we are reviewing might insist that "something exists" and "nothing exists" have as their common content that "*x* exists" is meaningful. On this proposal, all possibly true statements of the form "*x* exists" commonly assert "something is possibly true"—and with this common content, each in its own way combines some further content. Because this is the only available proposal, we can now see why the position cannot itself possibly be true, namely, because the assertion of it must beg the question. Begging the question has been discussed by some as "a dialectical, or dialogical" feature (Oppy, 53) of how arguments are used. On Graham Oppy's account, an argument fails in this way by including a premise that is contrary to some belief within a consistent set of beliefs held by the argument's recipient—for instance, in the case of theistic arguments, held by the atheist or agnostic (see Oppy, 53–57; see also Gale, 213).[7] In keeping with this account, we can say that a statement begs the question when it simply assumes something at issue. If we ask, for instance, whether there are universal human rights, a positive answer begs the question if it simply assumes the validity of Kant's moral theory.

In the present case, asserting as their common content the possible truth of "something exists" and "nothing exists" exhibits a similar failure. At issue is whether "nothing exists" *is* possibly true because it differs from meaningless statements of the form "*x* exists" by virtue of sharing with "something exists" a common content. Being possibly true, then, cannot be the common content required; to the contrary, something else is needed such that, given its presence, the possible truth of "nothing exists" would be established or confirmed. To the question of human rights mentioned above, the positive answer suggested may only happen to beg the question or may do so, we can say, contingently—if the positive answer can be given without simply assuming the validity of Kant's moral theory (or any other on which human universal rights are affirmed). In the present case, to the contrary, the proposed answer necessarily begs the question. Because the only available proposal for common content shared by "nothing exists" with "something exists" is being possibly true, the assertion that "nothing exists" is possibly true *must* simply assume precisely what is at issue.

Thereby, this supposed answer not only begs the question but is, by implication, self-refuting. Because it must beg the question, the position we are reviewing implicitly denies that the question itself is meaningful. In the sense relevant here, a question cannot be meaningful unless it has a true answer and thus includes or implies some basis or criterion for the difference between true and false answers. Perhaps we humans are, in fact, unable to determine the true answer (or answers) to some questions—for instance, certain questions about particularities of the past forever lost to memory or historical inquiry, or certain questions about the deepest motivations of a particular person. Still, a meaningful question must include or imply some way in which true and false answers are differentiated, even if we cannot, in fact, determine any answer thereby credited. Absent that differentiation, true and false could not characterize alternative answers, and the question could not be understood. But if we ask whether "nothing exists" is possibly true, a response that must beg the question by assuming precisely what is at issue denies, by implication, any such basis for the difference between true and false answers. In other words, " 'nothing exists' is possibly true" must be nonsense because, by implication, it purports to answer a meaningless question.

Perhaps this argument will be indicted for a similar failure. The view that "nothing exists" is possibly true, its advocates may say, cannot be defeated without also begging the question or simply assuming something at issue, and the disagreement becomes a stand-off. But this response is without merit. What, we may ask, is the statement supposedly assumed? That "something exists" is possibly true is not a statement at issue. Rather, its possible truth is transparent because it is transparently true; indeed, any denial of it is pragmatically self-contradictory because the act of denial implies the existence of a subject. With respect to the relevant question, in other words, "something exists" and "nothing exists" have different standings; the possible truth of the former, but not of the latter, is given. The relevant question is whether "nothing exists" is also possibly true because it shares with "something exists" a common content.

If there is a statement supposedly at issue, it must be that "something exists" is necessarily true. This statement is indeed asserted by implication when the possible truth of "nothing exists" is denied, and the implied statement, it might be said, is simply assumed. To the contrary, however, this implied statement is not merely asserted but, rather, defended by showing that "nothing exists" has no common content with "something exists" (the possible truth of which is not at issue) by which the former could be distinguished from a meaningless statement of the form "x exists." In its own way, then, this conclusion simply repeats the conclusion reached earlier: there can be no relevant difference between a putative thought whose supposed content is completely negative (that is, whose supposed content is "nothing exists") and a merely putative thought that has no content at all (that is, whose supposed content is a meaningless form of "x exists") because the content of each is completely negative. Thus, "something exists" is the common content shared by all possibly true statements of the form "*x* exists." In other words, "something exists" is necessarily true.

It now follows that all possibly true existential negations are, by implication, partially positive existential statements. Because "nothing exists" is nonsense, saying that something is absent is saying that something else, whose existence excludes the first, is present. For instance, "dinosaurs do not exist" implies "something exists" and thus implies that something other than dinosaurs exists under whatever conditions dinosaurs are said to be absent. Similarly, "Julius Caesar did not exist" implies that the relevant moments in Roman history were occupied by things or people other than Julius Caesar, and to say that something will not happen is to imply that some or other event incompatible with the first will occur. Indeed, it follows that every possibly true statement, whether explicitly about existence or not, implies a positive statement about existence. Were this not the case, some possibly true statement or statements would imply that "nothing exists" is also possibly true. Accordingly, possibly true mathematical formulations or, alternatively, statements about statements, if not themselves existential statements, imply (positive) existential statements—for instance, about possible states of affairs or possible states of human subjectivity. Necessarily, possibly true understandings are, at least implicitly, about something that did or does or will or might or must exist.

On my accounting, no decision in philosophical thought is more fundamental than whether or not "something exists" is necessarily true, and my hope is that subsequent chapters in this work will help to confirm this judgment. By way of anticipating the later discussion, however, I propose that a positive answer commits us to the following: the distinction some have drawn between ontological necessity, on the one hand, and logical necessity, on the other, is illicit. On some accounts, the ontological necessity of a given thing or feature of things does not entail the logical necessity of the corresponding statement "x exists" (see, e.g., Hick, 93–97; Post, chapter 3). In one application, this distinction appears in Kant's synthetic a priori principles of understanding. While they designate what is existentially necessary, because they constitute any appearing object as such, they are not logically necessary because they do not or may not designate the character of noumena. Again, the distinction has been used to discredit Anselm's so-called ontological argument for God's existence. It may be, we are told, that "God" as "that-than-which-nothing-greater-can-be-conceived" is itself conceivable or logically possible and designates an ontologically necessary being, that is, a being possible in all logically possible worlds and thus not dependent on specific existential conditions; still, this does not imply that "God exists" is necessarily true. The only legitimate conclusion is "if God exists, God exists necessarily," and it may be the case that under all possible existential conditions there is no God.

But this critique implies that "God does not exist," said to be logically possible, is an existential negation without any positive implication, since "all possible existential conditions" or "all logically possible worlds" otherwise remain the same independently of whether God exists or not. Hence, "God does not exist" is completely negative and, if the argument developed above is sound, is not possibly true. With that conclusion, it remains open whether God does exist, because an assessment of Anselm's argument also depends on whether "that-than-which-nothing-greater-can-be-conceived" is itself conceivable and does indeed designate a necessary being, and these questions will be postponed for later discussion. The point here is simply to discredit refutations based on the supposed distinction between ontological and logical necessity. As in Kant's formulation of it, this distinction in all of its uses assumes that "nothing exists" is possibly true, because the sheer absence of what is (or would be) ontologically necessary is said to be logically possible. Against that assumption, the argument above seeks to show that "something exists" is necessarily true, and thus the distinction is illicit.

The Task of Metaphysics

If "nothing exists" is not possibly true, we have grounds on which to depart from the metaphysics of Aquinas even while rejecting Kant's denial of metaphysics in the strict sense. Neither the assertion, with Aquinas, of some completely eternal existent nor the assertion, with Kant, that metaphysics excludes knowledge of existence as such is credible—because both implicitly affirm, each in its own way, that "nothing exists" is possibly true. We are now also in a position to formulate a third alternative. Throughout this section, I will, unless otherwise noted, use "metaphysics" in the strict sense, and we can summarize the third alternative by defining the metaphysical task as follows: *metaphysics is the critical study of what must be the case because the complete absence of existence is impossible*. Or, again: *metaphysics is the critical study of what must be true because "nothing exists" is not possibly true*. Since the impossibility of complete nonexistence implies that something must exist, we may also say: *metaphysics is the critical study of what must be the case because something must exist*. Or, again: *metaphysics is the critical study of what must be true because "something exists" is necessarily true*. This means that all other true metaphysical understandings are necessarily true understandings implied by "something exists," and, thereby, all true metaphysical understandings imply each other.

To be sure, one might allow that "something exists" is logically necessary and then conclude that little, if anything, follows from it. In

Why there is Something rather than Nothing, Bede Rundle argues in his own way that "something exists" is logically necessary. Asking "why?" disappears, he notes, if it demands an explanation and concerns a point where this demand "is seen to be misconceived" (Rundle, 185),[8] and he argues "that *something* is always presupposed when existence is affirmed or denied" (117). Moreover, he continues, "if anything exists, matter does; therefore matter exists" (109); that is "matter exists" is logically necessary and thus does not demand an explanation. This does not mean, he clarifies, "that everything is material" (166) and, specifically, he does not deny that mind or minds exist (see chapter 7). Rather, only matter has "the necessary independent existence," such that anything else that does exist or might exist is inseparable from "material substance" (166, 130). Still, if Rundle agrees that something or other must exist, little else beyond the independence of "material substance" and a "spatio-temporal setting. . . . broadly conceived" (129) seems, for him, to follow, so that metaphysics as critical study of those implications is a rather thin inquiry. But whether "something exists" has less or more significant implications is a question only metaphysics in the sense we have defined can answer. For the moment, then, we may set that question aside and proceed simply with the recognition that those implications, however extensive they may or may not be, are what this critical study pursues.

In that pursuit, we may speak of "metaphysical necessity" in two senses that also imply each other. The term means that certain conditions or characteristics of existence cannot fail to obtain or cannot fail to be exemplified; that is, such failure is impossible. Correspondingly, the term also means that true understandings of these conditions or characteristics are necessarily true, and their denials are not possibly true. Such understandings are logically necessary because metaphysical conditions or characteristics are ontologically necessary, and vice-versa. On my accounting, the metaphysical task as conceived by this third alternative is given classic formulation in Alfred North Whitehead's definition of "speculative philosophy": "Speculative Philosophy is the endeavor to frame a coherent, logical, necessary system of general ideas in terms of which every element of our experience can be interpreted" (1978, 3).

"Interpreted" here means that every element of experience may be so understood as to "have the character of a particular instance of the general scheme." Moreover, "every element in our experience" does not mean merely "such items as happen to have been considered" (1978, 3) but, rather, those in all possible experience—and, since we can experience something simply by understanding it as a possibility, the items of all possible experience include all possibility, whether actualized or not. This becomes apparent when Whitehead explicates "necessary": "The philosophic scheme should be 'necessary,' in the sense of *bearing in itself* its own warrant of universality throughout all experience" (1978, 4; emphasis added).[9] No scheme could bear such warrant unless "universality throughout all [items of] experience" means universality throughout strictly all actuality and possibility or universality definitive of the possible as such. In other words, "necessary" means that the scheme of ideas or understandings is necessarily true. One might object that some possibilities may not be possible items of experience, and thus universality throughout experience does not imply necessity. But "the unknowable," Whitehead writes, "is unknown" (1978, 4); that is, the supposed possibility of something we cannot experience (for instance, noumena, as Kant proposes) is a supposed possibility that, in truth, we cannot think.[10] The unknowable, we can say, is inconceivable, and on my reading, this is Whitehead's statement that "nothing exists," whether intended as a denial of all existence or the assertion of some possibility whose designation is solely by negation, is not possibly true. Hence, true understandings of what is universal throughout all possible experience are implied by all possibly true understandings, that is, are necessarily true.

"The philosophical scheme," Whitehead continues, "should be coherent, logical, and, in respect to its interpretation, applicable and adequate" (1978, 3). "Adequate" is a criterion repeating that all possible experience and thus the possible as such is to be interpreted. "Applicable," Whitehead says, "means that some items of experience are thus interpretable" (1978, 3) and is implied by "adequate"; an adequate scheme is a fortiori applicable. If I understand correctly, the latter criterion is added as a methodological counsel to fallible human thinkers who pursue the philosophical task. Clarity about application to at least some objects of experience protects metaphysical ideas, maximally abstract as they are, from being hopelessly vague and thus only apparently adequate. Indeed, a hopelessly vague notion is in no relevant way different from a notion whose designation is completely negative.

Applicability, we can say, means that each of the concepts marking true metaphysical statements as metaphysical meets one or both of the following conditions: (1) The concept designates a feature exemplified clearly in some object or objects of widespread human experience—and here it is assumed that the possible objects of widespread human experience include the experiencing itself as an object of self-consciousness. In Whitehead's scheme, for example, the metaphysical concept "quality" designates a feature exemplified in a perceived object of color (that is, the object as colored exemplifies the metaphysical feature), and the metaphysical concepts "relation to the past" and "relation to the future" designate, respectively, features exemplified in an experience of memory and an experience of anticipation. (2) The concept designates a feature that implies and is implied by a feature exemplified clearly in some object or objects widespread human experience. In Whitehead's scheme, for instance, the concept "relation to God" designates a feature that may not be exemplified clearly in widespread human experience but, in any event, is said to imply and be implied by, among other things, "relation to the past" and "relation to the future." In sum, phenomenological applicability, dependent finally on clear and widespread human experience, is essential to metaphysics. It is not a sufficient condition for the truth of a metaphysical statement, but inapplicability entails that metaphysical ideas are hopelessly vague.

"Logical" has, Whitehead says, "its ordinary meaning," and it serves in relation to the criterion of "coherence" a methodological function similar to that served by "applicable" in relation to "adequate." "Coherence" here has an emphatic meaning. It stipulates that ideas or statements in a metaphysical scheme, beyond being logically consistent, should also "presuppose each other so that in isolation they are meaningless" (1978, 3). True metaphysical statements in the strict sense are coherent in the emphatic sense that all implications of any one imply it; such statements are, all implications included, mutually implicative. This reasserts that true statements of this kind explicate what must be the case because the complete absence of existence is impossible, or what must be true because "something exists" is necessarily true.[11]

The criterion of coherence, we can say, repeats with respect to logical or conceptual form what the criterion of adequacy requires with respect to designation; that is, the criteria of adequacy and coherence are redundant; either, properly understood, defines the task of metaphysics. Adequacy means that every possible item of experience can be so understood that the general scheme is implied, and thus the concepts or statements of any adequate scheme must be, all of their implications included, mutually implicative; correspondingly, such mutual implication means that all true metaphysical statements designate features of all possibility, whether actualized or not. Hence, stipulating both criteria is also methodological in the aforementioned sense, that is, as counsel about how the inquiry should be pursued by fallible thinkers. A scheme that seems to be adequate can be properly criticized as only apparently so by showing that its statements are not coherent, and vice versa.

Some might propose that a set of statements about possibility could be coherent without being adequate, that is, without designating the possible as such. Given the emphatic meaning of "coherence," however, reflection shows this proposal to be mistaken. If there are true metaphysical statements, they will be implied by any possibly true statement; but a possibly true statement that is not metaphysical will designate the specification of metaphysical features to some but not all conditions or states of affairs and thus will not be implied by true metaphysical statements. Hence, any set of existential statements, one or more of which is not adequate, will not be a coherent scheme; at least one statement will have implications that do not imply it.

Because all true statements of this kind imply each other, the designation of any one, all implications taken into account, includes the designation of all others. In this sense, metaphysical truth and falsity characterize the whole system rather than individual statements. Correspondingly, the character of reality such a system seeks to explicate is an abstract singular. "Singular" here does not mean simple, in the sense that excludes differentiations. Rather, the point is that metaphysical differentiations must be self-differentiations, in a way similar to the self-differentiation of time into past, present, and future. In doing metaphysics, then, we pursue critical understanding of this single character by way of explicating its self-differentiations. In contrast to Rundle's account, on which the implications of "something exists" seem to be few, I will outline below a neoclassical metaphysics on which the self-differentiations of metaphysical necessity are extensive. If we assume that metaphysical explication requires this more complicated kind of scheme, then no set of self-differentiations can be final. Because our thought is inescapably fragmentary, the relevant metaphysical ideas depend in part on which distinctions are required for clear understanding by the subjects in question, given their historical context and the terms in which important philosophical problems are formulated. Hence, finality is prevented because alternative or further analysis may be required by another intellectual context in which clarity is sought.

It then follows that validation of claims to metaphysical truth can never be complete. Only the explication of all implications and a defense of their coherence as self-differentiations could fully validate any given metaphysical statement. For this reason, among others, this account of the metaphysical task is thoroughly consistent with the fallibility of metaphysical proposals. A metaphysical proposal is fallible not only because one or more of its concepts may be hopelessly vague or because there is incoherence among its explicitly formulated statements but also because implications not yet formulated may, if explicated, disclose incoherence that is otherwise not apparent. Moreover, metaphysics may be especially susceptible to such errors because it seeks understanding of maximally abstract conditions or characteristics.[12] In the nature of the case, then, metaphysical discourse is always an attempt to formulate a more successful scheme than those heretofore proposed and requires comparative judgments about the relative success of alternatives.[13]

But if these considerations introduce caution, they do not mean that doing metaphysics is impossible. Were that conclusion implied, adequacy and coherence would not make sense as criteria of critical thought, and thus "something exists" would not be necessarily true. As the above defense of that necessary truth intends to illustrate, moreover, relatively more complete validation of some individual statements or sets of statements is possible, so that relative metaphysical success and thus metaphysical progress can be recognized, even if, in the last analysis, metaphysical systems, not individual statements, are true and false. Any given metaphysical statement or set of statements is validated by showing that its denial is not possibly true.[14] This argument, as we have noted, can never be fully explicated because we cannot exclude the possibility of further analysis through which the denial is so restated as to be possibly true. In some cases, however, arguments offered for a given metaphysical statement or set of statements may be sufficiently convincing as to warrant confidence that additional attempts to contest it will differ only verbally, so that validation is relatively complete. Accordingly, there are relatively good reasons to say that a true metaphysical scheme will include a statement or set of statements substantively equivalent to the one in question. On my accounting, "something exists" is one such statement.

Whitehead's definition of "speculative philosophy" is, I judge, destined to stand as an unsurpassed formulation of the metaphysical task. If "nothing exists" is meaningless, then some statements designate existence as such and do so because they belong to a system of such statements that is adequate and coherent. Following others indebted to Whitehead, I will call metaphysics so understood neoclassical and thereby distinguish it from the traditional or classical form Kant discredited, namely, an account of existence as such to which designation by complete negation is essential.

Kant, as we have reviewed, held that an existent designated by complete negation could not be known, even while he affirmed its possibility, and thus he restricted metaphysics to the conditions of human subjectivity independently of existence as such. As also mentioned previously, many recent philosophers have rejected both classical and Kantian metaphysics without affirming the necessary truth of "something exists" and thus have remained committed, at least by implication, to the possible truth of "nothing exists." Given that premise, along with the rejection of Kant, some philosophers restrict generalizations about possibilities to the contingent or empirical features of "such items as happen to have been considered" (Whitehead 1978, 3), in distinction from the metaphysical characteristics of all actual and possible items in experience. On my reading, John Dewey is one such philosopher. For Dewey, metaphysics is part of an empiricist "reconstruction in philosophy" (see 1957) and seeks "cognizance of the generic traits of existence" (1958, 113). Philosophy is properly empirical because "the standpoint and conclusions of modern science" are the consequence of "the most revolutionary discovery yet made," namely, that what alone is "actually 'universal' is *process*" (1957, xiii). For modern science, the world is "infinitely variegated," so that "change rather than fixity is now a measure of 'reality' or energy of being; change is omnipresent" (1957, 61). Hence, for Dewey, "generic" means "most general" in the sense of empirical generalization; metaphysics is empirical "thinking at large" (1958, 27), and there are no necessarily true statements about traits of existence.

So far as I can see, Dewey's proposal is fundamentally problematic because, by implication, it undermines the possibility of empirical knowledge in the sense modern science typically purports to pursue. I have in mind understandings whose truth is independent of anything by which the individual or community who understands is distinguished from other subjects. In that sense, the truth of empirical understandings is universally true. Absent both metaphysical necessity and Kant's alternative metaphysics, scientific pursuit of such understandings is impossible, as I will now try to explain.

The problem appears once we recognize the following implication: if "nothing exists" is possibly true, then any statement of the form "x exists," where x is designated by complete negation, is possibly true. The latter follows because there is no way to distinguish among such statements, such that some would be possibly true and others not so, any such difference being positive. Now posit some set of empirical generalizations that is formulated and, so it seems, successfully tested—for instance, those in some version of relativity physics. The possibility remains that a set of features exclusive of those designated by these generalizations is, in truth, exemplified by some or all of the relevant existents or events because these features can be designated only by negation. Perhaps, in other words, the formulated generalizations stand to the relevant existent or events in the manner Kant's theoretical principles stand to the noumenal sources of phenomena. Moreover, there can be no procedure for ruling out this possibility precisely because the contrary set of features can be designated only by negation.

At this point, one might argue for the kind of empirical knowledge in question by appealing to the kind of universality Kant himself defended: while we cannot deny a possible difference between appearances (and thus empirical formulations tested) and things-in-themselves, empirical understandings are nonetheless true independently of any distinctions among subjects because they depend on certain synthetic a priori principles, those necessary to the understanding of a rational creature who experiences in the way universal to humans. But Dewey cannot agree to this without introducing "fixity" with respect to objects of human experience and, therefore, violating his empiricism, so that his proposal implies the impossibility of empirical knowledge in the relevant sense.

Moreover, Kant's solution is also problematic for similar reasons. If designation by complete negation is possibly true, nothing that appears counts against the statement that other subjects do or could properly understand the things in question with a contrary set of synthetic principles—other subjects whom we, that is, "we" who understand in terms of some given set of concepts and principles, can designate only by negation. To be sure, Kant allowed the possibility of such beings but insisted that they are not human, that is, cannot understand by way of sense experience. In truth, however, this does not protect empirical knowledge whose understandings are universally true unless one posits an account of sense experience. If "nothing exists" is possibly true, nothing that appears counts against the statement that others have sense experience of a kind that we, that is, "we" who experience in accord with a certain kind of sense experience, cannot know. In other words, Kant's own proposal cannot yield synthetic a priori principles without positing an understanding of human cognition—and this is, so far as I can see, what Kant did.[15]

I recognize that this analysis of Dewey's empiricism and Kant's critique of theoretical reason is summary and cannot be fully convincing without extended further argument. But perhaps enough has been said to give initial reason for the following assertion: without metaphysical necessity, empirical thinking can occur only within some conceptual context by which the philosopher or the community of understanding is distinguished from other subjects. In this respect, the logic of Dewey's view leads to the critique of universal reason by which contemporary philosophy is so widely characterized and for which some, who read Dewey as explicitly rejecting claims to universal truth, take him to be a basic resource. Whatever Dewey's own intentions, one can understand why, for instance, Richard Rorty appropriates Dewey's thought in presenting his own neopragmatism, on which "truth is not the sort of thing which has an essence" (1982, 162). Empirical generalization and, indeed, all other interpretation, becomes only what a given individual or group of individuals says is the case; that is, "truth" is "simply a compliment paid to sentences that seem to be paying their way and that fit with other sentences which are doing so" (1982, xxv).[16] Truth becomes merely "truth for me" or "truth for us." More generally, the critique of universal reason, however its presentation may differ from that of Rorty, holds that meaning and truth are circumscribed by, or dependent in all respects on, some specific location in the human adventure, with its inheritance of interpretations that are, to use Martin Heidegger's term, "thrown" into account. Although there are many meanings of "postmodern thought," most philosophical views that claim this name or can be plausibly designated by it have in common, I venture, this conviction.

On my reading, a critique of universal reason is so widely asserted or implicated in contemporary philosophy largely because thinkers are explicitly or implicitly persuaded that classical and Kantian metaphysics exhaust the alternatives. If the discussion to this point has been successful, that accounting is mistaken because it ignores the possibility of neoclassical metaphysics. But the course taken by most postmodern philosophy is not the consequence of simple oversight or neglect. To the contrary, the critique of universal reason is advanced on grounds that do or would also indict neoclassical metaphysics and thus constitutes a profound challenge to it. In my judgment, no expression of these grounds has been more influential than Martin Heidegger's, and the next chapter, therefore, will take up Heidegger's challenge.

Chapter 2

The Metaphysics of Subjectivity

Totality and Meaning

Heidegger's analysis is especially pertinent to the discussion here because he critiques, in effect, the central argument that "nothing exists" is nonsense. The reasoning in that argument is, on his account, superficial, failing to ask original questions. So far from redeeming the necessary truth of "something exists," one has merely refused to ask about nothing because one has not questioned the possibility of affirmation and negation. In proposing this objection, I have in mind specifically Heidegger's discussion of "the nothing" in his essay "What Is Metaphysics?" and I will approach through that essay the indictment he presents. As is well known, Heidegger's thought is immensely complex, with its own changes of mind and expression, and his interpreters disagree about how he is best understood, including the view that Heidegger's legacy is misrepresented as a philosophical proposal and is, rather, "a way of thinking" or "path of thinking" (see Pöggeler). In the nature of the case, attention to his thought here will be highly selective. Specifically, I will seek the sense in which "What Is Metaphysics?" and subsequent writings provide a critique of universal reason and, thereby, a challenge to metaphysical necessity.

Asking, "What is the nothing?" is, Heidegger agrees, "inherently absurd" because every answer "necessarily assumes the form: the nothing 'is.' " If subject-object or propositional thought is taken for granted, "the proposition that contradiction is to be avoided . . . lays low the question. For thinking, which is always essentially thinking about something, must act in a way contrary to its own essence when it thinks of the nothing" (1993, 96–97).[1] But this conclusion fails to ask about "the origin of negation" (108). In thinking "the complete negation of the totality of beings is impossible," one has assumed, as Heidegger says in his "Letter on Humanism," the possibility of a "no-saying," that is, has assumed the "not" as "the product of a subjective act" (1993, 261). But how is it that thought can negate—or, since negation negates something, how is it that something thought might negate can be affirmed? "How could negation produce the not from itself when it can make denials only when something deniable is already granted to it?" (105; see also 1993, 261).

A more original questioning asks how distinct somethings or beings are given. Whatever else the answer includes, beings are given as a whole. "As surely as we can never comprehend absolutely the whole of beings in themselves we certainly do find ourselves stationed in the midst of beings that are revealed somehow as a whole" (99); that is, they are differentiated from each other, and the one to whom they are given finds herself or himself within the whole. We are then led, Heidegger continues, to the following recognition: what gives beings as a whole cannot be a being, that is, something within the whole, and thus cannot be originally encountered as an object of thought. The totality of beings is, rather, presented in "the founding mode of attunement," which in "one way or another . . . determines us through and through" and "lets us find ourselves among beings as a whole" (100). In certain modes of attunement, our station among beings as such "irrupts" in experience. Heidegger mentions "genuine boredom" as one such occasion and "our joy in the presence . . . of a human being whom we love" as another (99). Nonetheless, attunement is "far from being merely incidental"; to the contrary, it is "the basic occurrence of our Da-sein" (100), even when we "cling . . . to our everyday preoccupations" (99), because it is the display or unconcealment of beings as a whole.

Attuned to the totality of beings means that human existence as Dasein "is in each case already beyond beings as a whole," including itself, or is essentially "transcending" (103). But what does it mean to transcend beings as a whole? "Da-sein means," Heidegger answers, "being held out into the nothing" (103). In other words, "the nothing makes possible the openedness of beings as such," and thus "the revelation of the nothing" belongs "essentially to Dasein" (104, 105). The mode of attunement with which "man is brought before the nothing itself" is "the fundamental mood of anxiety" (100), the sense of meaninglessness, wherein "all things and we ourselves sink into indifference," and "the receding of beings as a whole . . . oppresses us" (101). When this mood irrupts, "the nothing reveals itself," and "in the clear night of the nothing of anxiety the original openness of beings as such arises: that they are beings—and not nothing" (102, 103). The Nothing[2] "nihilates incessantly," even when we lose ourselves in everyday preoccupations. However "fragmented our everyday existence may appear to be, . . . it always deals with beings in a unity of a 'whole,' if only in a shadowy way" (99), and thus also deals with the Nothing. "The original anxiety in existence is usually repressed"; but "anxiety is there. It is only sleeping" (106). Given this recognition, "the old proposition *ex nihilo nihil fit* is . . . found to contain another sense . . . that runs: *ex nihilo omne ends qua ens fit* (From the nothing all beings as beings come to be)" (108).

This experience of the Nothing, then, is presupposed by all propositional understanding. If the understanding is a "no-saying," some affirmation is negated, and thus the negation depends on presentation of beings as a whole. But beings as a whole appear only by way of attunement to the Nothing. "The nothing is the origin of negation, not vice-versa" (105). Indeed, the negation of "no-saying" is also involved in propositional affirmation, in the sense that understanding a being means its presentation as "not anything else" in the whole. This is, I suggest, why Heidegger says: "The nothing nihilates incessantly without our really knowing of this occurrence in the manner of our everyday knowledge" (104). If this "origin" of understanding cannot be stated in a proposition without absurdity, so much the worse for traditional logic, which assumes the possibility of subject-object thought. "The idea of 'logic' itself disintegrates in the turbulence of a more original questioning" (105). In its most proper sense, "metaphysics is inquiry beyond or over beings, which aims to recover them as such and as a whole for our grasp" (106). But, then, "metaphysics is the basic occurrence of Dasein," its "being held out into the nothing" and, thereby, "surpassing beings as a whole" (109, 106). Hence, failure to question how thinking of beings is possible or to question the possibility of affirmation and negation results in a deficient mode of metaphysics that cannot account for understanding beings as a whole.

Metaphysics in its deficient sense, Heidegger also says, fails truly to ask about Being. In this deficient mode, metaphysical inquiry takes Being to mean the most general character of beings and thus assumes the presence of what is presented without asking how it can be present (see 1993, 432). But the latter is the metaphysical question in its original or proper sense. Thus, "What Is Metaphysics?" concludes, as Heidegger's *Introduction to Metaphysics* subsequently begins, with the question: "Why are there beings at all, and why not rather nothing?"

(110). On one reading, this question appears to ask why one of two conceivable alternatives—namely, the existence of things or complete nonexistence—is the case. That is the question Bede Rundle, as mentioned above, addresses. The demand for an explanation is, he argues, here misconceived because *"something* is always presupposed when existence is affirmed or denied" (Rundle, 117). Insofar, Heidegger agrees, because the question thereby treats the Nothing as a possible object of subject-object thought and remains within traditional metaphysics. Thereby, also, his point is missed. On Heidegger's intention, the question does not absurdly ask for why something is the case that cannot fail to be the case. Rather, "why" here asks what it means for something to be the case, that is, asks why beings can have meaning: why does Dasein find itself amidst a whole of beings—or, again, what difference does it make that there are beings rather than nothing?[3]

Understanding beings is, in other words, being-in-the-world, already engaged with beings by virtue of having a horizon of meaning or significance that constitutes beings as a totality. Our relations to particular beings, including the kind of relation involved in scientific cognition, presuppose this prior totality. "Heidegger's analysis shows," writes Karl-Otto Apel, "that the subject-object relation of scientific knowledge is always already embedded in the contextual structure of being-in-the-world as understanding the coherent significance of the world" (Apel 1998, 105). The question of Being, whatever else it includes, asks about the horizon, so that every understanding of beings depends on or discloses some understanding of Being. "Being is," as Richard Polt nicely says, "the difference it makes that there is something rather than nothing" (Polt, 3; emphasis deleted) and must be distinct from beings because anything within the totality presupposes a prior revelation or unconcealment of the whole. Being is what gives or makes beings a whole, and, in doing so, it differs from beings in the way a sense of significance differs from all things ordered by it.

In sum, we must speak of Dasein as attuned to the Nothing or "held out into the nothing" because Being and thus meaning are inseparable from negation of the whole. In *Being and Time*, Heidegger defines meaning in terms of understanding. "When entities within-the-world are discovered along with the Being of Dasein—that is, when they come to be understood—we say that they have *meaning*" (1962, 192). Moreover, understanding an entity involves Dasein having something as something, that is, having it in terms of its significance and, thereby, within the whole. "Meaning is the 'upon-which' of a projection in terms of which something becomes intelligible as something" (1962, 193; emphasis deleted). But Being is given, so that beings as a whole are understood, only by standing "beyond beings as a whole" and thus by way of negation of the whole. Wherever there is understanding and thus meaning, there is significance by way of negation and thus by way of the Nothing. In other words, some or other meaning of Being is present in all understanding—even if the meaning present may prevent reflection on the truth of Being.

But if Being is inseparable from the Nothing, the point is also that totality is inseparable from meaning. We may formulate Heidegger's account summarily as follows: *totality presupposes meaning*, even if it is also true that meaning presupposes totality. There can be no totality except as it has meaning; that is, beings as a whole presuppose understanding in, or as, the being of Dasein. Just as there is no Dasein without Being, so, too, there is no Being, no horizon of significance, without Dasein, whose transcendence into the Nothing is required for the revelation of beings as a whole. We can also say that Being and thus totality presuppose the temporality of Dasein, for which the future as possibilities opens the past and the present. If meaning is "the 'upon-which' of a projection," what is projected is Dasein's future for which beings are significant and by virtue of which Dasein's past becomes effective. Meaning and thus totality, in other words, are inseparable from Dasein's self-questioning because Dasein is always practically engaged; the horizon of significance is pragmatic or teleological. Dasein as held out into the Nothing *is* this engagement, and there is no totality without it because there is no totality without some or other meaning of Being.

Heidegger can say, "Being itself is essentially finite" (108), because Dasein's engagement is situated or historically conditioned. Dasein is "thrown" into existence with a horizon of understanding already given by its historicity. "Dasein itself occurs essentially as 'thrown.' It unfolds essentially in the throw of Being as the fateful sending" (1993, 231). As Richard Polt summarizes, "we are *historical*: we are rooted in a past and thrust into a future. We inherit a past tradition that we share with others, and we pursue future possibilities that define us as individuals. As we do so, the world opens up for us, and beings get understood; it makes a difference to us that there is something rather than nothing" (Polt, 5). If Dasein's essential temporality makes it "ahead of itself" in the sense of a project, it is "always already ahead of itself" because being-in-the-world means a historically inherited prestructure of understanding, and thus " 'world' does not . . . signify beings or any realm of beings but the openness of Being," that is, "the open region that clears the 'between' within which a 'relation' of subject to object can 'be' " (1993, 252). In writings subsequent to "What

Is Metaphysics?" especially his "Letter on Humanism," Heidegger speaks of Dasein as the being who "ek-sists"; being-in-the-world is "the ecstatic relation to the clearing of Being" (1993, 231), such that Being is "essentially broader than all beings, because it is the clearing itself" (1993, 240). If I understand correctly, the notion of a "clearing" captures the historically dependent revelation of totality.

Perhaps in *Being and Time*, Heidegger pursued a "fundamental ontology" in the sense that analysis of Dasein could explicate its abiding or transcendental character as original temporality, toward the end of asking about the abiding meaning of Being disclosed therein. If so, then this is the project that was never completed. Similarly, Heidegger's attempt in *Kant and the Problem of Metaphysics* to reinterpret Kant's transcendental analysis, such that original temporality constitutes time as a succession of "nows" for the representation of objects, was apparently abandoned (see Apel, 110). A transcendental or quasitranscendental analysis of Dasein is inconsistent with Heidegger's persistent affirmation, present already in *Being and Time*, that the being whose understanding totality presupposes is finite. Accordingly, his later writings consistently assert that "Being itself is essentially finite" or itself has a history because its unconcealment is inseparable from Dasein's historicity. Perhaps "What Is Metaphysics?" written soon after *Being and Time*, is a transitional essay, but its statement that "metaphysics is the basic occurrence of Dasein" (109) is best read in terms of how he later spoke of the meaning or truth of Being.

Heidegger himself counsels this reading in a "Postscript" to "What Is Metaphysics?" written several years later. He there calls us to "experience in Nothing the vastness of that which gives every being the warrant to be. That is Being-itself" (1949, 353). If I understand rightly, "the vastness" means that "Being-itself" is not equivalent to the horizon of significance within which the totality of beings is given but, rather, includes Being as concealed. In other words, experience of the Nothing belongs to the experience of Being because unconcealment is finite or historical. The Nothing reveals the Being of beings because "this 'Nothing' functions as Being" (1949, 353) or is the abysmal character of Being. Hence, *the* Being of beings, in the sense of something the same everywhere and always, is nowhere to be found; beings appear in a "clearing" that itself belongs to a given time, and "Being can be meaningful only if there are limits to its meaning, a boundary where Being verges on meaninglessness" (Polt, 124–25). For this reason, Heidegger can speak of a mysterious happening of Being and thus of an epoch in the history of Being, by which our very ability to understand and thus to give true and false answers to questions is entirely circumscribed.

The account of unconcealment as also concealment, as a clearing in the surrounding forest, provides the basis for Heidegger's indictment of metaphysics in Western thought. At least since Plato, the metaphysical project has belied the truth of Being by assuming that unconcealment is complete, an assumption that misrepresents even while it depends on an originating disclosure. This is the assumption with which Being means merely the most general features of all beings (or, if there are fundamentally different kinds of beings, means the systematic relation among the general features of these several kinds) so that Being is a constant presence independent of time or history. Typically, this meaning of Being is perfected in a supreme being from which all others are somehow derived, and Heidegger often calls such philosophy "ontotheology." Metaphysics in this sense "thinks the Being of beings. But it does not think the difference of both" (1993, 226); it "recognizes the clearing of Being either solely as the view of what is present in 'outward appearance' (*idea*) [as in Greek philosophy] or critically as what is seen as a result of categorial representation on the part of subjectivity [as in Kant]. This means that the truth of Being as the clearing itself remains concealed" (1993, 235). Correspondingly, the Nothing is misconceived as solely the absence of Being (see 107).

In either case, metaphysics effects a "general objectivization" of what is; that is, such thinking imposes on beings an "is-ness" independent of the history of understanding by abstracting beings from the horizon of practical engagement, the difference they make for finite Dasein. Encounter with the Nothing or the abyss of Being is forgotten. Accordingly, Dasein itself is objectified, and the hegemony of modern science and technology or the "enframing" of human life is the "destiny" of such thinking. "Without the original revelation of the nothing, [there is] no self-hood and no freedom" (103). While "What Is Metaphysics?" could assert that "metaphysics is the basic occurrence of Dasein" (109), Heidegger's later writings no longer seek a proper use of "metaphysics" and surrender the term to the traditional project that effects a "deworldling."

On Karl-Otto Apel's account, Heidegger "discovered the lifeworld," and, for him, it "assumes the role of ultimate bedrock" (1998, 140). Summarily stated, "the lifeworld" here means the historically emergent context of interpretation that constitutes the prestructure of understanding on which all understandings depend. Apel's formulation, then, says again that totality presupposes meaning, and therefore the meaning of Being presupposes the Nothing. Since there can be no totality without Dasein's understanding, beings can be given only by virtue of the context of meaning a lifeworld provides, and the meaning of Being depends on Dasein's being held out into the Nothing. This is not to deny that creative appropriation or transformation of the lifeworld, an unfolding of Being's destiny, even to the point of a new beginning, is possible. But historically evolving interpretations are nonetheless historically located. So far as I can see, the point is repeated when Heidegger calls language "the clearing-concealing advent of Being itself" (1993, 230) or "the house of Being and the home of human beings" (1993, 262). As these citations suggest, Heidegger understood language itself as an event of unconcealment, not simply an instrument of subject-object designation. And language itself is a historical emergent.

In any event, the finitude of Being means that understanding is historically circumscribed at least in this sense: there are no abiding or transcendental features of understanding and thus no necessary features of beings in view of which one's inheritance can be critically appropriated. To the contrary, Heidegger says that Dasein is appropriated through the historical disclosure of Being even as Being is appropriated by Dasein in "the event of Appropriation" (2002, 19). Seeking necessary features of beings or existence obscures the event of Appropriation because it obscures experience of the Nothing or the limits to meaning and thus perpetuates "the oblivion of Being." On my accounting, the notion that totality presupposes meaning and thus all understanding is circumscribed by its historicity summarizes the basis on which the widespread contemporary critique of universal reason is advanced, although one must add to the pervasive influence of Heidegger's achievement the similar influence of Wittgenstein, whose account of meaning in terms of a "form of life" and associated language games also, in its own way, made the lifeworld "ultimate bedrock" (see Apel 1998, 140). As is classical or Kantian metaphysics, the neoclassical project for which I argued earlier is said to be ill-conceived because all claims to meaning and truth supposedly independent of a specific context are inconsistent with the dependence of totality on meaning and thus the lifeworld dependence of human understanding.

But if Heidegger speaks of the Nothing because the unconcealment of Being is finite, we may ask about this supposed "ultimate bedrock." On its face, it appears to express an understanding whose meaning and truth concern all occasions of Dasein. Totality presupposes meaning must be the case for any and every situated being-in-the-world or wherever and whenever the event of Appropriation occurs. Still, this very understanding must be circumscribed by a thrown context of interpretation. If or insofar as *Being and Time* pursued the meaning of Being by way of a "fundamental ontology" of Dasein, Heidegger's later thought followed a *Kehre* after which the meaning or truth of Being became historical. But this turn, if that is what occurred, leaves the entire account dependent on a given disclosure or clearing in the history of Being.

The apparent problem in so relativizing the account can be reached by asking whether the meaning of Being can be consistently placed within time. If totality presupposes meaning because beings appear in a clearing dependent on Dasein's transcendence, how can revelation of the totality itself be a finite event within time? Such an event seems to require a prior notion of time as a succession of presents, but an understanding of temporal ordering in this sense itself depends on the work of Being and thus can only be within the totality. If meaning and truth depend on a thrown context of interpretation, to make the same point, then a happening of Being in distinction from its constant or necessary presence appears to make sense only within a given happening. But can this notion of happening itself have meaning without implying more than one such event, that is, without thinking of something constant to all possible thinking, even while the truth of that thought is circumscribed by a given disclosure?

It will not help to say that Being as unconcealed in other happenings is, within the given disclosure, the abyss of Being and thus is only encountered, whether in anxiety or some other mode of attunement. Saying this is still speaking about that encounter as occurring in all happenings. Even if one thinks only the concealment that is inseparable from unconcealment, in other words, one thinks nonetheless of an experience of Being common to all events of Appropriation, but the meaning and thus the truth of this thought, too, depends entirely on a given disclosure. If one then embraces this relativity, so that the very notion of an unconcealing/concealing event is circumscribed, one implies inconsistently the possibility of some other context of interpretation in which Being is revealed without concealment. Nor is the problem solved by saying that talk of Being as a finite event is, like speaking of the Nothing, using language beyond the subject-object form of thought and, in this sense, speaking of a truth that can only be evoked or experienced. It remains that saying *this* asserts the supposed distinction between truths admitting of subject-object expression and truths that do not have an object of thought, and the meaning of that distinction remains circumscribed by a given disclosure. So far as I can see, Heidegger's account is, in the end, pragmatically self-contradictory, exemplifying the very noncircumscribed understanding it speaks against. Apel makes the relevant point: "Whoever seriously speaks of the conceptual meaning of 'meaning' and 'truth' as being in the last instance dependent on events or fate—that is, [asserts] that the *logos* of our discursive claim to meaning and truth is in principle subordinate to time—thereby cancels the claim to the meaning and truth of their discourse" (1996, 178).

Since experience of the Nothing is required because totality presupposes meaning, we now have reason to doubt whether speaking of this experience expresses anything about understanding and, thereby, whether it poses a tenable objection to the argument for metaphysical necessity. If we accept this conclusion and, thereby, sustain the previous argument for metaphysics in the strict sense against Heidegger's account of the Nothing, we are also bound to conclude that *totality is prior to meaning*; that is, meaning presupposes but is not presupposed by totality. But having reached this point, we are left with a challenge presented by Heidegger's achievement. If totality is prior to meaning, and therefore thinking presupposes but is not presupposed by metaphysical necessity, how can we avoid ontotheology in the sense indicted by Heidegger or what has come to be called a "metaphysics of presence," that is, metaphysics that understands Being as constant presence and therefore objectivizes beings, separating them from the difference they make and thus, in the end, objectivizing Dasein?

We may also present this challenge in terms of the Nothing because, whether or not one accepts Heidegger's account, there is good reason to agree with him in this: understanding affirms by way of negation. To understand something, x, in distinction from merely being related to it or affected by it, is to differentiate or discriminate x from what it is not. To have something as something is to have it *as* nothing other than what it is: "x and nothing other than x" is, we can say, the content of an understanding of x—and, if x is a being, "nothing other than x" discriminates x from all others within a whole. Hence, every understanding presupposes an understanding of the whole. But how can the whole have a meaning or be understood without its discrimination from the Nothing or its revelation through encounter with "the complete negation of beings"? How, in other words, can totality be prior to meaning when all meaning (that is, all understanding) presupposes a *meaning* for (or understanding of) totality? This question presents again Heidegger's challenge because it asks how metaphysical necessity can be affirmed without presupposing, against itself, a historically emergent prestructure of understanding or horizon of meaning and thus a clearing/concealing event of Being. The following seeks to articulate a response to this challenge and will do so by first explicating neoclassical metaphysics further in order to show its twofold or systematically ambiguous character.

Totality Is Prior to Meaning

Although not with Heidegger's intention, metaphysics in the strict sense has always affirmed or implied that human beings cannot ask about Being without self-questioning, and this remains the case with the metaphysical task as Whitehead defines it. The maximally general characteristics of reality are, in the nature of the case, exemplified by the subject of understanding who seeks to explicate them. At least insofar, the question about existence as such is a question about the questioner. This recognition provides the context in which to clarify that "metaphysics" has a broad as well as a strict sense. As reviewed above, Kant denied the possibility of knowing general characteristics of all possible beings and redefined metaphysics to mean critical thought about the necessary conditions or characteristics of theoretical and practical reason, understood to be independent of metaphysics in the strict sense. If many subsequent philosophers have rejected the project in both senses, "metaphysics," as we noted at the outset, might be used to credit explication of both existence as such and subjectivity as such, that is, to designate critical reflection on the most general characteristics of possibility and, as a specification thereof, on the necessary conditions of subjectivity.[4]

The latter I will call metaphysics in the broad sense. In this formulation, I use "subjectivity" to mean the specification of existence as such that occurs with understanding or, as has been said, existence in the emphatic sense. Such metaphysics, then, differs from Kant's alternative because the former specifies metaphysics in the strict sense. Also, this specification is not—as is Kant's metaphysics, at least in its explication of theoretical reason—equated with *human* subjectivity. Distinctively human existence, where "human" designates the earthly species to which each of us belongs, does indeed exemplify subjectivity. But human life is not the only conceivable form of existence with understanding, and thus metaphysics in the broad sense reflects on human existence as such only in the respect that it exemplifies existence with understanding as such.

Given that metaphysics in the strict sense is possible, at least the following is a true metaphysical statement in the broad sense: existence with understanding exemplifies maximally general characteristics of reality. Naturally, subjectivity is not thereby different from any other specification of existence as such and is distinguished by also exemplifying understanding. Hence, the metaphysics of subjectivity is metaphysics in the broad sense because it includes but is not limited to metaphysics in the strict sense. For this reason, the former is also the inclusive sense. Metaphysics, we can say, is critical reflection on subjectivity as such and, as an aspect of this, on existence as such, so that "metaphysics" is a twofold or systematically ambiguous term. This last formulation is instructive because it more readily makes apparent that doing metaphysics is, for us, important or significant by virtue of its contribution to human life. As I will seek to show, there is every reason to endorse Heidegger's insistence that asking about Being is inseparable from the practical engagement of Dasein, and the present work will focus on the pragmatic character of metaphysics in the later discussion directed specifically to the metaphysics of purpose and of democracy.

But the twofold formulation of metaphysics is also instructive because it implies that necessarily true statements about existence also exhibit another kind of necessity that marks all true statements about subjectivity as such. As previously defined, metaphysics in the strict sense is critical reflection on what must be the case because something must exist; all true understandings of existence as such are implied by "something exists" and thus are necessary in the strict sense; that is, the denial of such an understanding is logically self-contradictory or meaningless and, thereby, not possibly true. Clearly, no statement about the existence of subjects has this character, since the nonexistence of subjects is possible or, to say the same, existence in the emphatic sense is contingent. Nonetheless, all true statements about subjectivity as such also share their own kind of necessity, which I, following common practice, will call pragmatic necessity.

A statement is pragmatically necessary when what it asserts is implied by every act of subjectivity. Hence, every subject who denies, explicitly or implicitly, what the statement asserts thereby engages in a pragmatic self-contradiction—implying in the act of denial what is denied. For instance, "some subject exists" is pragmatically necessary because every act of subjectivity implies the existence of the acting subject, and every subject who denies this assertion implies in the act of denial what is denied. "No subject exists" is, while possibly true, pragmatically self-contradictory. Similarly, all statements asserting that the character of subjectivity as such is exemplified are pragmatically necessary. If, for instance, subjects as such are bound by the moral law, then "something bound by the moral law exists" is pragmatically necessary, and every subject who denies this assertion implies in doing so that it is bound by the moral law and thus engages in a pragmatic self-contradiction.[5]

It follows that "something exists" is also pragmatically necessary; what it asserts is implied by every act of subjectivity. To be sure, this statement is, if the earlier reasoning is sound, also necessarily true, and "something exists" is metaphysical in the strict sense. Hence, true metaphysical statements in the strict sense are pragmatically necessary existential statements that are also necessarily true. Thereby, they share the pragmatic necessity of true statements about subjectivity as such, even while they are distinguished from other such statements by their own peculiar necessity, and the systematic ambiguity of "metaphysics" is represented, with its strict sense presented as an aspect of its broad sense. We may also say that metaphysics is transcendental reflection, where this use of "transcendental" has the same systematic ambiguity. Such reflection seeks critically to explicate statements about subjectivity that are pragmatically necessary and, as an aspect thereof, statements about existence that are necessarily true. Henceforth, I will use the name "neoclassical metaphysics" to designate transcendental reflection in this twofold sense.

"Totality is prior to meaning" is, in effect, itself a statement of the systematically ambiguous sense of "metaphysics" because the statement asserts that subjects of understanding are not exhausted by understanding. If understanding presupposes but is not presupposed by beings as a whole, then exemplifications of subjectivity are constituted by prior or nonconscious relations to an order of actualities and possibilities. In this formulation, "prior" does not mean temporally prior but, rather, prior in constituting the subject, such that understanding is a consciousness of these relations. Thus, subjects are *distinguished* by understanding; that is, something can be a subject only if it is also nonconsciously related to an order of actualities and possibilities to which the subject belongs, while something can be so related without also being a subject. Being a subject, then, presupposes but is not presupposed by one's being constituted as something by relations to an order of the whole—and, fully explicated, this repeats that existence with understanding specifies existence as such.

True metaphysical statements in the broad sense imply true metaphysical statements in the strict sense (because some of the former *are* true metaphysical statements in the strict sense and thus are implied by all others and imply themselves), but some true metaphysical statements in the broad sense are not implied by true metaphysical statements in the strict sense (because some of the former designate the distinctive character of existence with understanding). This formulation offers terms in which to restate the difference between "totality is prior to meaning" and "totality presupposes meaning," at least as Heidegger presents the latter in "What Is Metaphysics?" Redefining "metaphysics" to designate his own project, he writes: "Every metaphysical question always encompasses the whole range of metaphysical problems. Each question is itself always the whole" (1993, 93). The neoclassical project has every reason to agree that each question about metaphysical conditions in the strict sense encompasses the whole, because all true metaphysical statements in the strict sense are necessarily true and thus mutually implicative or coherent. Still, metaphysics in the strict sense does not encompass "the whole range of metaphysical problems," because the latter includes metaphysical problems in the broad sense, and some true statements about subjectivity as such are not implied by true statements about the possible as such. Thus, totality is prior to meaning. To all appearances, however, Heidegger does not distinguish the question of Being from the question of Dasein in this way. In each case, what one asks about implies the other; that is, Being depends on Dasein just as Dasein depends on Being. In other words, totality presupposes meaning, even if meaning also presupposes totality. On the present account, then, to endorse Heidegger's view is to engage in a pragmatic self-contradiction because every subject who so asserts thereby denies what its act of assertion implies, namely, its own *prior* participation in the totality as that which may be understood. Whitehead expresses the point in saying "consciousness presupposes experience, and not experience consciousness" (1978, 53).

We can now add the following: subjectivity as such presupposes not only this prior participation but also an understanding of the totality in which one participates, at least with respect to its most general character. All existence with understanding, in other words, includes an awareness of the necessary order of actualities and possibilities that metaphysics in the strict sense seeks to explicate. This must be the case because, as we previously agreed with Heidegger, understanding affirms by way of negation. To understand x, in distinction from merely being related to it, is to discriminate x from what it is not. To understand any particular being or specific possibility for beings is to discriminate it from everything else. For instance, to understand a particular rose one is perceiving as a rose and a flower is to mark it off (not only from all other roses or all other flowers but also) from all other actual things and all unexemplified possibilities as just this actual rose and strictly nothing else. The content of an understanding

The Metaphysics of Subjectivity 53

of x is, we can say, "x and nothing other than x" or "x in contrast with everything else." Where x is a particular being or specific possibility for being, this content is equivalent to "x and no other exemplification or specification of what is common to the possible as such" or "x in contrast with the possible as such and, thereby, with every other exemplification and specification of it." Thus, the metaphysical character of existence must be understood whenever any understanding at all occurs—and, if this is so, then "something that understands the possible as such exists" is also pragmatically necessary.

For Heidegger, on the reading of him given above, an awareness of totality can occur only because Dasein is held out into the Nothing. If having something as something means discrimination of it from all others within the whole, an understanding of the whole requires encounter with "the complete negation of the totality of beings" or requires a clearing of Being as the difference it makes that there are beings rather than nothing, and this is why totality presupposes meaning. But neoclassical metaphysics rejects his notion of the Nothing, even while such metaphysics asserts that understanding anything at all includes an awareness of totality. Hence, the challenge presented by our review of Heidegger, at least in one of its formulations, may be recalled: if not by way of the Nothing, how can the character of the possible as such be discriminated?

So far as I can see, the answer is this: the metaphysical character of existence is discriminated in contrast to all exemplifications and specifications of it. Where x designates the possible as such, "x and nothing other than x" means "x and not any particular being or specific possibility for beings." Perhaps this seems to imply that one could not discriminate this x without understanding all actual beings and all specific possibilities for beings completely. But that reading is mistaken. To effect the contrast of existence as such with all exemplifications and specifications, a subject needs only a fragmentary consciousness of actual beings and specific possibilities because, given an understanding of some, all other actual beings and specific possibilities are implied as simply other than those understood. This contrast is similar to understanding human individual as such, which does not require consciousness of all actual humans and specific human possibilities but, rather, can occur if a subject understands one or more human individuals because this implies the possiblity of others. Hence, "x and nothing other than x," where x designates the character of the possible as such, means "x and not these or any other particular being or specific possibility for beings." In sum, the negation by way of which discrimination occurs always effects a contrast with all else that is real, and this occurs in our awareness of existence as such because the object discriminated is the most general character of possibility in contrast with every particular or specific real thing.

This answer may seem unconvincing because, with it, the account of understanding appears to be viciously circular. If awareness of certain particular or specific real things must be understood to imply actual and possible others, awareness of the possible as such depends on understanding one's own understandings as fragmentary. But the latter is not possible without presupposing awareness of the possible as such. In order to discriminate the possible as such, in other words, a subject must recognize its other discriminations to be a fragment of the whole, even while that recognition cannot occur unless there is a simultaneous awareness of a larger whole. Thus, the account given must simply posit the very thing (that is, awareness of the possible as such) for which an account is required. In contrast, it might be said, Heidegger escapes this circularity by insisting on Dasein's encounter with the Nothing, by way of which the whole is given.

But the circle is vicious only if one ignores the premise, against Heidegger, that totality is prior to meaning. Given this premise, a subject, prior to understanding, belongs to the whole and thus is related to the possible as such even while fragmentarily related to actualities and specific possibilities. Prior to consciousness, in other words, the fragment a subject will understand is already given in an order defined by, whatever else it includes, its metaphysical character. As a consciousness of relations already given, understanding discriminates certain things and recognizes these discriminations as a fragment precisely because it marks them off from all others by discriminating simultaneously the metaphysical order they exemplify or specify, marking it off by contrast with all possible exemplifications and specifications. "The origin of negation," to speak in Heidegger's terms, is not the Nothing but, rather, the metaphysical plurality of beings, which does not depend on understanding but, rather, is prior to it.

Still, this conclusion implies that understanding cannot be in all respects dependent on the context of a lifeworld, and that implication, I expect, provides for many contemporary philosophers the most telling reason to reject transcendental metaphysics. For many who have taken the linguistic or hermeneutical turns to which Heidegger so profoundly contributed, understanding as such is constituted by participation in language or culture or the inherited interpretations of a lifeworld, in the sense that all understandings depend on learning.[6] Against this inescapable fact about the human condition, we are told, transcendental metaphysics implies the impossible presence of understanding that is prelinguistic or universally prior to all learning. If an understanding of possibility as such is metaphysical in the broad sense, then it must be present whenever any interpretation is inherited and thus cannot be circumscribed by the context of a given lifeworld.

But whether a prelinguistic or universal understanding is possible is precisely the question at issue in the discussion we have pursued with Heidegger. Once the critique of universal reason is called into question, the reassertion that all understanding depends on learning begs the question in the absence of other considerations that count against transcendental metaphysics. If the critique involves a pragmatic self-contradiction, as I have argued, this fact provides a negative reason for so interpreting understanding that its dependence on participation in language or a lifeworld is qualified. Still, neoclassical metaphysics cannot be convincing unless a positive account of this kind can be given. Such an account, we should note, need not deny the transparent importance of the linguistic and hermeneutical turns, and these may be reaffirmed, I propose, by insisting that understandings cannot be *explicit*, that is, clear or perspicuous to conscious attention in the sense required for the focus of a speech act, without being mediated by lifeworld concepts and symbols. But our understandings should not be so understood that they are exhausted by what is or has been our perspicuous attention to objects.

In the nature of the case, such attention is most apparent. Still, phenomenological reflection reveals that a focus of discrimination in any given moment is surrounded by a dim and elaborate background, some of which may be lifted into focus in a subsequent activity. "Even at its brightest," Whitehead writes, "there is [in our consciousness] a small focal region of clear illumination, and a large penumbral region of experience which tells of intense experience in dim apprehension" (1978, 267). The complexity of human understanding, then, cannot be appreciated without a distinction between explicit understandings, those in the foreground of attention, and a background of understandings that are implicit, where "implicit" here means "contained in the nature of something although not readily apparent" (American College Dictionary). Moreover, the background is required in order for the foreground to be what it is. Focus on what one is doing in, say, going to the polls on election day would be impossible without an effective background of understandings that include, to name only some, the organization of space and time, social arrangements, and political procedures—understandings that are not readily apparent during the activity in question.

This illustration cites background understandings that are themselves mediated by a lifeworld, and similarly, most of what is implicit in any given moment of awareness requires the individual's focused attention in some previous moment of consciousness. These understandings were once explicit or, at least, depend on certain previous learning—and are now implicitly remembered or included. One could not, for instance, enter the kitchen to prepare breakfast without having learned the properties of certain foods, the working of a stove, and so forth—to which understandings one no longer needs explicitly to attend. One could not comprehend a reading of Lincoln's Second Inaugural Address without an immensely complex education in American history, politics, religion, and so forth, that is not presently in focus. Indeed, as the last example makes especially clear, the more extensive the learned background one has available, the more extensive the possibilities for explicit understanding and the more profound one's focus on any given object. A thorough explication of how learning mediates an implicit context for whatever presently centers attention, including the acquisition of skills or capacities for control of or expression through one's body, is, I expect, a daunting task (see Searle 1983, 141f.; Habermas 1987, chapter 6).

For present purposes, however, the important point is this: The complexity of human consciousness does not entail that everything now implicitly understood is mediated by some inherited lifeworld—unless one assumes that totality presupposes meaning. If, to the contrary, consciousness depends on a prior participation in the whole of beings, then something always included in the latter may be always understood notwithstanding the absence of prior explicit representation—and understood because its discrimination is necessary to the discrimination of anything at all. To all appearances, we cannot become actual subjects without understanding something explicitly and thus without communication with other human individuals by way of which we participate in language. But it may also be true that no such understanding could emerge unless simultaneously attended by an implicit understanding of totality, even if the latter cannot become explicit in a given subject without substantial further mediation by language. This inescapable implicit understanding qualifies our dependence on a lifeworld, occasions the pragmatic self-contradiction in the critique of universal reason, and makes transcendental metaphysics possible.

Given existence with understanding, then, metaphysical necessity implies not only the priority of totality to meaning but also the priority of an implicit understanding of totality to any explicit understanding thereof. If understanding presupposes but is not presupposed by nonconscious relations to an order of actualities and possibilities, so, too, explicit understandings of totality presuppose and are not presupposed by an implicit understanding thereof. Because explicit understandings are constituted by lifeworld concepts and symbols, it may be thoroughly appropriate to say that metaphysics, as it critically asks about and thus seeks explicitly to understand the possible as such, has a history. But this cannot be the history of Being, if that means a history of how beings as a whole are given. To the contrary, existence as such is given the same everywhere and always, and the history of critical reflection on it can only be the course of attempts to make fully explicit an implicit understanding of beings as such that constitutes subjects as such and thus is the condition of any and all history.

Nothing in what has been said denies the fallibility of any metaphysical proposal within this history, precisely because any such scheme claims to make explicit an understanding that is originally implicit. What has been defended, rather, is pursuit of metaphysics in the strict sense and thus the method of "speculative philosophy" Whitehead formulates, at least on the reading of him given above: the possible as such can be the object of critical reflection, and statements claiming to designate its character are properly assessed by the criteria of coherence and adequacy, where each criterion implies the other. Nor does the affirmation of this universally implicit understanding compromise the refusal of any claim to metaphysical finality or completeness, which is, indeed, another way to say that metaphysics has a history. For this reason, engaging the metaphysical task as Whitehead defines it typically involves critical assessment of inherited alternatives and, in relation to them, pursuit of a constructive contribution. Still, it follows that any given lifeworld must include concepts and symbols, or the potential for concepts and symbols, in terms of which existence as such can be explicitly represented. Hence, understandings of Being or the ultimate nature of things that occur in terms of differing lifeworlds can be in principle, however difficult in fact, sufficiently translated each into the others to permit common discourse about their meaning and validity—since finally they are all speaking about an understanding common to subjects as such. The truth of true metaphysical statements about existence is, we can say, realistic; that is, their truth conditions are independent of any given system of symbols for interpretation because those conditions are given in the prelinguistic understanding presupposed by all interpretations.

For all that has been said, however, some may yet insist that we have not met the challenge posed by Heidegger's achievement. On this challenge, metaphysics in the strict sense can only be a "metaphysics of presence" and thus cannot avoid ontotheology in the sense indicted by Heidegger: Being is understood as a constant presence, which effects the "oblivion" of Being by objectivizing beings, separating them from the difference they make and thus from the temporality of Dasein, its self-questioning in the sense of practical engagement. While nothing less than a systematic metaphysics will fully answer this objection, it involves, at least to first appearances, a non sequitur. The explication of existence as such is a metaphysics of presence only if the maximally general features explicated do not include temporality in the relevant sense. We may grant that Western philosophy has often been, at best, equivocal with respect to temporality, at least insofar as the difference between what is incapable and what is capable of change has been taken to distinguish the eminent being or kind of being from lesser beings. Given that time is inseparable from change, traditional metaphysics may well be ontotheological in the sense that eminent being conceived as completely changeless is inconsistent with the final significance of practical engagement or the inseparability of understanding from the difference beings make. At least to first appearances, however, it is fallacious to assume that metaphysics in the strict sense requires the eminence of what cannot change.

Indeed, understanding may be inseparable from temporality because beings as such are characterized by relations to the past as actual and the future as possible. Dasein's original temporality is, we might say, the original temporality of beings as such when it is specified by subjectivity, and "something temporal exists" is both pragmatically necessary and necessarily true. With Heidegger, then, meaning is "the 'upon-which' of a projection," namely, a projection of Dasein into the future, for which beings are significant and in relation to which Dasein's past becomes effective—and, for this reason, meaning is inseparable from a subject's practical engagement; that is, the horizon of significance for possible encountering of beings is teleological. But nothing in this account of subjectivity requires that totality presupposes meaning. To the contrary, the temporality of actualities and possibilities is prior to meaning, and the latter occurs when subjects exemplify the former. Every subject's projection into the future, we might say, includes an implicit understanding of the teleological character of beings as such without which no other meaning or understanding is possible. As subsequent chapters of this work will seek to explicate, just this account is implied by "something exists" and thus belongs to an adequate and coherent metaphysics.

Chapter 3

The Metaphysics of God and the World

Final Real Things

Denying that completely negative existential statements are possibly true, neoclassical metaphysics affirms that some set or scheme of positive ideas or necessarily true statements defines the character of existence or the possible as such. This part of our discussion will attempt to outline such a scheme. The overall conception is not original. It will be apparent to anyone familiar with the work of Alfred North Whitehead and Charles Hartshorne that the neoclassical view here presented is deeply dependent on both. I will not seek extensively to cite them in support of formulations offered nor to credit them for specific ideas introduced. My purpose here is to develop a metaphysical outline indebted to them. The term "outline" might be underscored. Nothing approaching a more or less complete metaphysics of existence will be offered, even while I hope to say enough that a basis for discussing the metaphysics of human purpose will be in place. Still, this neoclassical understanding will not be simply asserted. Special attention is given here to metaphysical necessity. In all essentials, the formulations offered will be defended as consistent with the transcendental character of metaphysics in the strict sense, whereby its statements articulate what must be the case because "something exists" is necessarily true.

From the affirmation that true metaphysical statements in the strict sense are all necessarily true and thus mutually implicative, it follows that there must be one kind of final real thing or one kind of metaphysically final thing, in the exemplifications of which existence as such is actualized. Because true metaphysical statements are coherent, anything to which any such statement applies must be, in some or other way, something to which all such statements apply. If "something exists" implies "something that is y exists" and "something that is z exists," then y and z are exemplified whenever and wherever something exists. For instance, if "something exists" implies "something that is temporal exists" and "something related to other things exists," then being temporal and being related to other things are always and everywhere exemplified. Accordingly, y, z, and any other features whose exemplification is necessary together define one kind of exemplification—and it is final in the sense that anything else conceivably called real is an aspect of one or more things of this kind or is an aggregate of them. Noting this repeats the earlier conclusion that a true metaphysical scheme explicates the single character of the possible as such. At least if read through the transcendental task, the Western metaphysical tradition has proposed various terms to designate such metaphysically final things, for instance, "substances," "atoms," or "monads"—although, naturally, each of these terms is typically used with some or other metaphysical content. Whitehead makes the point by formulating "the ontological principle," which asserts that "the final facts are, all alike, actual entities" (1978, 18), and I will simply call them actualities. For Whitehead, we can say, the ontological principle states substantively what the criterion of coherence states methodologically, and, in the end, the metaphysical task is nothing other than to explicate the necessary character of an actuality.

Actualities are, then, the metaphysically concrete singulars, and all other real things are either aggregates of such singulars (and, in that sense, also actual or concrete) or abstracts. An abstract is a possibility, a feature or characteristic, that two or more actualities may exemplify, and I will also call such possibilities indeterminates. Affirming abstracts as a metaphysical kind of entity is, I recognize, contrary to what at least some forms of nominalism may assert, and I will argue presently for the reality of indeterminates. Focusing here on concrete singulars, I judge that metaphysical discussion too often proceeds as if we have prior clarity about or can point to examples of them, so that our task is to give these examples a coherent interpretation. Premodern thought often took human beings, other animals, plants, and so forth to be unquestioned instances of the basic realities. Modern thought has often taken for granted that atoms or atomic elements or more fundamental particles are the basic units of the universe. But metaphysics seeks to explicate the most general abstract, the universal character of all actualities, and thus the possible as such. Hence, the task is not only to describe but also to discover what is finally real—or, to say the same, understanding the character of metaphysically final things is also understanding what counts as such a thing.

In neoclassical metaphysics, the idea of an actuality occupies the conceptual space given to the idea of a substance (that is, primary substance) in the thought of Aristotle and Aquinas. It may be useful here to compare the typical examples of both concepts. Examples of substances cited by Aristotle or Aquinas are typically things characterized by accidental change over time, for instance, individuals of a living species, and these are, for neoclassical thought, what I will later discuss as societies or aggregates of many actualities. In contrast, actualities are, at least typically, micro-occurrences, such that change is the transition from one or more actualities to another or others. Conceptually, however, the all-important difference between this idea of an actuality and the classical notion of a substance is this: there is no equivocity in the former, as there is, at least on some readings, in Aristotle's distinction between movable and immovable substances and Aquinas's distinction between material and immaterial beings. If the final facts are, all alike, actualities, they are also actualities of the same kind, to be characterized in univocal terms. By implication, then, metaphysical dualism is untenable, where "dualism" here means any proposal on which existence as such consists of two (or more) different kinds of final real things. For instance, Western metaphysics has long been haunted by the view that physical and nonphysical substances are two different kinds of metaphysically final things.

For Bede Rundle, as previously mentioned, "if anything exists, matter does" because only matter has "the necessary independent existence," such that anything else that does or might exist is inseparable from "material substance" (Rundle, 109, 166, 130), and this might be read to mean that "material substance" is the only kind of final real thing. This appearance seems confirmed when he argues that "mind" does not "name . . . a substance" because a mind is not "a disembodied being" (152) and thus there are no immaterial beings. Still, he also speaks of matter as "unthinking matter" (153), even "blind, unthinking matter" (130), and this provokes the question of whether these two kinds of "material substance," the unthinking and the thinking kind, are in the end two metaphysically different kinds of matter and thus of final real things. That implication can be avoided only if some more general meaning of "matter" allows unthinking and thinking specifications. I am not clear how Rundle intends to be understood. But if, as I suspect, he does not avoid metaphysical dualism, this might help to explain why his commitment to the logical necessity of "something exists" nonetheless leaves the implications of this statement rather thin.

Be that as it may, no metaphysical dualism can be coherent because it implies that each kind of final real thing can be designated by completely negating the other. Since they are metaphysically different, the two (or more) kinds have nothing in common, so that each is, in all respects, not the other (or others). Nonphysical substance, for instance, is properly designated by the complete negation of whatever characterizes physical substance as such. Contrary to the conclusion reached earlier, then, "x exists," where x is a completely negative grammatical subject, is possibly true. Another way to state the point is this: in asserting more than one kind of final real thing, dualism implies that all existents in fact may belong to only one of these kinds. If nonphysical things are defined by complete negation of physical things, for instance, presence of the latter does not imply presence of the former, and, in fact, all existents may be physical. But, then, the difference between kinds cannot explicate what must be the case because "something exists" is necessarily true, since the characteristics so explicated can never fail to be exemplified. A metaphysically dualistic difference, in other words, is not coherent in the emphatic sense. Conversely, were designation by complete negation possible, explication of existence as such would be impossible because there would be no way to determine how many kinds of final real things there are or could be. Not only would Kant's notion of "noumena" make sense, but also Kant could not tell us how many metaphysically final kinds of noumena are possible.

In Western metaphysics, the dualistic alternative has sometimes been countered by metaphysical monism, for which there is only one final real thing (not one kind of thing but, rather, a single final real thing), of which everything else we might properly call real is an aspect. Spinoza's argument for a single substance is a clear example. Indeed, if the notion of God or eminent reality as completely eternal has, in many expressions, dualistic implications, it also easily leads to monism. A completely eternal and thus necessary reality from which all else is somehow derived appears to imply that all is eternal and necessary. In any event, monism is equally untenable because the single final real thing must be in all respects changeless. Change would mean a new thing, something different, and a single final real thing does not allow anything else. In other words, the sole final thing *must be* conceived as completely eternal and necessary and thus can be designated only by negation. Monism asserts, in effect, that what must be the case because the complete absence of existence is impossible can itself be designated only by "nothing exists."

The metaphysical necessity of something, then, entails more than one actuality—or, as I will say, a plurality of final real things. Because true metaphysical statements are coherent, the plurality must be implied by the character of any one; that is, a given actuality must implicate others. This means that any given concrete singular must be internally related to other such things. Here, a relation is internal if it constitutes in part the actuality in question; were the relation absent, the actuality would not be what it is. In contrast, an external relation does not constitute the term. On an asymmetrical view of temporal relations, for instance, a present memory is internally related to the remembered event or experience, while that past event or experience is not changed by its now being remembered. Unless every actuality is internally related to others, the metaphysical necessity of something cannot entail metaphysical plurality.

Moreover, an actuality must be entirely constituted by its internal relations. Remove all of the colors from a painting and, typically, there remains the canvass on which they were set. But there cannot be a something to which an actuality's relations belong and that remains to be designated once analysis abstracts from them. In this sense, there cannot be a "substance" beyond the "accidents" of a final real thing, for the following reason: a substance of that kind would *not* be constituted by relations to actual or possible others, and thus its reality would not imply the plurality of final real things. In other words, the notion of something independent of internal relations that somehow has relations introduces incoherence into a metaphysical scheme because, were there any such reality, there would be no necessity that there be any other one; that is, monism could be, in fact, true. It then follows that "substance" in this sense is not relevantly different from a completely negative grammatical subject, having no designation beyond "not constituted by relations to others."

To be sure, an actuality cannot be a single thing and thus distinguished from other final real things unless something is constituted by the relations to others. Since this cannot be something that remains once analysis abstracts from them, those relations can only constitute singularity because they are somehow unified. What has internal relations is, in other words, the unification of them. Clearly, an actuality cannot be constituted by a single relation, since there would then be no difference between the two terms. Rather, each of multiple internal relations constitutes their unity in part, and thus each relation becomes in some respect what it is only by virtue of the unification. This means that no actual or possible other can completely determine a given actuality's relation to it, since it would thereby determine how its effect is unified with other effects and thus, absurdly, have an effect greater than its effect. If x is a concrete singular constituted by relations to y and z, then x unifies the effects of y and z, and neither y nor z can effect what is more than its effect.[1] "Causal explanation," Hartshorne writes, "is incurably pluralistic: on the basis of many . . . events, it has to explain a single . . . event or experience. It is, then, simple logic that something is missed by the causal account" (Hartshorne 1970, 2).

Concrete singularity requires, in other words, some measure of self-determination or self-creation by the actuality in question. The metaphysical necessity of something entails that complete determination of any final real thing by others is impossible. Decision, we may say, is a feature of actualities as such. On this formulation, "decision" does not imply consciousness. With Whitehead, "the word is used in its root sense of a 'cutting off' " (1978, 43); that is, actualization is by way of cutting off within or among the possibilities for unification. The self-creation of actualities is what introduces contingency into the nature of things. Although decision as such is a maximally general and thus itself a necessary feature, the outcome of any given decision within or among possibilities cannot be necessitated by anything else. It may be useful to stress the focus here on final real things or concrete singulars, whose full character is still being pursued. Hence, we should not assume ready familiarity with examples of them and conclude, for instance, that stones or trees or other usual things of experience are self-determining. To the contrary, as subsequent discussion will show, such things are typically spatio-temporal aggregates of actualities, such that self-determination occurs in the latter. Still, every feature or condition of reality that is contingent can only be the consequence of one or more decisions through which actualization occurs, and in this sense, we may say, with Whitehead: "Actual entities are the only *reasons*; so that to search for a reason is to search for one or more actual entities" (1978, 24).

We can also say that every final real thing is characterized by internality, in the sense exemplified by sentience in many animals and by the subjectivity of distinctively human existence—or the sense expressed when we speak of something as "for-itself" and not solely "in-itself." Because the object of any given relation is different from how that relation constitutes the concrete singular, the unification having the relations is distinct by virtue of its internal particularity. This does not gainsay that an actuality is also other-determined. If a relation is in some respect what it is by virtue of the unification, it is also what it is by virtue of its object, and thus a concrete singular is determined by its relations to other actualities. In other words, an actuality unifies itself within the limits of possibility determined by its objects and is, as Whitehead says, the consequence of both efficient and final causation (see 1978, 84). But if final causation is metaphysical, efficient causation may nonetheless be largely determining, such that nothing said here is inconsistent with the lawlike regularities among things or events by which our world or most of it is, in fact, characterized. Metaphysically speaking, the relative significance of final causation for differing actualities is variable, and the possibility for self-determination may extend from trivial to unimaginably profound. The measure of self-determination present in any given actuality is, in other words, contingent, and the variation is exemplified by the range found in our known world from existents in which other-determination is overwhelming to human life in which self-creation is prominent.

It now follows that self-determination requires a distinction within the things to which a given actuality relates: some are fully determinate and thus other actualities or concrete singulars, but others are indeterminate or merely possibilities for actualization. Necessarily, an actuality relates to other actualities. Relations to indeterminates alone could not account for particularity, and thus unification becomes something determinate only because it relates to other determinates. The given actuality, we can say, reenacts at least in part their particular internalities, the reenactments being different only insofar as the new unification requires—and thereby other actualities are efficient causes of the one in question. But the objects to which a final real thing relates cannot be exhausted by fully determinate things, else there could be no final causation. Hence, some relations of a new unification must be to mere possibilities, for whose actualizations it becomes an object. Clearly, the actualizations for which it becomes an object cannot be the actualities it reenacts, because reenactment requires that its objects be fully determinate. Thus, the final causation of a given actuality, we can say, causes it to become an efficient cause of what cannot be an efficient cause of it. Here, then, is the metaphysical reason for affirming the reality of indeterminates and for why nominalism, in any sense that denies the reality of abstracts, is untenable. Decision, we may say, is not only "decision to," that is, to become a determinate thing, but also thereby "decision for," that is, to become an object for other actualizations. Speaking metaphorically, we may also say that every actuality is both a self-determination and a self-expression, and in this sense, every actuality is pragmatic.

Setting aside for the moment the distinctive character of divine actualities and the relations between God and the world, to be discussed presently, this difference between others that help to determine a given actuality and others that it helps to determine is the metaphysical meaning of time. The past consists of others reenacted by the actuality in question, and the future consists of mere possibilities, for whose actualizations the given unification becomes an object of reenactment. The present, then, is the given unification—and, when exemplified by existence with understanding, is original temporality as Heidegger, unless I misunderstand him, describes it. If meaning is a projection of Dasein's future, for which beings are significant and by virtue of which Dasein's past becomes effective, a final real thing is a unification for the future, in which the past is effective through reenactment. But the original temporality of subjects is a specification of concrete singularity as such, and thus time as a succession of presents is not dependent on Dasein's projection, that is, on meaning. Rather, time in this latter sense is the difference constitutive of any final real thing between others that determine it and others to be determined by it, where each of the others was or is to be constituted by the same difference. That others are given in this temporal order is a necessary characteristic and thus prior to any contingent feature of an actuality. Thus, the metaphysical order of actual and possible things is prior to meaning, and meaning occurs in a concrete singular when it is characterized by understanding.

Temporal order as a succession of presents is, then, an abstraction from the concrete temporality of actualities, each relating to determinate others in its past and to possibilities for others in its future. It follows that temporal extension is infinitely divisible only as an abstraction. Were temporal extension concretely divisible in this way, a successor in the sequence would not be a finite addition; hence, the succession of final real things would not be extended, and the differences among determinate others, the given actuality, and indeterminate others would not be real. It also follows that concrete unifying is not itself temporal, that is, cannot be chronologically divided. Time as a succession of presents can only be a succession of actualities. But an indivisible actuality, considered in terms of time as an abstraction, occupies "all at once" some finite extension, even if, by an everyday measure of time, that extension is especially brief. Actual time, we might say, occurs as a succession of finite units, not instantaneous points. The metaphysical character of each such unit is eminently captured in Whitehead's summary description of a final real thing: "The many become one, and are increased by one" (1978, 21)—and, accordingly, we may also call actualities becomings. As Whitehead also writes, each "arises as an effect facing its past and ends as a cause facing its future" (1961, 194). Relations to the past are unified as a condition of the future.[2]

Because it is different from all others, a given actuality includes a particular past that is different from that of any other. It might be thought that two or more actualities each inclusive of the same particular past could be different because their decisions differ. But decisions cannot be determined, and thus the two or more could also be identical—and it is impossible that two different things so much as could be identical. Whatever else defines the uniqueness of an actuality, the particular past it includes is unique to it, this being a necessary condition of its distinct singularity. For this reason, at least some actualities are fragmentary; that is, inclusion of the past is only partial, although the extent to which others are reenacted may vary depending on contingent circumstances. Were fragmentariness not exemplified, existence as such would consist entirely of all-inclusive actualities. Moreover, no two of these actualities could be copresent or be contemporaries because, having the same past, they would be identical.[3] Hence, existence as such would be a solely temporal sequence of actualities, each of which includes the past in its entirety. But this is impossible because that circumstance would not allow any given actuality to be different from its immediate predecessor, there being nothing other than the all-inclusive predecessor with which its relations might be unified.

I will subsequently argue that existence as such implies a sequence of actualities whose relations to the past are all-inclusive. But if this divine sequence, as I will call it, exists, it requires fragmentary others by virtue of which it becomes a temporal order of differing occurrences. The reality of God, in other words, implies the reality of a world, just as, or so I will argue, the latter implies the former. Moreover, the fragmentary actualities cannot be ordered in a solely temporal sequence because, were that the case, there would be no metaphysical reason for fragmentariness, that is, nothing to prevent each actuality from relating all-inclusively to its predecessor.[4] In other words, there would be no metaphysical reason for a difference between the worldly sequence and the divine sequence. Fragmentariness, as far as I can see, requires limitation by others also present, such that each of many contemporary actualities is spatially located; that is, fragmentary actualizations are the metaphysical meaning of space.

Given that we still leave aside the divine sequence and relations between God and the world, the relations of an actuality both to other actualities and to possibilities for actualization constitute a temporal-spatial order of extension defined relative to the actuality in question. Determinate others have actualized this extensive order, which insofar consists in a fully concrete or fully particular set of past loci. The future for which the given actuality decides is extended as merely possible and thus exclusive of any particular loci. Those contemporary actualizations by which space is defined are also, for the given actuality, mere possibilities. This is because they are not, so far as the actuality in question is concerned, fully determinate, and a becoming cannot reenact another unless the latter has achieved unification. To suppose otherwise is to imply that some partial internality of a concrete whole (that is, the contemporary upon full determination) can be, in effect, independent of the whole (that is, reenacted prior to full determination). Still, if both future and contemporary worlds are, for a given actuality, indeterminate, this does not prevent a distinction between the two: although future possibilities cannot be reenacted by it, the given actuality will be reenacted by the future when future possibilities are actualized; in contrast, the spatial present consists of possibilities whose actualization neither is reenacted by nor ever will reenact the actuality in question.

To some, the relativity of temporal-spatial extension to a given actuality may suggest that apparent differences between past and future and thus processes of becoming and change cannot be objectively true but, rather, must be "illusions" of perspective. Objective truth cannot be relative to perspective; hence, the objective reality of space-time is such that nothing within it becomes or changes. This is John Post's conclusion and his reason for saying that objectively true sentences must be "invariant"; that is, they are "eternal sentences" (Post, 67–70). To be sure, the relativity in question is, for him, itself metaphysical in this sense: *that* the differences among past, present, and future are relative is itself nonrelative, and therefore a sentence expressing these differences as the perspective of a given actuality is objectively true. Still, if I understand Post correctly, becoming or change could itself be objectively true only if there is some nonperspectival difference between what is determinate and what is indeterminate, and this is precisely what the relativity of temporal-spatial extension precludes. In other words, the differing perspectives must be themselves compared or included within an all-encompassing order if each is to be an aspect of objective truth, and, for Post, the all-encompassing order can only be one in which all truth is eternally true, so that becoming and change are illusions.

So far as I can see, the assertion that all objectively true sentences are eternal sentences or, as others have said, are timelessly true is profoundly problematic because it requires the view that objectively true existential statements are either all necessarily true or all contingently true. Here, "contingently true" means "true but not necessarily true"; that is, the denial of a contingently true statement is not self-contradictory or meaningless. If Post allows that one or more objectively true existential statements are logically necessary, there seems no way except by stipulation for him to distinguish others as logically contingent. All alike are eternal sentences, and thus the distinction seems precluded by the complete absence of objective change. I will here assume that all objectively true existential statements cannot be necessarily true, because that account implies monism in the sense previously criticized. It is to the point, then, that all objectively true existential statements are, on Post's view, logically contingent (see Post, 98–106). But this implies, against the conclusion reached above, that "something exists" is contingently true and, therefore, "nothing exists" is possibly true.[5]

I will not further pursue the conversation with Post because I wish to affirm, with him, the following: relativity of temporal-spatial extension is consistent with the objective reality of becoming or change only if the differing perspectives are themselves compared or included within an all-encompassing order. But, then, Post's conclusion involves a non sequitur if, as I will subsequently argue, there is an all-encompassing order of change constituted by a divine sequence of actualities. The point will be that both God and the world are implied by the metaphysical necessity that there is something, that is, by a coherent and adequate metaphysics.

If the reasoning to this point has been successful, the fact that "nothing exists" is not possibly true entails that "some actualities occur" is necessarily true, and any possibly true existential statement is finally about actualities—those that did or might have, or do, or will or may become. The character of this becoming implies that change is a kind of difference between or among actualities; that is, an actuality itself cannot change. This follows because self-determination or decision determines a whole, the unification of relations, and nothing about a determinate whole can be altered without effecting a different whole. To be sure, we may call the unifying, the many becoming one, a process. But process in this sense should be distinguished from change, at least if change means that an actual difference in something has occurred—for instance, a plant grows, an animal travels, a person ages. As the process of becoming occurs, there is no "something" that can change. Hence, if becoming and change are both designated by the term "process," doing so involves a systematic ambiguity. Speaking of two or more actualities together, one may say that something is in process, but the metaphysically fundamental fact is that process is *in* the final somethings; that is, each actuality is a process of becoming a final real thing by way of decision.

Something that changes, then, must be something other than an actuality. If plants grow and animals travel and persons age, explication of these changes in any given case requires designation of several actualities. Those who take Whitehead as a principal resource typically speak of "societies" of actualities. A society is a temporally extended aggregate distinguished because its member actualities all (a) exemplify the same identifying characteristic or complex set of characteristics and (b) do so (at least if the society is not defined solely by metaphysical characteristics) genetically; that is, later members of the society are so characterized because they reenact and thus are determined by earlier ones. No such identifying characteristic, given that we exclude metaphysical features, can be timeless. If not necessary to all final real things, any such characteristic is a contingent abstract or feature. But all contingent aspects of reality depend on the decision of an actuality or the decisions of two or more actualities, and nothing dependent on a given decision or decisions can be timeless.[6] Strictly speaking, then, genetically enduring characteristics by which a contingent society is identified cannot be fully explicated without pointing to the actuality or actualities from which, and thus the thoroughly particular context in which, the society emerged—just as a human person cannot be identified without pointing to her or his birth and thus to her or his particular parents. In other words, an identifying characteristic is or includes "relation to x," where x is a given actuality or set of actualities.

In speaking of things that exist, we typically designate societies rather than actualities. For instance, a given plant or animal or person exists. Clarity is served, I judge, by retaining this usage, at least in the sense that actualities do not exist but, rather, occur. To say that something exists, then, is typically to say that some society and thus its identifying characteristic is presently actualized in the occurrence of one or more actualities. By extension, to say "x exists," where x designates a given feature or set of features (for instance, "courage exists" or "freedom exists") is to say that this feature or set of features is presently exemplified in one or more actualities.[7] On this usage, to speak of existence as such is equivalent to speaking of the possible as such, and both are equivalent to speaking of actuality as such or reality as such, because any one of these terms designates the necessary features exemplified whenever and wherever any other feature is exemplified in one or more actualities—and, for this reason, I have and will continue to use the several terms interchangeably in speaking of what metaphysics in the strict sense seeks to explicate.[8]

It remains, then, to distinguish between (a) societies in which no two-member actualities are contemporary (that is, all of the members are sequentially or serially ordered) and (b) societies in which some members are contemporaries of others. The former are individuals, and the latter are nonindividual societies. The metaphysical character of actualities sets no limits on the possible complexity of contingent societies, that is, of the identifying characteristics that may be actualized. Also, societies may have subsocieties, some of which may be individuals. Perhaps this is the case in a world where macroscopic things are composed of microscopic particles, with each particle being an individual subsociety.

A human being is an immensely complex society of societies of societies, distinguished from other kinds of living things known to us because it includes an individual whose member actualities occur (or, at least, there is the potential for member actualities that occur) with extensive understanding. Perhaps some other higher animals also live with at least rudimentary understanding. Still, humans are distinguished among worldly beings known to us by including an individual that is or has the potential to understand in comparatively dramatic measure. An individual exists in the emphatic sense, we may say, when its member actualities exemplify understanding, although this does not deny that its existence may well depend on inclusion within a society of societies of societies; to all appearances, a human individual's existence depends on relations to its body, most immediately to its brain. Decisions of human purpose occur with understanding, and it will be important at a later point in this work to interpret understanding as characterizing the interiority of certain actualities. But I will not further pursue distinctively human existence until having first discussed the consequences of this neoclassical metaphysics for philosophical theism.

The Divine Individual

If actualities are the final real things, then all metaphysical differences among real things (whether final real things or not) must be, in accord with metaphysical necessity, self-differentiations of actuality as such. Indeed, the previous discussion already articulated one such self-differentiation: actuality as such implies a difference between relations to actualities, on the one hand, and relations to mere possibilities, on the other. Because the differentiations are self-differentiations, they do not violate the mutual implication of all true metaphysical concepts or statements. To the contrary, self-differentiations imply each other because they imply and are implied by what is differentiated. In the example given, "actuality" implies two other concepts designating the two kinds of relations and thus two aspects of all actualities, such that the concept of each aspect implies and is implied by the concept of the other because each implies and is implied by the concept "actuality." Hence, we may speak either of self-differentiations in the metaphysical character of things (for instance, in actuality as such or in other characteristics it implies) or of self-differentiations in metaphysical concepts (for instance, in "actuality").

In addition, actuality as such is, at least to first appearances, self-differentiating because it implies two kinds of concrete singulars. Unification of relations to other things implies two possible exemplifications, namely, unification of relations to some other things and unification of relations to all other things—or, in the terms noted above, the metaphysical characterization of a final real thing implies a distinction between fragmentary relativity, on the one hand, and all-inclusive relativity, on the other. Unless the concept of an all-inclusive relativity is meaningless, the differentiation follows simply because "some x" implies "all x," and vice versa. To be sure, one may object that "all-inclusive relativity" *is* meaningless, and I will turn to such objections shortly. If, for the moment, we accept the concept, the metaphysical character of this differentiation means that every exemplification of fragmentary relativity implies one or more exemplifications of all-inclusive relativity, and vice versa, just as there can be no relations to a determinate past without relations to an indeterminate future, and vice versa. In other words, fragmentary actualities must include relation to one or more all-inclusive concrete singulars, and each of the latter must include relations to fragmentary ones.

The distinction between fragmentary and all-inclusive relativity might seem to entail merely the possibility, not the exemplification, of each, whereby the realm of actual things must include the one or the other but not necessarily both. But this proposal neglects the metaphysical character of the difference. It is a self-differentiation of "the many become one, and are increased by one." Because the possible as such must be exemplified, so, too, must its implications and thus its self-differentiations. Were it possible to have fragmentary actualities without all-inclusive ones, in the way that, say, life may be exemplified solely by plants and thus without animals, fragmentariness and all-inclusiveness would identify contingent specifications of the possible as such, and the differentia of contingent specifications cannot be implied by the necessary character of an actuality; that is, the difference would not be a metaphysical self-differentiation.

All-inclusive actualities can be ordered only sequentially because, as noted earlier, two contemporary actualities so defined would not be distinct. Difference between actualities depends on difference between the many to be unified. Hence, two or more actualities can be contemporaries only because at least one is fragmentary, whereby the many as included in one differ from the many as included in another. Accordingly, the self-differentiation of concrete singular as such implies the existence of an individual whose identity is all-inclusive relativity, that is, a sequence of actualities each of which exemplifies this metaphysical characteristic. The sequence in question is, we may say, a metaphysical individual, one whose identifying character is solely metaphysical in the strict sense, and this individual is distinguished from all others because the identifying characteristics of all others are contingent. Precisely because this individual is metaphysical, it exists necessarily; that is, there are no possible conditions under which it is not actualized somehow.

We may speak of all possible actualities as actual or possible members of a nonindividual metaphysical society, whose identifying characteristic is "the many become one, and are increased by one," and this metaphysical society includes two other metaphysical societies, the nonindividual society of fragmentary actualities, on the one hand, and, on the other, the metaphysical individual. In so speaking, however, we should recognize that "society" and "individual" are also self-differentiating concepts, since each implies the difference between contingent and necessary instances. Because a metaphysical society is necessary, moreover, exemplification of its identifying character by member actualities is not (or is not solely) consequent on genetic transmission. If the reasoning behind this conclusion is sound, the impossibility of sheer nothing entails the necessity of the world (the metaphysical society of fragmentary actualities) and the necessity of God (the metaphysical society of all-inclusive actualities).

Because there are no conditions under which all-inclusive relativity is not actualized, the existence of God cannot be temporally or spatially located. As a necessary sequence of actualities, the temporality of God is without beginning or ending. To be sure, the world as the society of fragmentary actualities is also necessary and thus also without beginning or ending, but this is not possible for any given worldly individual (or other society within the world).[9] Only the metaphysical individual is, as an individual, omnitemporal. It is also omnispatial; that is, a divine actuality cannot be spatially limited by the extension of its contemporaries. Such limitation defines fragmentariness; worldly contemporaries each unify a different many because each is restricted by others with respect to spatial location. In contrast, a given divine actuality is everywhere, in the sense that worldly actualities cannot actualize spatial possibilities that are not cooccupied by some actuality of the metaphysical individual.[10]

Speaking of a necessary individual calls to mind the long Western discussion of a priori arguments for God's existence and, specifically, the so-called ontological argument, where versions of the latter seek to show why the divine existence is implied by the concept or definition or essence of God. It is not my purpose to pursue an extended treatment of theistic arguments. Still, attention to some recent discussions may help to clarify the promise of neoclassical metaphysics.

On one accounting, indebted to Kant, only ontological arguments count as a priori, all others being a posteriori because they include as a premise or component some or other "contingent existential fact" (Gale, 239)—for instance, a causal order among beings or events in the universe or a complexity found in some of its creatures. Typically, those who endorse or, at least, work with this distinction have in view a particular concept of God. In *The Nature and Existence of God*, for instance, Richard Gale explicitly limits his analysis of theistic arguments to those for the supposed existence of "God, as conceived by traditional Western theism" (Gale, 1). On this conception, the existence of things other than God is the free creation of the completely eternal and changeless God, the view eminently presented by Aquinas. Only God exists necessarily, and thus every statement about the world is about a "contingent existential fact."

So far as I can see, the critical success Gale enjoys with respect to certain theistic arguments, all of which he finds unconvincing, is confined to reasoning about God conceived in ways neoclassical theism also finds untenable. Accordingly, he does not discuss theistic arguments within which God is so conceived that both the divine individual and the world are metaphysically necessary. Assuming the neoclassical context, one may say, with Hartshorne, that a priori arguments for God's necessary existence may be either ontological or cosmological, the former defending its conclusion as implied in the concept of God itself, and the latter pursuing the implications of some other metaphysical concept (see Hartshorne 1967).

Gale is aware of those he calls "process theologians" and, at one point, allows that their understanding of God may well be immune to certain criticisms he addresses to the " 'traditional' account" of divine omniscience (Gale, 177–78). Still, *The Nature and Existence of God* does not otherwise consider a neoclassical account of the divine individual, in keeping with Gale's focus on "traditional Western theism." That limitation is further confirmed by his most general critique of arguments for a necessary God, which reasons from the possibility of "morally unjustified evil" (an evil that God "could not be morally excused for permitting") or, alternatively, from the possibility of "a world in which every free person always freely does what is morally wrong" (Gale, 228, 229). Both possibilities are, Gale argues, intuitively more plausible than, and incompatible with, the possibility of a necessary God whose unsurpassable greatness includes unsurpassable benevolence (see Gale 228–37; 281–84).

Without analyzing the soundness of Gale's critique, we can see that its success depends on the traditional concept of God as omnipotent or sovereign creator of the world in the sense neoclassical theologians also criticize. I will not here pursue a discussion of evil in relation to divine existence. It is sufficient to note that "process theologians," precisely because they affirm both the world and God to be metaphysically necessary, have no reason to accept the traditional account of divine omnipotence. Instead, they typically hold that all individuals must, by definition, have some power because all actualities, worldly or divine, are necessarily self-determining. Hence, unsurpassable greatness can only mean the greatest power possible for any one individual—and, given this metaphysical understanding, any plausibility remaining in Gale's premises need not be incompatible with the divine individual (see Hartshorne 1966; Griffin 2004).

The significance of this metaphysical context may also be presented through focus specifically on the ontological argument. A version thereof is implied in what has been said, and this argument might be formulated as follows:

1. God, defined as the greatest possible individual, is possible. (Premise)

2. An individual having necessary existence is greater than an individual having contingent existence (where "contingent existence" means the possible nonexistence of the individual). (Premise)

3. God has necessary existence. (Implication of 1 and 2).

4. Hence, God exists. (Implication of 3).

Here, the modal term "necessary" and thus its contrary "possible" are used in the logical sense, such that the conclusion, "God exists," is logically necessary or necessarily true. Given this usage, the argument is, so far as I can see, valid; that is, the conclusion is implied by the combination of premises. A greatest possible individual, whatever other characteristics or properties it must have, must also have, given the second premise, necessary existence. Naturally, the logical use of "necessary" might be rejected as inapplicable to existential statements. But this usage is authorized by the argument above for metaphysical necessity, that is, for the logical necessity of "something exists." Still, one might contest either or both of the premises, and that is why the neoclassical context is significant.

The first premise stipulates a definition of God and asserts that, on this definition, "God exists" is logically possible. Many have, in one way or another, argued for the impossibility of God so defined, but typically such arguments have in view "God, as conceived by traditional Western theism," that is, the concept of God as entirely eternal and immutable. As discussed above, neoclassical metaphysics has no interest in defending the first premise so understood. "God" as a self-differentiation of the metaphysical concept "individual," such that God implies and is implied by nondivine individuals and is distinguished from them by virtue of member actualities exemplifying all-inclusive relativity, is a decidedly different concept. To be sure, one might also doubt the logical possibility of "God exists" on this definition of the divine—and, as noted, I will focus on that issue below. But it remains that arguments whose critical force depends on having the traditional concept as their object are not pertinent.

Even if one grants the first premise, however, the second might be contested. Why does having necessary existence make an individual greater; that is, why must the greatest possible individual have necessary existence, such that its nonexistence is impossible? I doubt that traditional theists can answer this question, because it requires a metaphysical meaning of greater or less great individuals (or beings) that is applicable to the idea of God. In any event, the neoclassical concept of God, if logically possible, also backs the second premise. Given that final real things are exemplifications of relativity, the meaning of greater and less great individuals can only be capacity for greater or lesser relativity. For this reason, actualizations of the greatest possible individual must exemplify all-inclusive relativity. But all-inclusive relativity, as noted or implied in the previous paragraph, is a self-differentiation of actuality as such and, therefore, must be exemplified. Hence, all-inclusive relativity defines an individual having necessary existence—or, what comes to the same thing, an individual having necessary existence is greater than an individual having contingent existence.[11]

We may also draw the following conclusion: at least on neoclassical metaphysics, the second premise, "an individual having necessary existence is greater than an individual having contingent existence," is itself valid only if "greatest possible individual" defines a possible individual. If God, so defined, is impossible, then no individual can have "necessary existence" because only all-inclusive relativity must be actualized somehow—or, to restate the point, an individual whose capacity to relate is limited must exist contingently. Thus, if the greatest possible individual is impossible, the second premise is false because the supposed concept of an individual having necessary existence is nonsense. Accordingly, the first two premises might be restated as one, namely, "the necessary existence of God, defined as the greatest possible individual, is possible," and this becomes the antecedent of an argument for which the consequent is "God exists." Moreover, the antecedent is validated if neoclassical metaphysics successfully defends the self-differentiation of "individual" into "individual whose actualities are fragmentary relativities" and "individual whose actualities are all-inclusive relativities."

For all that, some may find the conclusion (namely, "God exists" is necessarily true because the greatest possible individual has necessary existence) unconvincing because "existence" is not a predicate. I will not seek to engage the extended discussion of this Kantian dictum (for one detailed discussion, see Oppy, chapter 10). In its relevant sense, so far as I can see, its point is this: "existence" is not a predicate implied by the concept of a thing, in the manner that, say, "having angles whose sum is 380 degrees" is a predicate implied by the concept "plane triangle," or "being warmblooded" is a predicate implied by the concept "mammal." "Existence" cannot be this kind of predicate, a defense of the dictum runs, because the concept of a thing is the same concept whether the thing conceived exists or not. But this very way of making the point implies that "existence" is not a predicate when the thing conceived might not exist, that is, existence is not a property of something that exists contingently. It then follows, as Hartshorne has argued, that *mode of existence* is indeed a predicate. The concept of a thing whose existence, if it exists, is contingent implies the predicate "contingent existence." By implication, "necessary existence" is also a predicate, at least if "greatest possible individual" is logically possible.

It also follows that "existence" is a predicate implied by the concept of a thing *if* that concept is "greatest possible individual" (and "greatest possible individual" is logically possible). In other words, "existence" is a predicate in this one case. To all appearances, Kant took " 'existence' is not always a predicate' " to entail " 'existence' is never a predicate"—and the validity of that entailment is precisely what is at issue in asking whether "God exists" is logically necessary. Still, Kant or others convinced by his critique may find " 'existence' is never a predicate" credible because they identify existence with actuality. The concept of a thing never implies "actuality" as a predicate, that is, a given actuality, because concepts designate abstracts or indeterminates, and a given actuality is concrete or fully determinate—and what is indeterminate cannot imply any given exemplification. If "God" is defined as the greatest possible actuality, no ontological argument can be sound because "greatest possible actuality" is meaningless, a supposed concept that is merely putative because no concept can designate a given actuality.

With respect to the theistic tradition he inherited, which understood God to be the eternal and unchangeable actuality, Kant had good reason for his critique of the ontological argument. But this is simply because the idea of God he inherited is not logically possible. In contrast, neoclassical metaphysics defines God as the metaphysical individual, that is, the individual whose sequential actualities exemplify all-inclusive relativity. Thereby, the existence of this individual is distinguished from any one of those member actualities, each of which might have been other than it is because the worldly things to which it is relative might have been different, or it might have unified them in a differing way. It is the metaphysical individual that is metaphysically necessary.

At least to first appearances, then, an ontological argument set within neoclassical metaphysics adds to the discussion, and this perception may be confirmed by reviewing the relevant analysis in Graham Oppy's *Ontological Arguments and Belief in God*, namely, his treatment of "modal arguments involving necessity" (Oppy, 70). He finds these arguments, as all of those he considers, dialectically unsuccessful; that is, they beg the question against an atheist or agnostic by assuming a premise those interlocutors may, without inconsistency, deny. A modal argument for the existence of maximal excellence or greatness, Oppy proposes, might be formulated as follows: "It is possible that it is necessarily the case that God exists"; hence, "God exists" (70). The antecedent of this formulation, we can recognize, is an appropriate restatement of the first two premises in the argument presented schematically above and is, therefore, substantively equivalent to the restatement in which we also united the two, namely, "the necessary existence of God, defined as the greatest possible individual, is possible." Oppy affirms the validity of the argument he here formulates and, indeed, finds it "quite clear that there is a valid ontological argument—involving a suitably cooked up modification of the property of maximal excellence—based on any propositional modal logic" (Oppy, 72).

But "cooked up" is the relevant adjective because, the argument's validity notwithstanding, "arguments . . . to contradictory conclusions" are "equally plausible"—for instance: "It is possible that it is necessarily the case that God does not exist"; hence, "God does not exist" (Oppy, 70). The atheist or agnostic might allow that maximal excellence or greatness either necessarily exists or necessarily does not exist, but "the arguments give him no help in deciding which" (Oppy, 71). With respect to the substantive conclusion, then, the most one can say is this: *if* it is possible that it is necessary that God exists, then God exists. More generally, then, Oppy holds that any valid ontological argument depends on an "operator" (in the present case, the antecedent asserting the possibly that God necessarily exists), and thus its use against the atheist or agnostic begs the question (see Oppy, 114–15).

Recognizing that someone defending a modal argument for God involving necessity might seek to argue for its antecedent, Oppy asks whether "anything further . . . can be said in defense of the claim that it is possible that it is necessary that God exists" (Oppy, 72), that is, defense of a kind that does not beg the question. But he finds, with some dispatch, no such defense (see Oppy, 72–74). This result is, I suspect, indicative of how he understands his project, namely, as "a thoroughly general treatment of ontological arguments" that "should, if possible, remain neutral between the various ontological positions" (Oppy, 160). Moreover, that project may commend itself because most who have advanced ontological arguments take the being whose existence is in question to be "God, as conceived in traditional Western theism," that is, the God to whom the terms designating ontological features of nondivine things do not apply.[12] Be that as it may, asking whether the antecedent in one's modal ontological argument can be defended opens the door to argument for a metaphysical individual as an implication of metaphysical necessity: necessarily, individuals are actualized as relativities, and necessarily, individuals actualized by fragmentary relativities imply an individual actualized by all-inclusive relativities. If this neoclassical metaphysics can be sustained, then the antecedent of what Oppy calls an "equally plausible argument"—namely, "it is necessarily the case that God [understood as an individual actualized by all-inclusive relativities] does not exist"——is shown to be impossible. In sum, metaphysical necessity as explicated neoclassically provides the basis for an ontological argument whose antecedent does not, for all Oppy has shown, beg the question.

As we have previously discussed, Rundle affirms metaphysical necessity, at least in the respect that "something exists" is logically necessary. Still, he, too, doubts the necessary existence of God. On one argument, this is because "something" here means "something or other," while "God" designates a given individual. "There is clearly a difference between the claim that there has to be something or other, and the claim that there is some particular being which has to be. The latter, of course, posits a being, but the former rests content with a more abstract *principle*" (Rundle, 109). While Rundle is quite correct to note the difference, he apparently denies that the "more abstract *principle*" implies the necessary existence of God. But given a neoclassical account of "something" as an individual and the metaphysical self-differentiation into fragmentary individual and all-inclusive individual, "something exists" does, against Rundle, imply "God exists."[13]

In any event, Rundle appears not to credit that implication because he has in view the traditional concept of God as completely eternal and unchangeable. This is especially clear when he argues from his conclusion that "something," whatever it ranges over, is inseparable from matter and thus from spatiotemporal setting. This "rules out the existence of God in at least two ways: First, if reality without matter is unthinkable, then God does not enjoy the position of supreme existential independence that his nature requires; there is something other than him which must exist. Second, if the only genuine substances are material substances, if there is no place for immaterial agents, then there is no place for God" (Rundle, 192). But a divine reality as alone having supreme existential independence, in the sense that all worldly or material things exist contingently by way of God's immaterial agency, is God conceived in a way neoclassical metaphysics rejects. Being "outside space and time" and "the source of all being" (Rundle, 17, vii) is not, on this metaphysics, a nature being divine requires. In any event, it is apparent that Rundle has not considered the understanding of metaphysical necessity on which "something exists" implies "God exists" because the concept "individual" is self-differentiating, implying a world of individuals, on the one hand, and the greatest possible or metaphysical individual, on the other.

Still, if these brief comments on some recent literature suggest that neoclassical theism merits attention beyond what it has received, a defense of it will be incomplete without a convincing account of its own concept of God. Ever since Whitehead introduced the notion of a divine reality as necessary to his metaphysical system, philosophers have debated whether any neoclassical idea of God is self-consistent, and, if so, how it should be explicated. A central issue in this controversy is whether the divine reality should be conceived as a metaphysical individual, that is, a succession of all-inclusive actualities. In fact, that conception was introduced, not by Whitehead but, rather, by Hartshorne in his appropriation of Whitehead for a systematic philosophical theology. On Whitehead's own apparent belief, God is a single becoming whose unifying is contemporary with strictly all others and, therefore, a becoming that does not arise subsequent to any others and is never completed—and several neoclassical thinkers have sought to clarify and affirm this account. The concept of a divine individual faces its own problems, some of which it shares with this notion of a single, all-inclusive relativity that is with all time. But the latter is, I believe, problematic in its own distinct way, and it will be useful first to clarify why it prevents a coherent metaphysics.

The distinct problem may be formulated in terms we have recently reviewed. Neoclassical metaphysics argues that mode of existence is a predicate and that "necessary existence" is implied by the concept of God. Still, God cannot be metaphysically necessary if "God" is used to name a given actuality because no concept can imply a given "actuality" as a predicate. Concepts designate abstracts or indeterminates, and a given actuality is concrete or fully determinate (or becoming fully determinate)—and indeterminates cannot imply any given exemplification. Hence, metaphysical conditions cannot include any given actuality. To the contrary, the notion of greatest possible actuality must itself be meaningless, precisely because it is or purports to be a concept—indeed, a metaphysical concept—and no concept can name a given concrete singular. But just this notion of a greatest possible actuality is what the understanding of God as a single becoming contemporary with strictly all others would have to be. That understanding, then, must be a misunderstanding, and "greatest possible thing" designates, if it designates anything at all, a necessary individual.

This conclusion may also be reached in another way: explication of what must be the case because the complete absence of existence is impossible requires, as discussed above, a univocal designation of final real things or actualities. Philosophy, Whitehead himself says, should not pay "metaphysical compliments" to God (1963, 179), and he later takes this to mean "God is not to be treated as an exception to all metaphysical principles" (1978, 343). Given the coherence of metaphysical principles in the strict sense, understanding God as a single, all-inclusive relativity requires a univocal designation of this actuality and all others. As those who affirm this understanding agree, all nondivine actualities are designated by "the many become one, and are increased by one." On the proposal in question, however, this cannot designate all final real things because the divine actuality does not become one and, thereby, increase the many by one. Hence, the metaphysical definition of all final real things can only be "the many become"—and this concept must be self-differentiating, implying "the many become one, and are increased by one" and "the many become but do not become one and are not increased by one." We may now ask: what does "become" designate such that "become one" and "become but do not become one" can be alternative meanings, in the way that "fragmentary relativity" and "all-inclusive relativity" are meanings of "relativity" as a defining feature of final real things?

In the latter case, "relativity" itself designates in a manner relevantly neutral to the alternative meanings, just as "others" in "relative to others" is neutral to "some others" and "all others"—and the self-differentiation of "relativity" as a characterization of final real things occurs because "relative to others" not only may but also must be exemplified by actualities relative to "some others" and actualities relative to "all others." But there is no similarly neutral designation of "become" that allows "the many become one" and "the many become but do not become one" as alternative meanings. To the contrary, "do not become one" is, so far as I can see, the negation of "become." "The many become" differs from "the many," that is, a mere multiplicity, only by way of unification, so that absence of unification is the absence of becoming. Internal relations constitute an actuality, in other words, by way of its interiority, and there can be no particular "how" of such relations absent the unity of which each relation is a part and in which they are together. Accordingly, the proposal we are reviewing is, by implication, either monistic (because the all-inclusive actuality is the only final real thing, and all other realities are solely aspects of it) or dualistic (because the all-inclusive and other final real things have nothing in common). Since neither alternative is tenable, "the many become one, and are increased by one" must be the univocal designation of actualities.

But if the divine reality cannot be a single actuality, questions have also been raised about the concept of a metaphysical individual. One of these asks whether the concept is consistent with the findings of relativity physics. A sequence of all-inclusive actualities constitutes before and after in a universal or absolute sense and, therefore, defines an absolute meaning of simultaneity. On some accounts, however, relativity physics has established that simultaneity is always relative to some or other perspective within our universe, so that cosmic simultaneity is, at least in our universe, impossible. This issue is not one I can pursue with sophistication in the relevant scientific theories. But the discussion will be confused if it fails to credit the difference between theories in physics, which concern the contingent characteristics of observed events, and metaphysical theories, which are properly transcendental because they seek to explicate the character of existence as such.

Clearly, no true metaphysical theory can be inconsistent with any empirical theory that is so much as possibly true, because the former explicates the possible as such. Still, the metaphysical task is not to formulate a scheme of ideas consistent with what are said by contemporary science to be empirical truths or empirical possibilities. Kant took Newtonian physics for granted and, thereby, assumed that judgments a priori must be consistent with it. Hence, Kant concluded, necessary principles of theoretical reason must define events as, among other things, completely determined by temporally prior causes, and one consequence was his separation of theoretical and practical reason. His account of theoretical principles has not survived, in part because developments in physics have shown the Newtonian scheme to be inapplicable to very large and very small phenomena. But metaphysics has it owns reasons, quite apart from developments in empirical science, to deny in all conceivable worlds the complete determinism Newtonian physics was thought to require. At least if the argument previously presented here is sound, what must be the case because the complete absence of existence is impossible includes the self-determination of all final real things, that is, of effects as fully concrete.

The metaphysical task, in other words, is bound only by its own transcendental criteria. Even if we grant that widely held scientific theories are inconsistent with a metaphysical individual, the conflict does not determine whether the metaphysical or the empirical understandings are in need of revision. Empirical theories in physics are themselves attempts to explicate very abstract features of realities or events and may themselves be internally problematic, so that, in some respects, they may not describe any possibility. Thus, metaphysics is not bound to accept without criticism the reigning scientific theories, and whenever they are inconsistent with a metaphysical proposal, the latter can be at fault only if, in some respect, it is incoherent or hopelessly vague. Although transcendental metaphysics is finally required to confirm the adequacy of its statements and, therefore, their consistency with all physical possibilities, theories in physics cannot be so much as possibly true if inconsistent with transcendental understandings authorized by the criteria of applicability and coherence. "Philosophy," Whitehead says, "is the critique of abstractions which govern special modes of thought" (1938, 67).

To the best of my understanding, the absence of absolute or cosmic simultaneity in our universe is not a secure theoretical conclusion in contemporary physics (see Griffin 2007, 179–81). Still, even if an empirical theory asserting that absence describes a possible universe, it is far from clear that a metaphysical individual is thereby contradicted. The conclusion would follow only if a divine sequence requires two of more member actualities that together are coterminous with a universe in which absolute simultaneity is impossible. But nothing in the concept of a metaphysical individual implies any limits on the extension of a divine actuality. To be sure, I have already argued that God cannot be a single becoming throughout all time. But this impossibility leaves open the possible duration of a divine actuality or, to say the same, leaves open what world is contemporary to an all-inclusive becoming.

The extension of a given divine actuality is, in other words, contingent and thus must be determined by a decision or decisions. So far as I can see, nothing prior could set contingent limits for this extension except the divine decision immediately preceding, that is, the immediately previous actuality in the sequence of divine becomings or in the divine existence.[14] Moreover, any general character to the contemporary world with which the present divine extension must be consistent is also determined by the previous divine decision. Let us use "the natural laws" to mean the set of ordered possibilities generic to this contemporary world, such that this set at least includes the most general regularities empirical physics seeks to explicate. The natural laws, then, are not themselves necessary in the metaphysical sense, and a contingent order of possibilities generic to a universe depends on a decision influential throughout it. If this order defining a certain possible universe—or, in Whitehead's term, a "cosmic epoch"—precludes a concurrent sequence of all inclusive actualities, the conclusion to draw may be this: the immediately prior divine decision determined (or would determine) for the contemporary divine becoming an extension coterminous with that universe.

Given that circumstance, there is no absolute time within the given universe, in the sense of time constituted by relations of reenactment, where one actuality is before another. Absolute before and after is then constituted by the contemporary divine internality in relation to its divine predecessor, which is absolutely before the universe in question, and will be further constituted by the relation of a successor divine becoming, which will be absolutely subsequent to the universe in question. Thereby, the impossibility of a divine sequence within that universe is fully consistent with a metaphysical individual whose all-inclusive actualities exemplify, as do all others, "the many become one, and are increased by one."

God and the World

The possibility of divine actualities whose durations vary relative to actualities of the world provides a context in which to formulate and address the question of relations between God and the world. Affirming the necessity of the world as well as God and refusing to "pay metaphysical compliments" to God, neoclassical metaphysics claims for itself a capacity to clarify these relations, and this is central to the claim for superiority over traditional or classical metaphysics. Because the latter conceives of God as completely eternal and changeless and thus, finally, designated only by complete negation, real relations of God to the world and of creatures to God cannot be explicated without equivocation. In contrast, the concept of God as the eminently temporal individual is said to imply real interaction with worldly individuals.

Nonetheless, a problem or set of problems with respect to these relations appears to arise within neoclassical metaphysics. As previously discussed, an actuality unifies reenactments of the past as a condition for the future and thus, on most neoclassical accounts, cannot relate to the internality of contemporaries. Indeed, we have already affirmed that reenactment of another depends on the other's completion because nothing about a final real thing, as it unifies, is determinate, and therefore there is nothing to reenact. If one asserts to the contrary, one supposes that some aspect internal to a concrete whole can be, in effect, independent of the whole. Does it follow that relations between a given divine actuality and its contemporary world are impossible? For Hartshorne, if I understand his considered view correctly, the answer is yes. Relations to others of any given actuality, divine or worldly, are always reenactments of the past. But is this mutual isolation convincing, especially when the temporal extension of a given divine actuality is large relative to those in its contemporary world? A discussion responding to this complex question will, as I hope to show, be metaphysically instructive whatever the duration of any given divine actuality.

In approaching this response, we need to underscore the self-differentiation of actuality as such into kinds of actualities, whereby divine actualities exemplify all-inclusive relativity and, therefore, differ metaphysically from all nondivine becomings, which exemplify fragmentary relativity. We have noted previously the implied self-differentiation of individual as such, namely, the distinction between contingent individual, on the one hand, and necessary individual, on the other. Further implications will, I think, prove pertinent to our present problem. I will first consider the relation of an all-inclusive becoming to its contemporaries and, subsequently, the relation of worldly becomings to the copresent divine actuality.

The two metaphysical kinds of actuality imply, I believe, a difference with respect to reenactment of contemporaries. While no actuality can be reenacted as it unifies, this consideration alone does not exclude all reenactment of contemporaries because one or more of the latter may be completed as the given becoming occurs, and it remains a question whether this becoming may then reenact them. Now, the many become one by way of the actuality's own decision or self-determination. Indeed, a becoming *is* its decision to integrate reenactments. Hence, we may posit the following general rule: reenactment of a completed contemporary is impossible if doing so increases the range of possibility determined by reenactment of the past.

Because the unifying originates with or simply is the becoming, the decision is for something within the range of possible unification presented by reenactment of the past. Subsequent reenactments by which this range of possibility would be increased would, then, require another decision; that is, extended possibility cannot truly be possibility for self-determination without another decision. To illustrate by way of a specifically human instance, let us assume, with Robert Frost, his arrival at a fork between the road less traveled and the well-worn path. Now add to his situation a third alternative, so that the fork is three-way. The range of possibility having been increased, another decision is required. Notwithstanding that the added alternative is consistent with what was previously decided—for instance, to take the road less traveled—the third path was not an alternative for that previous decision and thus cannot be an alternative without another taking of the decision. Hence, reenactment of a completed contemporary cannot occur if it increases the range of possibility within which a becoming decides.

By virtue of its spatial location, a worldly actuality reenacts a fragment of the past, and the range of possible integrations is limited by this reenactment. Because different from anything in the past, a contemporary could not also be reenacted without adding to the fragment a given becoming unifies, thereby increasing that becoming's range of possibility and defining another decision. Fragmentariness thus prevents relation to the internality of any contemporary, completed or not. Fragmentary becoming, in other words, requires closure on reenactments as the becoming originates. This is, if I understand correctly, at least one reason for Whitehead to write: "Space expresses the halt for attainment" (1938, 139). Contemporaneity of worldly actualities *is* mutual independence, so that decision and thus a completed occasion can occur.

But a present divine becoming is not fragmentary. Hence, it is not apparent that reenactment of completed actualizations in the contemporary world increases the range of possibility and requires another decision. To be sure, a worldly contemporary is different from anything in the past. Let us assume, however, what the present discussion seeks to render self-consistent—namely, the relevant past for any given divine actuality is solely the previous divine actuality, which was also all-inclusive. The possibilities for a present divine becoming are then limited only insofar as full inclusion of its divine predecessor determines. That preceding actuality is also influential on all worldly actualities contemporary to the divine present, having decided their most general order of contingent possibilities (the natural laws). Because everything that happens in the contemporary world is thereby limited by the previous divine decision, nothing that happens in the contemporary world can increase the range of possibility derived by the present divine becoming from its predecessor. Hence, reenactment of contemporaries can only add further determination for the one decision by which the divine integration occurs. Nor does divine reenactment of contemporaries prevent a divine "halt for attainment," because the extension of present divine becoming (or, at least, limits on this extension) was also an aspect of the previous divine decision.

On this account, to be repetitious, the past reenacted by a given divine actuality is exhausted by the previous divine actuality, with its decision for the most generic contingent character of the present world—although the present all-inclusive becoming thereby includes strictly all of the past, since its predecessor was all-inclusive of its divine past and its completed contemporaries. What the current divine becoming decides is precisely how its reenactment of everything completed in the contemporary world will be unified with this past as a condition of the subsequent divine actuality.[15]

In his reflections on the divine reality, expressed in his own technical vocabulary, Whitehead writes: "God is to be conceived as originated by conceptual experience with his process of completion motivated by consequent, physical experience." Or, again: "For God the conceptual pole is prior to the physical, for the World the physical poles are prior to the conceptual poles" (1978, 345, 348). Restated in terms we have been using, this means: unlike nondivine becomings, which arise through relations to actualities and are completed through relations to possibilities, the divine becoming originates in relations to possibilities and is completed by relations to actualities. On my understanding, this contrast expresses Whitehead's apparent conception of God as a single becoming contemporary with strictly all others and originating in a metaphysically primordial "envisagement" of strictly all "eternal objects" or "pure possibilities" (see 1978, 44, 343–44). That understanding of God has been criticized above. Still, we are now in a position to appropriate Whitehead's formulation in a qualified sense. At its origination, each divine actuality "envisages" (along with the future as such) its contemporary world as defined by the generic order of possibilities its predecessor decided, although this "conceptual experience" depends on a prior "physical" experience, namely, reenactment of the previous divine actuality. That its originating physical experience relates to a single past actuality does not prevent a new divine becoming because there is something with which relation to the predecessor is unified, namely, the contemporary universe of worldly actualizations.[16]

But if divine reenactment of completed contemporaries follows from the metaphysical self-differentiation into kinds of actualities, both the closure on reenactments required for fragmentary attainment and the impossibility of reenacting a becoming as it unifies appear to preclude relations of worldly actualities to a divine contemporary. Clearly, there must be some relation of a nondivine becoming to the divine, again because actuality as such is self-differentiating. Metaphysical self-differentiations characterize every final real thing, and this means in the present case that any instance of fragmentary relativity or all-inclusive relativity must relate to at least one instance of the other. And we have already mentioned at least one respect in which reenactment of the divine occurs in the world. Given that divine decision effects the natural laws in a given world, every worldly becoming must be determined by the relevant divine decision—although this relation to the divine may be indirect, that is, occur by way of or through relations to other worldly actualities that directly or indirectly reenacted the relevant divine decision. Still, relations to God in this sense are not relations to a divine contemporary, and if the present divine duration is large relative to actualities in the world, reenactment of God is or could be, from a worldly perspective, relation indirectly to a distant past—at the extreme, something like indirect relation to the "big bang" with which, it is said, our universe originated.

For many, this conclusion will be religiously troublesome because religious experience appears to involve an immediate relation to God. But we can, I believe, affirm worldly relations to the contemporary divine becoming by way of underscoring metaphysical necessity. The presence of some or other worldly actuality does not beg for explanation in the manner that contingent features of any given one are explained only by reference to some decision or decisions—either the decision of the becoming in question and/or the decisions of other actualities to which it relates. In one formulation, Whitehead expresses the ontological principle as "no actual entity, then no reason" (1978, 19), but he cannot consistently mean that occurrence of a concrete singular, in distinction from its contingent characteristics, has no reason except its own decision and/or the decisions of those to which it relates. What is metaphysically necessary does not in that sense require a reason. To the contrary, some or other actuality occurs because the complete absence of existence is impossible.

We simply repeat the point in saying that each worldly actuality exemplifies metaphysical characteristics by necessity. Let us now note that metaphysical features, like contingent ones, are abstracts or indeterminates, distinguished as those of greatest possible generality—and exemplifying an abstract is, in its own way, an internal relation because the exemplification is something other than the indeterminate itself.[17] If the abstract is contingent, exemplification occurs only through reenactment; that is, the feature is either genetically derived from relations to the past or exemplification depends on the present decision, and contingent possibilities for this decision are derived from relations to the past. But exemplifying metaphysical features must have another reason—because relations of reenactment presuppose a present actuality. Relations to the past are already aspects of a process in which the many are becoming one, and there is no such process without the exemplification of metaphysical characteristics.[18]

I will formulate the point as follows: in contrast to exemplifications that only occur through reenactment, exemplifying relations to metaphysical indeterminates are, or are also, relations of *enactment*. We need not deny that these relations do occur through reenactment. Every present becoming reenacts other actualities and, thereby, may necessarily reenact their exemplification of metaphysical characteristics. Still, present exemplification of these relations cannot occur only through reenactment—because reenactment itself presupposes the occurrence of a present actuality.[19] Every actuality, therefore, also occurs through internal relations of enactment to its own metaphysical features. To be sure, these relations also presuppose a process of becoming one, but this is simply to say that being an actuality presupposes being an actuality. Occurrence through relations of enactment is occurrence by metaphysical necessity.

This concept of enactment, then, allows a coherent statement of how every worldly actuality is constituted by an immediate internal relation to God. Because the divine cooccupies the locus of all contemporaries, worldly enactment localizes the divine. To enact metaphysical indeterminates is to localize God; that is, the metaphysical character being exemplified by the divine is simultaneously exemplified in the manner possible within some part of the divine extension.[20] The qualifying phrase "in the manner possible" simply means that localization is fragmentariness of reenactments, whereas the divine actuality reenacts all-inclusively. Still, localization *is* an internal relation of enactment. Correspondingly, a divine actuality has, in addition to its reenactment of the divine past and of all worldly becomings whose completion is contemporary to it, a relation of enactment to contemporary actualities as they become, and we may call this the relation of omnipresence.

In accord with the metaphysical differentiation into worldly and divine actualities, then, every instance of each kind is constituted, in the way appropriate to its character, by a relation or relations of enactment to one of more instances of the other. A worldly relation to the divine as a contemporary is problematic only if all internal relations to other actualities are thought to be reenactments. To the contrary, the relation to God as a contemporary is one of localization, a relation presupposed by all worldly reenactments, including direct or indirect reenactment of a previous divine decision by way of which the natural laws or scope for natural laws in the current world are effected. Actualization occurs in the world through unification in which the past is reenacted, and this unification is, whatever else it is, localization of God.

We can even say that every worldly actuality exemplifies "the many become one, and are increased by one" *because* each localizes the divine—and thus say that each is caused by this relation to God. To be sure, enactment is a metaphysical necessity, and, accordingly, we can also say that God is caused by the world; that is, every divine becoming occurs because it has the relation of omnipresence to its contemporary world. But the divine becoming alone exemplifies metaphysical necessity by cooccupying the locus of every actuality contemporary to it. Given that causal dependence is more properly understood as relation to an actuality, there is special reason to call God the metaphysical or first cause of all things. In doing so, however, we must recognize the implication of using "cause" to designate metaphysical dependence on

God, namely, that the term is self-differentiating, implying the difference between causal relations of reenactment and those of enactment. The divine actuality is the first cause of all contemporaries through their relations of enactment to God.

Some may object that the self-differentiation of concepts in neoclassical metaphysics appears so to escalate as the scheme is explicated that one is led to doubt whether insistence on the univocal designation of terms maintains any importance. If we speak of an internal relation to God in a different sense than internal relations to the past, and we speak of God as the cause of all things in a different sense than we speak of some worldly things as the cause of others, how is this proposal finally distinct from Aquinas's assertion that metaphysical terms apply to God and creatures analogically? The all-important distinction is this: a self-differentiating concept, unlike an analogical name in Aquinas's sense, has a univocal meaning that implies and is implied by its differentiations. "The many become one, and are increased by one" designates univocally all possible concrete singulars and may mean either "the many in some respects become one, and are increased by one" (a fragmentary concrete singular) or "the many in all respects become one, and are increased by one" (an all-inclusive concrete singular). Similarly, the concept "internal relation to x," where x is another actuality, has a univocal meaning, namely, "concrete singular partially determined by x," the other actuality. But the concept is self-differentiating because the feature thereby exemplified may be contingent to some or necessary to all actualities. In the former case, the relation is one of reenactment; in the latter case, the relation is or is also one of enactment.

On Aquinas's proposal, to the contrary, analogical terms applicable to God and creatures have no univocal meaning because, in application to God, they designate what can be univocally designated only by complete negation of their application to creatures. Indeed, his attempt to affirm such analogical terms seeks, one might say, a metaphysical account that only the self-differentiation of univocal terms can credibly provide, and the distinction is all-important because, finally, it marks the difference between a classical notion of God as completely eternal and changeless and the neoclassical concept of an eminently temporal individual that again and again unifies strictly everything. Moreover, the fact that many metaphysical terms turn out to be self-differentiating is precisely what one should expect if, as also argued above, the metaphysical concept of a final real thing or concrete singular implies two kinds thereof—because the metaphysical scheme as a whole is nothing other than an explication of actuality as such.

But the metaphysical gain, some may say, exacts an unacceptable price. If relation to God as our contemporary is localization of God's metaphysical character, anything we might call our experience of God is thin and cold, and this account, therefore, remains inconsistent with religious, especially mystical, experience in which a profound sense of immediate communion with God is present. This, I submit, is a misunderstanding. Localization of the divine means relation to a becoming that cooccupies one's place in the world and, therefore, means a communion unlike any other, so that God, we may say, is "closer than hands or feet." As the metaphysical individual, God is literally the one "in whom we live and move and have our being"; our relation to God defines our very existence in the world and thus our presence as creatures who act to make a difference. Because making a difference is becoming something that, in all of its uniqueness, is then immediately received and reenacted by God, whereby we make our everlasting contribution to the all-inclusive and ever-enriching unity of all things, the subjective sense of enactment is also the appetition on which all other zest for life depends. When this relation to the divine becomes prominent in consciousness, there is every reason to call it a union experienced with a profound sense of peace and harmony.

Chapter 4

The Metaphysics of Human Purpose

Decision for a Self-Understanding

We are now ready to focus on a metaphysical understanding of human purpose. According to the previously outlined metaphysics, in which becomings are the final real things, a worldly individual exists in the emphatic sense or as a subject when its member actualities do or may exemplify understanding. So far as we know, such an individual depends on intimate interaction with a complex order of actualities or complex of societies. In the case of human beings, this is the human body and, most immediately, the brain. Metaphysics in the broad sense asks about the characteristics of subjectivity as such, and this means, we can now say, the characteristics of a final real thing that exemplifies understanding. In common discussion, however, "subject" so readily refers to individuals that I will, in what follows, use "subjective activity" to mean an actuality that understands, or simply "activity" when its equivalence to "subjective activity" is clear from the context, and also use "human activity" to mean a human subjective activity. I will use "subject" and "subjectivity" to mean, respectively, an individual that exists in the emphatic sense and its distinguishing feature—although I will also use both terms when the difference between individuals and activities is irrelevant to the point. When I wish to emphasize that I am speaking about an individual who exists with understanding, I will use "subjective individual."

Because totality is prior to meaning, I have argued, subjective activities are not exhausted by understanding but, rather, are also constituted, as are all worldly actualities, by nonconscious relations to an order of actualities and possibilities. In a subjective activity, the latter relations are prior to understanding, such that understanding is consciousness of these nonconscious relations.[1] Consciousness, we may say, is a certain kind of internality, namely, the internality of a fragmentary becoming insofar as it discriminates what is first present nonconsciously, and discrimination occurs by way of negation. If a nonconscious relation to x may be called simply relation to x, a conscious relation to the same thing is "relation to x and nothing other than x" or "relation to x in contrast with everything else."

This means, as we previously discussed, that understanding involves relation to a contrast between some given object and existence or the possible as such. All actualities are related to this metaphysical character because each enacts it. In understanding something actual or some specific possibility, an activity contrasts relation to it with the relation to existence as such, and the latter is required because no more specific contrast could define everything other than the object discriminated. "Not a color other than yellow," for instance, does not discriminate yellow, since many things have no color at all and, accordingly, are also "not a color other than yellow." Again, "not the previous cosmic epoch" fails to discriminate this cosmic epoch, since epochs prior or subsequent to both are also "not the previous comic epoch." Summarily, then, "relation to x and nothing other than x" (where x is something actual or some specific possibility) requires relation to an indeterminate of which strictly everything is an exemplification or a specific possibility for exemplification. Still, this consciousness does not require omniscience, a contrast with all other things in their detail. Rather, "relation to x in contrast with everything else" means "relation to x in contrast with the possible as such and, thereby, with whatever other things there are or could be," so that most other things are not discriminated.

This accounting implies that activities, in understanding anything at all, also understand the possible as such, precisely because relation to it is involved in the contrast whose internality is consciousness—and that conclusion may seem counterintuitive. But we may now recall the difference between explicit understanding, in which objects occupy the focus of attention, and the "large penumbral region of experience . . . in dim apprehension" (Whitehead 1978, 267), consisting of background understandings that are implicit in the sense of "not readily apparent" but are nonetheless essential to explicit awareness being what it is. Awareness of the possible as such may be implicit in a subjective activity, whether or nor it has ever been explicit in the subjective individual in question. Indeed "totality is prior to meaning" entails the necessity of this implicit understanding whenever explicit understanding occurs and thus the priority of this implicit understanding of totality to any explicit understanding thereof.

The discussion here has proceeded without distinguishing consciousness and understanding. On my accounting, the latter is a higher form of consciousness, such that understanding presupposes consciousness but not consciousness understanding. To all appearances, some conscious creatures in our world are not subjects. In these creatures, I speculate, consciousness does not discriminate specific possibilities as possibilities and thus does not include a discrimination of the specific future. Instead, awareness is restricted to the presentation of past actualities and aggregates, given consciously in the nontemporal immediacy of perception, although such perception may be of the creature's own body, and thus consciousness without understanding may include bodily pain. These creatures cannot be self-conscious or be aware of themselves as a particular present—because, as I will discuss in a moment, such consciousness requires awareness of the difference between a particular past of which one is an effect and a specific future of which one becomes a cause.[2]

In its metaphysical sense, I propose, understanding occurs when an actuality is conscious of a specific future and, therefore, of specific possibilities or abstracts or indeterminates. Because possibilities are indeterminate, we can here appropriate the classical Western view that humans are distinctive by virtue of an "intellectual soul" and thus may have in the soul universals as universals. I use "universal" to mean any indeterminate or abstract. Understanding, then, is consciousness by way of universals, where this involves the consciousness of specific possibilities and thus of things or states of affairs as actual or possible exemplifications of specific universals. To understand a given yellow rose, for instance, is to be conscious of it as exemplifying the specific universals "yellow" and "rose," which means that one is simultaneously conscious of or understands "yellow" and "rose." Recurring to the scheme used previously, we can represent understanding of a universal as "relation to x in contrast with all actualities and all other possibilities." As one instance of it, moreover, this formula represents understanding of the possible as such, which is contrasted with all actualities and all specific universals. Consciousness of some actuality and some specific universal is sufficient to draw the contrast, since any one of each implies that there are others.

Consciousness by way of universals is, on this account, relation to meaning, and thus understanding involves, we may say, meaning-intentions. Because the future is the realm of unactualized possibility, meaning-intentions are inseparable from relation to the future, which characterizes all actualities and becomes conscious in subjects. So far as we know, moreover, awareness of a specific future and thus meaning-intentions do not occur, at least beyond minimal measure, without the subject's participation in a language or lifeworld, whereby universals are consciously symbolized, ordered, retained, and opened to creative extension. For this reason, to continue restating things previously said, advocates of the linguistic and hermeneutical turns in recent philosophy have rightly insisted that all explicit human understanding (and thus all implicit human understanding of specific universals), at least beyond minimal measure, is mediated by such participation. The same reason at least suggests that subjectivity is not possible unless the actuality in question belongs to an individual or sequence of actualities having the capacity to cumulate learning in dramatic measure. But it does not follow that implicit understanding of the possible as such must be linguistically mediated. To the contrary, every understanding depends on the presence of this meaning-intention, even if it cannot become explicit in consciousness except in the terms provided by a language or lifeworld.

Completing the metaphysics of purpose now requires recognition that subjective activities include an understanding of themselves; to exemplify understanding is also to exemplify self-understanding. To understand a determinate world, on the one hand, and specific worldly possibilities, on the other, is to understand the difference between the past and the future and thus to understand the present. This present, moreover, cannot be simply generic to oneself and one's contemporaries. Understanding is consciousness of one's own nonconscious relations to the past. Hence, the determinate world one understands is inescapably the past as given to oneself, the past in the perspective of one's own spatial location. The present understood is, then, the difference between one's own past and the future—and this particular present is oneself becoming an addition to the many.

On first reflection, perhaps, the notion of self-understanding seems paradoxical, implying a distinction between the self as subject and the self as object even while the two are the same self. But this apparent impossibility can be clarified as merely apparent if we recall again that every actuality unifies itself by way of a "decision for," that is, a decision with respect to how the future will be conditioned. "The many become one, *and are increased by one*"; what a becoming becomes is a cause of the future. Every actuality, Whitehead writes, "arises as an effect facing its past and ends as a cause facing its future" (1961, 194). In the case of existence with understanding, we can say, every self (using "self" to mean the actuality in question) is also a self-expression, whereby the self that expresses and the self that is expressed are distinct, and yet what is expressed is the same self that expresses. To complete one's becoming as a subjective activity *is* to express oneself. Self-understanding, then, is a "decision for" with understanding, and the self as subject takes as object the expression for which it decides. The relation of self as subject to self as object is not, in the first instance, retrospective, a consciousness of something prior; it is, rather, prospective, a consciousness of what one is to be. What one understands when one understands oneself is the difference to others one decides to make.

Still, understanding is, we have said, consciousness by way of universals. In terms of what universals, then, is an activity conscious of its own particular expression? So far as I can see, the self can understand itself only in relation to the end for which its expression is chosen. Decision with understanding, in other words, is decision for a telos, some future possibility, at the realization of which the self-expression is aimed. The end in question, moreover, is chosen from among alternatives, possible states of affairs defined by characteristics or sets of characteristics that actualities might exemplify in some future extension, that is, some future time and place. Hence, a subjective activity, *s*, understands itself as the exemplification of a universal, where *s* is distinguished from all else by given relations to the past to be unified, and the universal is "pursuit of *t* (the telos chosen) instead of t_1 or t_2 or . . . t_n" (some other available alternative)."[3] Subjective activities enjoy the distinctive freedom they do, we can say, because they are able to think about ends. Moreover, "*s* as pursuit of *t* instead of t_1 or t_2 or . . . t_n" is a self-understanding because the self in question *is* the self-expressed unification of its relations and thus, given the particularity of relations to the past, is its purpose—and the internality or subjective sense of this relation to an end is that of conscious choice. The becoming of an activity occurs by way of a purpose chosen with understanding, and this means by way of deciding for a self-understanding.[4]

We are now in a position to appropriate within transcendental metaphysics Heidegger's assertion that subjectivity is inseparable from temporality: meaning is inseparable from a projection of Dasein's future, for which beings are significant and in relation to which Dasein's past becomes effective; the horizon of significance for possible encountering of beings is pragmatic or teleological. Reinterpreted in the present context, this formulation articulates a moment of subjectivity as an exemplification with understanding of "the many become one, and are increased by one." A self-understanding must be an activity's inclusive understanding, in the sense that all of its other understandings are included in what the activity, given its particular past, becomes and thus what is expressed. But a self-understanding is a decision with understanding to actualize one among more than one alternative for purpose. Hence, the inclusive understanding is indeed teleological, and the past as understood is unified for the sake of "Dasein's future"—assuming that the latter means the future of which Dasein will be a cause.

If meaning is in this sense teleological, then so, too, is the truth of understandings. I will not attempt here the extended treatment any adequate discussion of truth requires. Still, a word about the approach implied in what has been said may be useful, and the focus here on subjects counsels focus on truth as a feature or characteristic of (some) understandings. Truth may also be a feature of propositions but thereby is derivative from truth as a feature of understandings having those propositions as their content. Given that its self-understanding is an activity's inclusive understanding, any other understanding the activity includes is an aspect of that self-understanding, and a self-understanding is an understanding of the self as expressed. It then follows that truth as a feature of understandings should be understood in the following pragmatic sense: to call an understanding true is to say that something is the case when the understanding is expressed.

Insofar, neoclassical metaphysics has reason to agree with pragmatic accounts of truth formulated by, for instance, Jürgen Habermas and Karl-Otto Apel (see Habermas 1984; Apel 1979). On their accounts, however, what is the case when a true understanding is expressed is confined to a possible effect within the community of subjects, namely, consensus in the "ideal speech situation" (Habermas) or agreement in the "indefinite argumentation community" (Apel). So far as I can see, that accounting is incoherent because, in the end, it equates what *is* the case (namely, the understanding *is* true) with what, at best, *may become* the case (namely, consensus or agreement in some future community of subjects).[5] Within the context of neoclassical metaphysics, in any event, the truth of true understandings entails the divine relativity, that is, the metaphysical individual, each of whose actualities is all-inclusive. What is the case when a true understanding is expressed is the following: as an object of a divine relation, the expression corresponds to the divine inclusion of what the understanding is about. Metaphorically, we can say that a true understanding is one with which the divine, on receiving it, agrees. This effect in the divine relativity *is* the feature of a self-understanding and understandings within it marking them as true.[6]

Self-understanding, along with an understanding of existence or the possible as such, is implied whenever subjective activity occurs. Because activity with understanding is conscious of a particular past and a specific future, awareness of oneself as a choice among possible ends or purposes cannot be absent whenever understanding is present, and a subjective activity understands itself whether or not the subjective individual in question has ever explicitly discriminated itself or any of its purposes. Implicit understanding of self, we can say, is prior to any explicit understanding thereof. "The primitive stage of discrimination," Whitehead writes, "is the vague grasp of reality, dissecting it into a threefold scheme, namely, The Whole, That Other, and This-My-Self" (1938, 150). Whatever else Whitehead intended by "The Whole," it includes existence as such, and this statement makes clear that understanding cannot discriminate anything other than the self without awareness of the possible as such and in distinction from the self.

Understanding both itself and "The Whole," moreover, every activity inescapably understands itself, even if only implicitly, as an exemplification of the possible as such and, thereby, in relation to totality. Self-understanding includes an understanding of the self's own enactment. Also, every activity at least implicitly understands this enactment to be subjective. To decide with understanding what one becomes is to understand one's self-expression *as* this decision and thus as a subjective activity. It now follows that every activity is constituted by an implicit understanding of subjectivity as such. Understanding oneself as a decision requires a universal or universals; because this understanding characterizes subjectivity as such, it cannot be entirely dependent on learning, and thus the universals must include "conscious decision as such." The primitive grasp of "This-My-Self" discriminates the self not only from everything else within the whole but also from all other subjective activities, actual or possible. If the self as subject takes as object its own expression, then the object is at least implicitly understood as the self's own enactment specified as subjectivity.

Mindful of the distinction between understanding something and believing it, where the latter involves assent to or affirmation of the understanding, we can also say that every activity believes a true understanding of the possible as such and subjectivity as such. So far as I can see, understandings without which there could be no understanding at all are also beliefs without which there could be no understanding at all. This is because every activity, in deciding for a self-understanding, decides for its own expression as a subject and thereby affirms its implicit understanding of its own enactment specified as subjectivity. With this recognition, we can amend the earlier account of true metaphysical statements in the broad sense. They are, I previously argued, pragmatically necessary in the following way: every subject who denies, explicitly or implicitly, what such a statement asserts thereby engages in a pragmatic self-contradiction because the act of denial implies what it denies. The pragmatic self-contradiction also occurs, we can now say, because any subject who denies what a true metaphysical statement asserts simultaneously *believes*, at least implicitly, what it denies, namely, its own enactment specified as subjectivity. Because this belief is constitutive of subjectivity as such, I will call it the "original belief" or set of beliefs.

Some have objected that such beliefs are not, simply by virtue of being original, true. What any subject must believe is one thing, this objection holds, and what is true is something else. Perhaps, for instance, all subjects inescapably believe that God (defined, say, as the greatest possible individual) exists. This says something only about subjects, and it remains that this belief may be false because, in reality, there is no God. But this objection is not convincing. If a belief whose content is p is false, then "p is false" can be the content of a true belief. But if the belief whose content is p is necessary to subjectivity as such, anyone who believes "p is false" does so inconsistently because she or he simultaneously believes "p is true." Hence, she or he says, in effect, "I believe p, and I do not believe p" and, thereby, engages in a pragmatic self-contradiction. Indeed, if p is the content of a belief necessary to subjectivity as such, anyone who believes "p may be false," where this means "it is possible that p is presently false, and thus I neither affirm nor deny p," engages in a pragmatic self-contradiction, because suspension of belief, like denial, is also inconsistent with assent. This believer also says, in effect, "I believe p, and I do not believe p."

The pragmatic self-contradiction occurs because the content of beliefs necessary to subjectivity as such can only be what believing itself, that is, every act of subjectivity, implies. This does not deny that p might be the content of such a belief, and yet "p is false" is still logically possible. For instance, if all subjects inescapably believe their own enactment specified as subjectivity, then all subjects inescapably believe that some subject exists—and yet there might be a world without subjects. But "p is false" cannot be the content of a true *belief* because the world cannot be without subjects so long as there is some subject who believes. What every subject must believe must be a true belief, given that there are subjects who believe. Hence, if subjects must believe that God exists, then "God does not exist" is pragmatically self-contradictory and cannot be true so long as there are subjects—and if subjects must believe that God exists necessarily, then "God does not exist" cannot possibly be true. But this is simply to repeat that original beliefs characterize subjectivity as such because their content is implied by every act of subjectivity. What is implied by the occurrence of subjectivity cannot be, if there is such an occurrence, false. Our original beliefs, the next section will seek to explicate, include a belief in the moral law.

The Comprehensive Good

Self-understanding also means that subjective activities necessarily affirm some understanding of the good, in terms of which alternative ends are discriminated as better and worse. This follows because a self-understanding is consciousness of one's purpose as chosen. To be sure, such awareness requires a descriptive discrimination of possible ends and, thereby, a comparison of them in terms of descriptive similarities and differences by which they are characterized. Indeed, as alternatives for conscious choice, ends *are* future possible states of affairs in the respects that or insofar as they are understood. For instance, one decides to vote for and, thereby, pursues the election of one of two or more senatorial candidates, described, say, in terms of their own political commitments. But one cannot understand the choice, pursuit of t instead of t_1 or t_2 or ... t_n, unless the ends are compared *with respect to choosing*, and a comparison of possible purposes in this respect is an evaluation. To understand some future possibility as a chosen telos is to affirm it as good and thus to compare it with alternatives in terms of better and worse.

At least implicitly, then, every activity understands itself in terms of some principle of purpose, that is, a principle of good purposes in view of which alternative ends are compared with respect to choosing. In this sense, we may say, with Kant, that rational beings understand their exercise of freedom in terms of a maxim for action. Also with Kant, the principle of evaluation is itself chosen, at least if differing choices among the alternatives exemplify differing evaluative comparisons, because the decision by which a subjective activity is constituted is a decision about the good and thus for the terms of evaluation. Such principles may be of greater or lesser specificity. One may decide that voting for a certain candidate is good because one decides that the candidate's commitment to civil rights is good, and one may decide that the candidate's commitment to civil rights is good because one decides that a democratic society is good. Against Kant, however, principles of evaluation must always be or imply principles of *purpose*, by which I mean those that compare possible ends or tele' in their entirety, as marked by all of their descriptive similarities and differences. Decision for some possible future cannot choose it solely in some aspect because the choice can only be among alternative ends as whole things.

For this reason, no feature in terms of which ends are compared only in part can be adequate for evaluation. This is, so far as I can see, the mistake in all nonteleological ethics, of which Kant's conception of the moral law is the preeminent example. Here, nonteleological ethics are those on which the supreme principle of evaluation defines a partial comparison of alternatives for purpose. On Kant's moral theory, for instance, good action respects the freedom of all other persons, that is, treats them as ends withal, never merely as means, where this categorical imperative defines a partial comparison of alternative tele' and, in that sense, defines a constraint or limitation on future possibilities one may pursue. Regard for "every rational nature" as "*an end in itself*," Kant writes, constitutes "the supreme limiting condition of all our subjective ends," and thus rational nature "as an *independently* existing end. . . . is conceived only negatively, that is, as that which we must never act against" (1949, 48, 54).

As Kant recognized, however, one does not simply choose whether or not to respect an end conceived only negatively; rather, one determines whether to treat others as ends withal as one chooses among possible subjective ends or decides for some telos in its entirety. Because it assesses subjective ends partially, Kant's moral law implies that similarities and differences among alternatives for purpose in other aspects are morally indifferent, that is, make no difference with respect to better and worse. But this supposed moral indifference is itself a *moral* conclusion; that is, the implication *is* a moral comparison or evaluation of those other aspects and thus of the alternatives as whole things. Marking a difference between respects in which decisions can be moral or immoral and those in which they are morally indifferent implies a moral comparison of alternatives in all respects. If possible purposes are in some respects morally indifferent, this can only mean that they are insofar morally equal, that is, equally good.

Thus, the categorical imperative presupposes another principle by which alternatives for purpose are evaluated in their entirety.

Mutatis mutandis, the same is true of any other nonteleological ethic—and this is just to repeat that a decision among alternatives for purpose is a decision among them as whole things. In this respect, Hume's characterization of moral evaluation has it right: "In moral deliberations we must be acquainted beforehand with all the objects, and all their relations to each other; and from a comparison of the whole, fix our choice or approbation. No new fact to be ascertained; no new relation to be discovered. All the circumstances of the case are supposed to be laid before us, ere we can fix any sentence of blame or approbation" (1975, 290).[7] All nonteleological theories, we can say, commit "the partialist fallacy," asserting that comparison of alternative ends in some partial way is sufficient for moral evaluation, and the assertion is fallacious because it implies "a comparison of the whole" such that the aspects supposedly beyond moral comparison make no difference with respect to choosing.[8] Whitehead coined the phrase "fallacy of misplaced concreteness" to name the mistake committed when one equates a given thing or kind of thing with some abstract aspect of it—as, for instance, when final real things are said to be fully described in terms of efficient causation in accord with the kind of laws physics seeks to explicate. The partialist fallacy, we can say, is the fallacy of misplaced concreteness as it appears in moral theory.

Decision with understanding, then, implies a teleological definition of the good, that is, a measure in terms of which possible futures as alternatives for decision can be compared in their entirety as greater and less. Such a teleological measure need not be an ideal in the sense of some consummate or perfect state of affairs whose realization would be an actualization of all possible good or, at least, the elimination of all evil—in the manner that, perhaps, Augustine understood the eternal city of God or some Marxists have understood the classless society. Indeed, the neoclassical affirmation of a divine individual and a world of fragmentary others as both without beginning or ending gives every reason to reject any such ideal realization as incoherent. To the contrary, then, a teleological principle evaluates alternative possible ends in terms of something to be realized insofar as possible; that is, it calls for decision that pursues the maximization of something.

Amoralists will reject the assertion that some principle of this sort is true or valid, in the sense that it defines what an activity ought to choose. For them, there is no character to "better" and "worse" to be understood or misunderstood, and the terms designate whatever the activity in question determines in taking its decision. Saying that some alternative is good cannot be true or false but, rather, is solely another way of saying that decision was for it. "Good, evil, and contemptible," wrote Thomas Hobbes, "are ever used with relation to the person that useth them: there being nothing simply and absolutely so; nor any common rule of good and evil, to be taken from the nature of the objects themselves" (1962, 48–49). "Ought," therefore, is a meaningless term except insofar as prescriptions are, in Kant's sense, hypothetical, that is, prescribe something to be done because the activity simultaneously decides for some future state of affairs to which the doing is a means. In relevant respects, the same account is expressed in "emotivist" theory (see, for instance, Ayer) and some forms of twentieth-century existentialism (see, for instance, Sartre) and is at least implied in a considerable tradition of social science indebted to Max Weber.

But this objection has, in effect, already been addressed in the analysis of self-conscious decision. Any such decision is for an evaluative understanding of the alternatives. Were there no character of better and worse to be rightly or wrongly understood, one could not affirm the chosen alternative as good and thus could not understand the several alternatives with respect to choosing. Such an understanding would make no sense, just as understanding or misunderstanding the descriptive similarities and differences of the alternatives would make no sense were there no valid descriptive comparisons. On the objection, in other words, the consciousness of possible ends among which choice is made is exhausted by understanding those descriptive comparisons, and the choice is, so far as understanding is concerned, a void.[9] But this implies that self-understanding makes no sense, because what a self understands in understanding itself is its *decision* among and thus its evaluative comparison of alternatives for purpose.[10]

Precisely because ends must be evaluated in their entirety, moreover, nothing can finally define the good except the necessary character of existence. In truth, all future states of affairs are, whatever else they are, specific possible realizations of existence or the possible as such, and any other feature they may have is a contingent specification of what defines existence necessarily. In that sense, any other measure in terms of which alternatives for purpose might be compared—for instance, contribution to the power and success of a nation or to an equalitarian society or to maximal happiness—is partial. Hence, comparing ends evaluatively in terms of any other characteristic assumes that doing so coincides with comparing them in terms of the metaphysical character of possibility, since the latter is the measure of all things in their entirety. To understand alternatives with respect to choosing is always to assert, at least by implication, that any other evaluative principle is a specification within the given circumstances of maximizing the realization of existence or the possible as such.

To first appearances, calling existence or the possible as such the supreme measure of good may seem problematic. Any possible state of affairs is, on the present account, a possible realization of the good; how, then, can the necessary character of existence compare things with respect to moral and immoral choosing? But this problem is merely apparent because realizing the good is one thing, and maximizing it is another, and the difference can be defined metaphysically if the most general character of possibility is a variable, such that its actualizations can be in some sense greater and less. On neoclassical metaphysics, final real things are all alike concrete singulars in which "the many become one, and are increased by one," that is, unifications in which other unifications are reenacted by way of a decision for future unifications in which this decision will be reenacted. Metaphysically, then, greater and lesser good can mean, and can only mean, greater and lesser unification and, since unity differs with the relations unified, greater and lesser unity-in-diversity.

Whitehead speaks of actualities as exemplifications of "creativity," which is, in his formulation, the metaphysical term defined by "the many become one, and are increased by one." Appropriating this concept, we can say that creativity is the comprehensive good, and greater and lesser good is, in the most general sense, the realization of greater and lesser unity-in-diversity or greater and lesser creativity. A true evaluation of alternative ends, then, compares them in terms of maximizing creativity in the future—and since there can be no metaphysical distinction between creativity realized somewhere and that realized elsewhere, in the future as such. The moral law is: *maximize creativity in the future as such*. This supreme law may also be formulated: decide in accord with the comprehensive purpose, that is, the purpose defined as conscious pursuit of the maximal comprehensive good.

The original belief or set of beliefs constituting subjectivity as such includes, then, belief in the comprehensive purpose and thus in creativity as the comprehensive good. This purpose defines, we may say, the most general character of self-understandings that ought to be chosen. Moreover, our original belief in the comprehensive good also includes or implies a belief in God, in keeping with, as previously argued, the self-differentiation of actuality as such into divine and worldly actualities. The argument from the comprehensive good to God is this: As a variable defining the good, creativity implies real similarities and differences that make no sense absent an individual whose actualities are all-inclusive. Two or more actualities can be greater and lesser (or equal) realizations of the good only by way of comparison between them, in the manner, say, that two or more memories can be more or less vivid only if a present moment of subjectivity includes and thereby compares them. Because realization of the good characterizes any given actuality in its entirety or its full concreteness, the implied comparison must itself be an actuality in which the exemplifications of good are fully included. Hence, the very idea of a comprehensive good implies the universal individual in whose actualizations all actualities are included or unified.

The same point may be stated with focus on the comprehensive purpose: Absent the reality of God, the maximal good to be pursued would be creativity to be realized in a multiplicity of fragmentary actualities. But realization in that sense alone is inconsistent with the purpose to maximize. One's success or failure has no meaning unless the worldly multiplicity is somehow summated, since maximal good in the future as such means all realizations together—and because realization of the good occurs in actualities as wholes, the togetherness of all realizations must itself be actual. Hence, belief in the comprehensive good implies belief in the metaphysical or universal individual, in whose actualizations all that has become actual is again and again unified. In this sense, the future as such whose maximal good all subjects inescapably affirm *is* the future of the divine individual. If every subjective activity believes a true understanding of its own enactment specified as subjectivity, this belief is or includes an original belief in the God whose maximal future defines the comprehensive purpose.

We may also call our original belief an attachment, precisely because its object is or includes the good. If Kant separated the moral law from human inclination or desire because he took all objects of purpose to be in all respects contingent, the moral law as a comprehensive purpose entails that conscious appetition for the good is constitutive of human subjectivity. Accordingly, the issue between Heidegger and neoclassical metaphysics is not whether understanding presupposes attunement, an inclusive attitude or sensibility by virtue of which beings are understood as a whole. The two disagree, rather, on the character of this attunement and, in that sense, phenomenologically. For Heidegger, at least in "What Is Metaphysics?" Dasein is constituted by anxiety because Dasein is held out into the Nothing, and totality presupposes meaning; that is, Being, the difference it makes that there are beings rather than nothing, is finite. In keeping with that explication, our constitutive attunement is not itself an understanding; the Nothing is not itself understood. For neoclassical metaphysics, in contrast, humans as such are attached to the comprehensive good and, thereby, to the divine individual, and this constitutive attunement is an original belief. Totality is prior to meaning.

Human Purposes

Because the good is metaphysical, pursuit of its maximal future realization also maximizes the good realized in the present, that is, in the activity choosing that purpose. An activity (and, indeed, any actuality) maximizes its own unity-in-diversity, realizes the greatest creativity its circumstances allow, by deciding for maximal creativity in the future as such. Were this not the case, a present activity in pursuit of maximal creativity might not maximize its own—and since every possible future, if and when it occurs, becomes present, the good to be pursued would not be creativity but, rather, pursuit of creativity. In other words, the moral law would be: maximize the pursuit, not the realization, of unity-in-diversity. But if the point were not to realize creativity, there would be no reason to pursue it.[11] As the metaphysical character of good defining the moral law, creativity implies a coincidence between pursuit of its maximal realization and its maximal realization in the activity that decides for this purpose.

To avoid misunderstanding, we might underscore here that "subjective activity" designates the actuality in question, in distinction from the subjective individual of which the present becoming is a member. The metaphysical coincidence explicated is not between decision for maximal future good and for maximal unity-in-diversity in the given individual's own future. What maximizes good in the present activity is a decision to pursue maximal creativity in *the future as such* and thus in the future of God, and there is no reason to say that this will coincide with maximizing creativity in one's own future as an individual.[12] Further, nothing we have said implies that greater or lesser creativity in the present depends solely on present decision. To the contrary, the measure of creative achievement possible in the present depends on the past to which it relates. Were that not the case, there would be no point in deciding for creativity in the future, since the latter implies that one's decision can affect the measure in which good may subsequently be achieved.

The potential unity-in-diversity of a given actuality is, in other words, greater or less depending on what other actualities have done for it, that is, depending on the actualities it reenacts. Insofar as a more ordered diversity is received, the potential for present creativity is the greater. For this reason, actualities belonging to a living thing, that is, those within a living society, at least typically realize greater unity-in-diversity than those located within the existence of something inorganic. Further, human activities have immense potential compared with other known creatures of the world because a human individual exists within the massively complex order of societies composing the human body, including the human brain and nervous system, and within communities that order the creative achievements of other human individuals. Accordingly, the moral decision of any given human activity is whether to realize the maximal unity-in-diversity made possible by its particular past or, instead, some lesser possible good.

We should, then, speak of human freedom, the human capacity to be creative, in two senses: On the one hand, there is the freedom of emancipation or empowerment, the greater or lesser potential given by the past. The empowerment enjoyed by a human individual can vary dramatically depending on the biological conditions of her or his body, the larger nonhuman setting, her or his own past achievements and failures, and the communal or associational contexts, including the justice or injustice of larger social and political orders, to which she or he relates. On the other hand, there is moral freedom, the decision with understanding that does or does not pursue the maximal good in the future as such. In itself, this freedom does not vary; it is nothing other than a subjective activity's inalienable privilege and responsibility to decide for a self-understanding. Insofar as the relevant future is the human future, we can add, pursuit of the maximal good is pursuit of maximal emancipation or empowerment for subsequent human activities, including those of the individual who is presently actualized by the decision in question.

Given that subjects may fail to pursue the maximal good, a decision with understanding is an exercise in *moral* freedom because every subject believes, whatever else it believes, a true evaluation of its alternative ends in terms of creativity. Subjectivity necessarily includes, on the argument above, an original belief in the comprehensive purpose in terms of which one's chosen evaluation of possible purposes ought to occur. Absent that belief, no decision could be moral or immoral—because "ought implies can." On its more typical explication, this dictum means that action cannot be prescribed if it is impossible, that is, if the subject for whom it is said to be prescribed does not have the action as an alternative for choice. But "ought implies can" also has another meaning, namely, that a decision cannot be obligatory if the activity in question is ignorant of what is morally required.[13] Unless one understands one's obligation as one's obligation, one cannot decide for it because one ought to do so—and, correspondingly, one cannot be responsible or at fault for failure to meet one's obligation. Were there a decision with understanding without a necessary belief in the comprehensive purpose, the subjective activity would be neither moral nor immoral because the decision would be taken in ignorance of what is morally required. Subjectivity is an exercise of moral freedom because it includes an original belief in the moral law.[14]

As moral or immoral, then, a subjective activity decides among its specific alternatives for purpose by choosing an understanding of the comprehensive good and thus the comprehensive purpose. Since moral and immoral decisions involve differing evaluative comparisons of specific possible ends, they also involve decisions concerning differing terms for comparison. In one sense, this is a choice between only two alternatives. Since the terms for moral comparison are defined by the comprehensive good, one's decision can only be for or against the comprehensive purpose. Deciding for an evaluation of one's specific alternatives in terms of maximal creativity in the future as such, insofar as the future is understood, is the moral decision, and immoral decision can only mean that one has chosen some false understanding of the comprehensive good—even while necessarily believing also the true understanding one has denied. But, naturally, there are many false alternatives, and, in that sense, the decision to be moral or immoral may choose among a plurality of possibilities.

An immoral decision occurs when, necessarily understanding the comprehensive good and also understanding other, specific universals, a subjective activity decides as if one of the latter were the former and, thereby, evaluates specific alternatives for purpose by way of a false comparison. For instance, one might take the good as such to be the pleasure or profit of the individual presently making the decision or the power or success of a given group or nation. Because an immoral decision is not taken in ignorance of one's moral obligation, the decision is self-convicting. However difficult it may be to explain, one cannot decide immorally without knowing, in the sense that one necessarily believes implicitly, that one is deciding to be duplicitous.[15] In this sense, an immoral decision may be called an implicit lie to oneself, and it introduces, however far it may be kept from explicit awareness, a sense of discord, an uneasy conscience.

Clarity may be served by noting that "moral" and "immoral" are used here with a more inclusive meaning than is sometimes the case in other discussions. Some may limit application of these terms to decisions for some specific end or purpose, so that decision about the proper terms for all decisions is not included. In contrast, I take the constitutive choice of a self-understanding, by way of which a given subjective activity unifies itself, to be the primary designation of "moral" and "immoral"—and I understand this to be a systematically complex decision: a choice about the comprehensive purpose determines the evaluation of specific alternatives and is expressed in the choice for a specific purpose, and the latter implicates the former. I also take this usage to agree with Kant in the following respect: the only thing morally good without qualification is a good will, that is, the decision for the moral law as one's fundamental maxim, which is expressed in the decision for a specific maxim in accord with that law.

But if morality in the primary sense concerns this systematically complex decision, specific purposes or maxims may nonetheless be considered in abstraction from decisions about the comprehensive purpose thereby expressed. Considered concretely, the specific purpose of a given activity expresses its decision about the comprehensive good; the former is an aspect of the chosen self-understanding wherein the latter determines the terms for evaluating specific alternatives. Considered abstractly, however, the same specific purpose may, at some important level of specificity, express more than one of the activity's alternatives for understanding the comprehensives good. In given circumstances, for instance, a certain individual may have her or his own maximal pleasure and her of his own maximal power as alternative ways to misrepresent the good, and either choice may be expressed in deceiving another person with whom she or he is interacting. Or, as another example: decision for maximizing creativity in the future as such or for maximizing one's own long-run financial advantage may both require the specific purpose to keep a given promise.

Accordingly, an activity might be called moral or immoral in a secondary sense, whereby the evaluation concerns specific purposes in abstraction from decisions about the comprehensive good and typically designates whether these purposes do or do not accord with specific moral rules and norms, for instance, a norm prescribing promise keeping of proscribing theft. Perhaps one might call an activity immoral in the secondary sense even if the activity is moral in the primary sense. But doing so could only assess the specific purpose as contrary to what most people in relevantly similar circumstances would be morally bound to do, for instance, contrary to a specific rule or norm by which most people in relevantly similar circumstances would be obligated. In their cases, the specific purpose would express immorality in the primary sense. Nonetheless, the assessment is false with respect to the particular agent in question. If she or he does in fact decide for the comprehensive good, the atypical specific purpose means that this agent's possibilities are atypical, whereby doing what most people in relevantly similar circumstances would be morally bound to do is not among her or his specific alternatives for purpose or is prevented by some specific ignorance. In that case, the activity is not in any sense immoral.[16] Debasing treatment of another person is typically immoral, for instance, but it may be that an individual who acts in this way toward members of a certain race has never learned that all persons are full persons—a circumstance that may still be all too common in the education or miseducation of young children.

On the other hand, an activity may clearly be moral in the secondary sense even while it does not express a decision for the comprehensive good—because at some important level of specificity, the same expression would have been chosen were the activity moral in the primary sense. Considered concretely, the expression implicates whatever decision about the metaphysical good was taken; considered abstractly, the specific purpose may conform to the comprehensive purpose without being informed by a decision for it. Here, we may recur to the example cited a moment ago: a person may keep a promise as the maximal good requires because thereby she or he expects to maximize her or his long-term financial advantage, where the latter is taken to be the comprehensive purpose. In Aristotle's terms, one acts as a just person would act but is not a just person. Given this possibility, one can never infer from a specific purpose properly called moral in the secondary sense that the person—either oneself or another—is moral in the primary sense.

Having in mind this twofold use of "moral" and "immoral," we may call decision for or against the comprehensive purpose the essence of moral freedom. If that decision is moral, the specific purpose it informs will be also. But a moral activity in the secondary sense may still fail to be morally good without qualification. I will call the unifying decision for a self-understanding, which includes both a decision about the comprehensive good and its expression in the choice of a specific purpose, a subjective activity's "original decision." Alternatively, one might reserve "original decision" for that aspect of an inclusive self-understanding in which one decides about the comprehensive good—and this more limited meaning might be counseled by the previous use of "original belief" to designate a subject's affirmation of its own enactment specified as subjectivity. In order to preserve the fundamental importance of a self-understanding in this respect, I will reserve the terms "authentic" and "inauthentic" to mark whether an activity embraces with integrity or denies with duplicity its original belief or set of beliefs and thus the comprehensive purpose. Still, I will use "original decision" to designate the inclusive self-understanding with which a subjective activity originates, wherein decision for or against one's authenticity is expressed in or implicated by decision for a specific purpose, and thereby one unifies one's given past in this fully particular activity or deed for the future. This inclusive self-understanding can never be fully explicit. As unifying the activity, the original decision unifies all understandings present, and it must remain in part implicit because explicit understanding is always a fragment of the understandings present. "In fact we can never, even by the strictest examination, get completely behind the secret springs of action, since, when the question is of moral worth, it is not with the actions which we see that we are concerned, but with those inward principles of them which we do not see" (Kant 1949, 25).

Indeed, the decisions we take through much of our lives are not explicit at all. Explicit attention is focused, rather, on some ongoing practice in which we are engaged—for instance, performing a task or engaging in conversation—and our participation proceeds through a series of cumulating, explicitly nonreflective decisions. Even when we focus on some choice to be made and deliberate about it, the deliberation is a process occurring in moments leading up to the decision in question and thus marked by other decisions. Strictly speaking, then, the choice may remain implicit during the moment in which it is taken, although influenced by the explicit deliberation immediately preceding. Nonetheless, there are certainly occasions when focus on a decision includes a clear sense of explicitly choosing. The recognition that original decisions can never be fully explicit does not deny this obvious fact of our existence, since original decisions may be partially explicit or explicit in some respects.

So far as I can see, our focused attention to some decision or set of decisions typically concerns the specific alternatives for purpose or specific ends (or some aspects of them) among which, given the situation, a choice must be made. What remains implicit, then, includes especially the decision for or against one's authenticity. This does not preclude our explicit attention to differing conceptions of the comprehensive good and a decision that one among those being considered is more convincing—as can occur, for instance, when we discuss moral theory or metaphysics. But these are occasions when focus on such conceptions is itself the specific practice in question, chosen from among other specific ends we might then be pursuing, and our decision about the comprehensive good expressed on those occasions may or may not be the same as the conception of it we explicitly endorse. It seems apparent, for instance, that a person engaged in sound philosophical thinking is not necessarily a moral person in the primary sense as she or he is so engaged, and the same is the case with people engaged in specifically religious practices. Perhaps there are also moments, of which certain kinds of mystical experience may be illustrations, in which a person's attention is focused on how her or his originating choice decides about the comprehensive good. If so, they are, I expect, rare.

It remains that one's original decision, inclusive of both the choice about authenticity and its specific expression, is implicit. But this does not mean that an individual has no explicit responsibility for her or his decisions or moral character. The original decision is one decision, and it is as true to say that a decisive evaluation of specific alternatives implicates a decision about the comprehensive good as it is to say that the latter is expressed in the former. In a given moment, therefore, the decision taken explicitly may, as it were, constrain the decision about the comprehensive good. As an example, let us return to the person who, in a given situation, explicitly decides whether to keep a promise, and let us assume that she or he ought to do so. Choosing explicitly to keep the promise does not necessarily implicate a decision for authenticity, since the specific decision or purpose may be in service to, say, maximizing her or his reputation among people from whom later advantage is sought. Nonetheless, choosing this specific purpose may mean that understandings of the good among which she or he simultaneously chooses are correspondingly limited. Beyond pursuit of the maximal comprehensive good and a larger purpose inclusive of gaining some subsequent social advantage, let us suppose, the person might also decide for a comprehensive purpose in which her or his immediate pleasure is especially important, and this purpose could only be expressed in breaking the promise. Hence, the explicit decision to keep the promise excludes an implicit decision for this latter understanding of the comprehensive good.

There is nothing morally good *without qualification* except a good will, that is, an original decision inclusive of a decision for authenticity. But it does not follow that an immoral decision in the primary sense cannot be morally good *with qualification*, that is, better than what it would have been had it chosen another immoral alternative, precisely because the former in contrast with the latter is decision for greater rather than lesser creativity in the future as such. Given the moral obligation to pursue maximal good, we are also morally bound to pursue the greater good, because what matters in the end is greater or lesser contribution to the divine good—and thus, in the present example, the person is bound explicitly to decide for keeping the promise.

In addition, our explicit decisions for or against certain specific alternatives have consequences for the situations in which subsequent moments of our lives occur. Let us assume, as previously noted, that subjectivity, at least beyond rudimentary form, requires an individual who can cumulate learning in dramatic measure. We can then derive a prima facie prescription for a human individual to develop her or his own capacity for effective moral judgment, and we can speak of explicit responsibility to decide accordingly. A decision for the comprehensive purpose, in other words, can be expressed only insofar as specific alternatives for purpose are included within what is then understood, and our explicit decisions today may enhance our relevant understandings tomorrow. This may happen when we explicitly pursue learning about circumstances or situations in which our future decisions will or likely will take place, so that specific purposes then chosen may be more informed and, thereby, have a greater possibility for good. Such learning is, in other words, emancipating or empowering for the individual in question. This will be more the case insofar as the understandings we decide to acquire include explicit understandings of the comprehensive purpose and of specific moral norms that typically apply it to situations of some specific kind. Such knowledge aids in focusing what we learn about contingent circumstances on those most important to maximizing the good—as seems to be the case especially when understandings of institutional norms, including norms of justice, help direct our learning about complex patterns of social and political life.

Moreover, the learned understandings of specific norms may themselves be present when we subsequently choose, explicitly or implicitly, our specific purposes—and if we then choose those purposes accordingly, we may make a greater difference to the future and constrain our decisions about the comprehensive good. Something like this, I judge, occurs in the formation of moral habits. For instance, to continue the previous illustration, learning the specific norm of promise keeping may aid in developing a habit of choosing in accord with it, and thereby one's specific purposes may be better for others and also effective in shaping one's larger understanding of the good. Although one may have begun the practice because one sought certain social advantages, belief in the norm may subsequently evoke a choice against immediate pleasure even in a situation where it is apparent that longer term personal advantages will not be served.

The relation between implicit and explicit aspects of human decision making is, I expect, complex and becomes more so if we consider its dynamics through a temporal sequence of an individual's activities, during which what was previously implicit may become explicit and vice versa. In any case, subjects are always responsible for their original decisions precisely because they are decisions with understanding, inclusive of a necessary belief in the comprehensive good, and we are explicitly responsible for what we become in whatever measure our decisions occur explicitly.

The Good of Human Rights

Norms by which the comprehensive purpose is applied include, I now wish to argue, those that define morally required or permitted social practices. As here used, the term "social practices" does not mean simply any human interaction but, rather, designates a specific kind. These are patterns of interaction constituted by rules, whereby the rules or norms define rights and duties of the participants, so that each understands both her or his proper role and those of the others with whom she or he interacts. For instance, the making of contracts or of promises or the playing of baseball is a social practice, but so, too, are every institutional and virtually all associational interactions in our life together—including the practice of democratic politics, whose basic norms are stipulated by the political constitution.

Saying that such interaction is *constituted* by its rules means that, when one engages in the practice, the very definition of what one does implicates the norms. A person can slide into a bag but cannot steal a base except when playing and implying the rules of baseball; one can mark a card or pull a lever but cannot vote in the United States without implying its principles of democratic government (see Rawls 1955; Searle 1995; Barry). Participation in a morally required or permitted interaction of this kind, therefore, commits one to observe its norms, and a participant who simultaneously decides whether to do so by assessing whether her or his action directly serves the best consequences overall engages in a kind of performative self-contradiction. For instance, making a promise commits one to keeping the promise, and deciding whether to keep it by asking whether this act directly maximizes good overall is the simultaneous affirmation of two inconsistent obligations.

They are inconsistent because, should each prescribe a different decision, there is no moral principle for resolving the conflict. It may seem that assessment in terms of directly serving the maximal good is always overriding. On that account, however, the rules of a social practice would no longer constitute the interaction. A supposed act of promising, for instance, would not, in fact, be promising, with its commitment to keep the promise; rather, one could only say that one will subsequently do something, this being one way in which directly to pursue maximal good. We might formulate a rule calling one subsequently to do as one has said, but one's initial act no longer implies one's commitment to observe the rule. Instead, the latter can only be a guiding rule or "rule of thumb," a counsel with respect to subsequent actions that is thought to identify in many or most circumstances what will continue to maximize good overall. Analogously, "play to tie if at home and to win if on the road" is a guiding but not constitutive rule for the later innings of baseball, a counsel about maximizing one's chances in the game. In contrast to guiding rules, then, norms that constitute morally required or permitted social practices are, we can say, obligatory whatever the consequences.

This does not mean that no social practice can consistently allow exceptions to its standard norms, as if, for instance, promises should never be broken under any conditions. The rules of a practice may be so defined as to include possible exceptions, but the definition of exceptions is, in principle, specific—even if precise formulation of all exceptional circumstances is difficult. For instance, one ought to keep one's promises, but one may be released from many promises if, as it turns out, one's own health will be seriously compromised—and, some may hold, even the moral rule prohibiting theft may not apply if the life of one's child is at stake and the theft meets certain other conditions. Typically, perhaps, exceptional circumstances involve a situation where the rules of another practice also apply, and the second practice is overriding. Having contracted with an employer to work for a wage, for instance, one is bound to do so on certain days, but one is released from this obligation when called to jury duty because, at least in this respect, the obligations of citizenship are overriding. In complicated ways, then, social practices themselves may be hierarchically ordered. But however they may be defined, exceptional circumstances cannot be determined by a *nonspecific* principle, that is, by appeal to an assessment of consequences overall.

For this reason, some hold that a comprehensive purpose cannot be applied or specified in social practices. An ethics directing human purpose to a comprehensive good is, a common objection maintains, exclusive of any principles or norms to be observed whatever the consequences. At the most basic level, teleological ethics are said to exclude all principles of human rights, and this indictment often persuades thinkers to seek a nonteleological moral theory. To be sure, the preceding discussion sought to show that Kantian theories of human rights commit the partialist fallacy because evaluating alternatives for purpose in one respect presupposes a principle in terms of which they are evaluated in all respects. But if that critique is successful against nonteleological theories, the issue now is whether it also precludes the affirmation of human rights in anything other than a provisional sense, that is, as a guiding principle. In terms of a traditional distinction, a teleological moral theory is said to deny all perfect duties, duties "not to do, or not to omit, an action of a certain [specific] kind," whatever the consequences, because all such duties can be canceled by the imperfect duty "to promote a certain general end" (Donagan, 154). Hence, the duties correlative to basic human rights, including the right to life and to control of one's own body, become at best provisional because they are subject to rebuttal by the overriding obligation to create the best consequences.

That human rights of the innocent can be morally canceled seems counterintuitive. In addition, the indictment continues, the exclusion of inviolable rights betrays a more pervasive problem: a comprehensive good finally prevents social cooperation and coordination. Because all rules of social interaction may be overridden by the imperfect duty to maximize the good, no person can have settled expectations about what others will do, even assuming they act morally. Having received a promise, for instance, one cannot count on its being honored, because maximal good at the time when the promise falls due may require or permit its maker to act otherwise. Moreover, the unpredictability is, as it were, cumulative. Once all actors must decide without settled expectations regarding the actions of others, what any given actor can expect of others becomes radically indeterminate. In other words, an orderly social life requires social practices and thus principles and norms to be observed whatever the consequences. A teleological ethic, one might say, self-destructs because, on any plausible account of the comprehensive purpose, maximizing the good requires the social cooperation and coordination an ethic of this kind prevents (see Barry, 217–21).[17]

Naturally, the supposed need for social practices may itself be contested. Guiding rules, some may argue, are themselves sufficient to insure cooperation and coordination, given only the general recognition that circumstances in which they (or, at least, the most important ones) are overridden by the maximal good are rare. Even principles of human rights may be considered guiding rules because the situations in which they are morally canceled will be especially rare—and in those thoroughly exceptional circumstances, a teleological ethic may rightly bite this bullet. If guiding rules are generally understood to apply "by and large and for the most part," each actor will have good reason to expect that others will generally act on them, thus establishing cooperation and coordination, even if each also knows that, in rare circumstances, others may act contrary to such expectations.

This account of teleology then depends on the following assertion: pursuit of the maximal good permits actions in violation of certain guiding rules only in rare circumstances (I will assume that the rules in question have been specified; they might include, for instance, certain rules of human rights). This assertion might be understood as a descriptive statement about the consequences of action, something like: for actions generally, the probability is high that violating certain guiding rules will, given a certain definition of the good, lessen realization of the good. On this reading of the assertion, the account depends on an empirical generalization because the probable consequences of any given action are contingent on particular circumstances. Accordingly, the assertion cannot itself be derived from the comprehensive good and thus can be justified only as a generalization derived from past moral experience. On that interpretation, however, the assertion becomes itself a guiding rule, and consistency now requires that this rule, too, can be overridden by an assessment of consequences overall—and with that implication, the account becomes incoherent.

Alternatively, the relevant limitation on violations may be advanced as itself a universal moral principle, something like: act in accord with the guiding rules (again assuming that these have been specified) except in rare circumstances. But this principle constitutes a social practice—indeed, a universal social practice. To be sure, one might now give up the refusal of all social practices, allowing this one but only this one, and affirming it precisely because the good cannot be maximized without social cooperation and coordination. I will subsequently argue that social cooperation and coordination do indeed require a universal social practice and, further, that such a practice is authorized by the telos of maximal creativity. But this cannot be a practice constituted by the principle "act in accord with the guiding rules except in rare circumstances," because that principle is hopelessly vague or indeterminate absent a universal standard of "rare." Since the probable future effects of any given action are, as previously mentioned, contingent on particular circumstances, no definition of the probabilities for maximal good that marks when violation of the guiding rules is permitted can be authorized by the comprehensive purpose. Hence, any determinate character given to "rare" and thus to this supposed deontological principle can only be arbitrarily asserted.

Nor can this problem be avoided by appeal to inadequacies of understanding. Assessing the probabilities for maximal good attached to differing alternatives can often be immensely complicated. Given the fragmentariness of human understanding, it might be argued, guiding rules are required, and "rare" in the relevant sense means circumstances in which greater good is clearly served by acting against the rules. But this account of the principle remains indeterminate without a defined measure of "clear." Because the relevant probabilities for any given action are contingent on its specific circumstances, so, too, is the relevant meaning of "clear," and thus a universal definition of that term can only be stipulated.

I conclude that a credible comprehensive purpose requires application through (determinate) social practices. In their absence, any such purpose self-destructs by removing the moral basis for social cooperation and coordination, and the contention that no teleological ethic can consistently avoid this implication is a serious challenge to the metaphysics advocated in this work. As an indictment of all teleological ethics, however, the critique depends on the following assumption: a comprehensive purpose prescribes its own direct application to each action; that is, the alternatives open to each and every decision should be assessed without attention to the social consequences of how all possibilities for action are assessed. All teleological ethics, to rephrase the point, entail that each action should be "separately taken" (Barry, 224). But the validity of this assumption is not transparent. At least to first appearances, a teleological ethic would *not* so prescribe, precisely for the reasons on which the critique depends; namely, direct application to each action would prevent the social coordination and cooperation required by the maximal good. Perhaps, then, a teleological ethic prescribes its own *indirect* application to some actions, that is, application through social practices, including a practice constituted by human rights, because such application is essential to maximizing the good.

If the difference between direct and indirect applications of a comprehensive purpose can be sustained, it commends a refinement of the common distinction in recent moral theory between teleological and deontological ethics. On a typical account, the former grounds morality in some good to be maximized, and the latter asserts principles of the moral life to be honored whatever the consequences because they are independent of any inclusive telos. Given the difference between direct and indirect applications here under consideration, we require a more nuanced set of terms. Principles or norms said to be independent of any inclusive good should be called nonteleological. In distinction, deontological principles or norms prescribe duties to be honored whatever the consequences. In a given ethic, deontological norms may or may not be nonteleological, depending on whether they are said to apply indirectly some inclusive purpose, because such a purpose may itself prescribe or permit one or more social practices.

The issue, then, is whether an understanding of maximally good consequences can be so formulated as consistently to prescribe such indirect application. To the best of my reasoning, this is not possible without a universal deontological principle or set of principles and thus a universal social practice, such that both the comprehensive purpose and the principles of this universal social practice are conditions of existence with understanding as such, implied by every act of subjectivity. If we assume such transcendental conditions, pursuit of the maximal good and conformity to the practice imply each other; that is, transcendental conditions specific to subjectivity are mutually implicative, and thus the comprehensive purpose prescribes the practice as an indirect application. The comprehensive good, we may say, is so defined that pursuit of it is essentially a common enterprise among subjects. But a teleological ethic cannot, to repeat the point for which I will now seek to argue, consistently prescribe indirect application without a universal social practice. In other words, morally valid social practices cannot be exhausted by specifications of the comprehensive purpose to some or other circumscribed social context; rather, such specifications must be mediated by a social practice whose norms are morally binding in all social contexts.

Suppose, for instance, that a teleological ethic purports to prescribe for some (but not all) social contexts a democratic form of politics and thus action in accord with a democratic constitution whatever the consequences, but the ethic does not prescribe a deontological principle, for instance, a principle of human rights, by which action is bound in all social contexts and of which a democratic constitution is, in some contexts, a fitting specification. The ethic is, so far as I can see, internally inconsistent because it violates the logical rule that specifications of a general character or principle cannot include features contrary to those defining it. If, for instance, the general character of human activities defines them as self-conscious, then no specific set of human activities can be nonconscious. In the supposed teleological ethic described, the general principle prescribes activities pursuing maximal consequences of a certain kind and does not imply or include deontological requirements for this pursuit. Hence, no specification of this comprehensive obligation can prescribe certain actions whatever their consequences "separately taken." So far as I can see, in other words, teleology is consistent with deontological norms only if the maximal good to be pursued itself includes and thus prescribes universally a certain social practice.

Another way to make the point is this: were all morally valid social practices specifications of the comprehensive purpose to circumscribed social contexts, there would be, in effect, no difference between direct and indirect applications of the comprehensive purpose. In the absence of a universal social practice, the supposed rules of a specific social practice could be observed by all supposed participants if each applied the comprehensive purpose directly and with sufficient awareness of the specific circumstances in which application occurs. The proposal implies, for instance, that all people in a given political community would be able to act in accord with a democratic constitution given only that they sought to maximize good consequences and had adequate knowledge of their situation—since precisely the situation itself, independent of any universal deontological principle, would warrant the democratic practice. But this proposal can arrive at its point only by assuming what it purports to show, namely, that a teleological ethic authorizes social practices. In fact, no person could conclude that her or his action in accord with a democratic constitution will maximize the good unless the supposed knowledge of the situation on which this conclusion is based includes knowledge that other people will act likewise, and knowledge of what other people can be expected to do is not available without social practices. "The optimal course of action for me depends upon what I expect others to do, while the optimal course of action for others depends upon what they expect me to do. . . . Expectations can be coordinated only by a system of rules," such as those stipulated by a democratic constitution, "which are adhered to regardless of consequences" (Barry, 220). Without a universal social practice, the comprehensive purpose can only prescribe its direct application to every decision, and the indictment of teleological ethics reviewed above is in force.[18]

On my reading, the assumption that all teleological ethics prescribe direct application to all decisions is more convincing to critics who advance it because they assume that social practices could only be applications of a comprehensive purpose to some or other specific circumstances.[19] In any event, I am persuaded that pursuit of maximal creativity in the future as such is essentially a common enterprise; that is, this comprehensive purpose implies and is implied by a (determinate) deontological principle constituting a universal social practice.

Because this deontological principle prescribes indirect applications of the comprehensive purpose, authorization of the former by the latter cannot be established by showing that actions prescribed by the principle directly maximize the good. Still, the principle will be implied by the purpose if both are transcendental conditions of subjectivity. Accordingly, the argument here can be in its own way indirect—first showing that subjectivity as such implies a universal social practice constituted by respect for all subjects and then confirming that pursuit of maximal creativity is also transcendental by showing that it includes and thus prescribes that universal social practice. I will here present the argument in summary form and will revisit both steps during the discussion of democratic justice in chapter 6.

The argument for a universal social practice is based on the claim to moral validity made or implied by every activity. Decision for a self-understanding is decision for a self-expression, whereby a subjective activity makes or implies a claim for itself as morally valid, that is, as morally permissible or morally required. Because it thereby includes a claim to express the comprehensive purpose, the activity claims validity for its understanding of the original imperative by which all subjective activities are morally bound and, in that sense, claims validity for a moral prescription applicable to all subjects. Thus, every subjective activity implies that all other subjective activities affected by its self-expression should respond to these effects in accord with the same understanding of the comprehensive purpose. But "ought implies can," which now means that recipients must be able to obey the implied prescription because it is valid.

It then follows that every subjective activity is morally bound to respect the freedom of all recipient activities—and thus morally bound to respect every other activity as subjective. To be sure, no activity can respect another without understanding which recipients of its expression are indeed subjective, but this merely repeats in the present context that no activity can decide in accord with a general moral obligation except insofar as the contingent future is understood. If the relevant understanding is present, so, too, is the moral obligation to respect subjective recipients as subjective. In keeping with the previous discussion, this conclusion has been reached in terms of actualities that occur with understanding. We can then derive from it a principle formulated in terms of subjective individuals, assuming only that subjective activities depend on being member actualities of individuals: every subjective individual is always bound to respect the subjectivity of all other subjective individuals. Given that effects on subjective recipients caused by claims to validity may be called communicative effects, we may reformulate the principle: every subject is bound to respect the communicative rights of all subjects and, thereby, to participate in a universal practice of communicative respect.[20]

The principle of communicative respect is transcendental.[21] Belief in it is original because implied by the claim to moral validity of every decision for a self-understanding, whatever the purpose for which validity is claimed. This moral belief is, in other words, an aspect of our original belief in subjectivity as such as a specification of the possible as such. The required respect, we can say, is implied by the metaethical form of subjective decision; that is, the principle can be derived without explicit assertion of any other normative principle. For this reason, the communicative rights of subjects cannot be overridden by the comprehensive purpose. If one asserts that one's direct pursuit of maximal good cancels the obligation to respect all subjects, one engages in a pragmatic self-contradiction, precisely because the obligation is transcendental; in claiming to be released from it, one simultaneously affirms it as universally applicable. Thus, the principle of communicative respect is deontological, to be observed whatever the consequences, and no teleological ethic can be valid that does not consistently include or imply this principle as an indirect application of maximizing the good.

To be sure, every teleological ethic implies the principle, simply because the latter is transcendental. Still, the given teleological ethic may not be implied by the principle, and thus the ethic is not self-consistent because its conception of the comprehensive good to be pursued is not implied by subjectivity as such. If pursuit of maximal creativity in the future as such *is* a principle implied by subjectivity as such, then it will consistently imply the principle of communicative respect, because both are transcendental moral principles. But we may also explicate that consistency in terms of creativity as the good. Toward this end, I will simply assert what more extended metaphysical argument could, I think, establish: within the world, the existence of subjects is marked by possibilities for unity-in-diversity dramatically greater than any kind of existence without understanding. This does not mean that only existence with understanding is intrinsically good, such that all other creatures are solely instrumental to subjective creativity. To the contrary, all actualized unity-in-diversity is intrinsically good. Further, we may here leave open whether pursuit of greater creative possibilities for subjects is properly constrained by responsibilities to other worldly creatures. However that question is answered, the distinctive capacity of subjective existence does entail that subjects as a community are not teleologically subservient to creativity actualized by some other kind of creature or community of creatures. Hence, insofar as human decision properly aims at the good realized by subjects, our activity properly seeks to create a common world of self-expressions, in which diversity is maximally emancipating for all.

In other words, the maximal good may constrain but nonetheless includes a communal order in which every subjective achievement becomes maximally empowering for all other subjects—or, we may say, a common world of relations among subjects maximizing the creative possibilities of all. Such an order is transparently a common achievement or, to say the same, pursuit of the maximal good consistently prescribes a certain determinate kind of social interaction as a universal social practice. This prescription, moreover, fully embraces the metaethical form of subjective community, because giving and receiving communicative respect is always empowering, whatever other social practices we should create within the community of subjects.

A substantially longer discussion is needed to sustain this summary argument and to explicate its implications for or applications to our life together. But if original belief in the comprehensive good can be successfully united with original belief in communicative respect, it does not follow that all human subjects necessarily understand and affirm the content of *human* rights. This is because subjects are not necessarily human subjects; that is, individuals who exist by way of self-understanding do not necessarily inhabit the kind of body marking the human species. In drawing this distinction, we may seem to echo Kant's assertion that the moral law "must be valid not merely for men, but for all *rational creatures generally*" (1949, 26; see also 42). On my reading, Kant means that some rational creatures may be noumenal and thus unknowable, and in this sense, his assertion is untenable. We can know that possible rational creatures we do not otherwise experience can only be possible subjective individuals, whose subjectivity exemplifies the same metaphysical characteristics and thus includes the same original beliefs as our own. But we should agree that subjectivity does not entail human existence and thus does not entail life within a human body. That existence with understanding has emerged in our world within the human species is an empirical fact, not a transcendental or metaphysical (in the broad sense) condition.

The difference between subjects and human subjects is important because the content of most human rights is inseparable from the distinctive characteristics of human beings. Chapter 6 will argue and, therefore, I will here simply assert that human rights include formative rights to public and private liberties, by which the principle of communicative respect is specified to human existence. Rights to private liberties include rights to life and control of one's own body, and rights to public liberties include (wherever democracy is possible) rights to freedom of speech and freedom of assembly and, summarily, to democratic political participation—and the content of these rights cannot be explicated without reference to the human body. The human rights to life and to control of one's own body transparently illustrate the point, but rights to public liberties or democratic participation cannot be explicated so as to distinguish permitted and prohibited actions without reference to how human decisions are expressed in bodily movements.

As chapter 6 will also argue, moreover, human rights are not exhausted by these formative rights because the latter imply certain substantive human rights, and the content of these substantive rights is also inseparable from the requirements of distinctively human creativity. Insofar as it depends on nonmetaphysical conditions, the content of human rights cannot be within the content of original belief. Still, the principle of communicative respect is transcendental, so that principles of human rights can be derived given only the empirical conditions of distinctively human subjects. These principles are, therefore, deontological, and the rights of all humans are to be honored whatever the consequences.[22]

Insofar as human rights are nonmetaphysical, understandings of them must be acquired, and therefore the norms of all social practices, universal and specific, through which the comprehensive purpose is applied indirectly to human life depend on learning. Recognition of this fact makes especially apparent how central moral learning is within the human adventure. Social practices are pervasively important to maximizing creativity in the future as such. Empowering human subjects through the ordered diversity of human communities requires political governance that stipulates a complex social practice or set of social practices, and virtually all of the associations prescribed or permitted by such governance are constituted by deontological norms. This simply confirms that insistence on the metaphysics of human purpose in no way elides the significance of explicit attention to the moral character of our lives. The argument in this work is solely that our moral hopes and strivings make no sense absent an original belief in our relation to the good, without which there could not be a moral enterprise and, indeed, without which we could not exist with understanding. Because we necessarily understand the comprehensive purpose, all of our decisions are taken by way of an original decision for a self-understanding, and whether we are moral or immoral in the primary sense is determined by this implicit decision.

For this reason, our explicit attention to the moral enterprise may also include religious activities. On its broadest definition, the distinctive purpose of these activities is to represent explicitly the metaphysics of human purpose in expressions through which we humans seek to cultivate in our own future activities original decisions for this understanding. Perhaps philosophical reflection functions for some in this way, and we might then speak of philosophy functioning religiously. Typically, however, a religion is a cultural formation or set of concepts and symbols and associated communal practices in terms of which or through which its adherents explicitly affirm as decisive an understanding of their relation to existence as such, seeking thereby to persuade their own subsequent activities to take original decisions accordingly. The distinctive function of religion, we may say, is to mediate original decisions that are authentic and thus moral in the primary sense. If the understanding of existence as such previously developed in this work is sound, a true religion is one that decisively represents in this way our original belief in our existence as a coenactment of the divine and thus a communion with God, who empowers us to decide for maximal creativity in the future as such and, thereby, to maximize our worth to the all-inclusive and ever-enriching unity of all things.

Chapter 5

The Metaphysics of Democracy, Part 1

Introduction

During the past several decades, political theory in the West has been inseparable from democratic theory. Stretching back to classical Greece, "democracy" has been used with diverse meanings. In part because some of these have been disparaging, it has not always been the word of choice for those modern thinkers whose political theories or commitments have nonetheless contributed to the democratic advance. Instead, thinkers have endorsed, for instance, "constitutionalism" or "constitutional liberalism" or "republicanism." Whatever the possible differences these terms may express and the importance thereof in other contexts, I will use "democracy" in a summary sense to name the reversal in which modernity turned its back on the long Western tradition of rule by the one or the few, who were supposedly authorized by special gifts of wisdom or virtue or divine appointment, and affirmed rule by the many—so that governing power is accountable to the citizens.

To be sure, who counts as a member of the many was, at least in earlier democratic expressions, decidedly restricted, and how best to make power accountable has been contested, and thus a continuing debate about what democracy means and requires has occurred. Still, precisely this question has become central to political theory because the summary reversal is profound and rightly understood as a triumph. While political proposals may go by other names—"liberal" or "communitarian" or "republican" or "Marxist" or "feminist" or "postmodern"—no contemporary Western theory will be convincing unless it can also claim to explicate or, at least, to be consistent with the proper character of democratic politics.

Within this context, recent proposals, notwithstanding extensive disagreements among them, largely perpetuate a consensus dominating moral and political theory in the West for two centuries, namely, that democratic principles of the good and the right are properly separated from any understanding of existence or reality as such. Thereby, most democratic theory since 1800 shares with pursuit of the philosophical task generally during this time a profound suspicion of metaphysics in the strict sense and thus departs from virtually all premodern and early modern Western thought. This chapter and the next offer an alternative by formulating democratic principles for which the metaphysics of human purpose previously explicated is the essential backing, and these principles will be developed through asking about the relation of democracy to religion.

The previous chapters argued that life with understanding becomes what it is by way of original decision for an understanding of ourselves in relation to totality and the purpose it defines. Those chapters ended by defining the distinctive function of religion as concerned with this original decision: a religion is a cultural formation or set of concepts and symbols and associated communal practices in terms of which or through which its adherents explicitly affirm as decisive an understanding of their relation to existence as such, seeking thereby to persuade their own subsequent activities to take original decisions accordingly. Those who seek a "postmetaphysical" political theory, to borrow a term from Jürgen Habermas (see Habermas 1992), will not accept the essential reference in this definition to original beliefs and, by implication, to both broad and strict metaphysical necessity. Still, virtually all who discuss modern politics will agree that religions, whatever else they do, typically represent and seek to mediate some or other comprehensive orientation for human life and do so in relation to an understanding or supposed understanding of ultimate reality.

This latter statement is sufficient to recognize why the relation of democracy to religion is a basic problem in democratic theory. On the one hand, rule by the many has emerged in the modern world coincident with the emergence of religious plurality *internal* to political communities, so that religious freedom or, at least, religious toleration has typically characterized democratic politics. Indeed, some have argued that religious diversity, leading in the sixteenth and seventeenth centuries to ruinous religious wars, was a central cause of modern democracy, whose beginnings were historically inseparable from the attempt to find neutral terms for peaceful coexistence (see, for instance, Rawls 2005, introduction). On the other hand, political principles consistent with legitimate religious plurality must be those all citizens can endorse, whatever their religious commitment—and if each religion claims to represent the comprehensive orientation, it is not immediately clear how any citizen who is also a religious adherent can consistently affirm principles for political life that do not finally depend on the convictions her or his religion expresses. More briefly stated, then, the apparent problem is this: because a religion represents a comprehensive orientation, differing religions in the same political community appear to threaten political conflict that cannot be composed or civilized because there is nothing more fundamental to which politics might appeal.

Given focus on this problem, it may seem obvious that John Rawls's achievement, especially the "political and not metaphysical" (Rawls 2005, 10) proposal of his later thought, is the proper conversation partner for making here a contribution to democratic theory. Still, I am persuaded that Rawls is more appreciative of the need for neutral political principles than he is of the apparent problem they present to citizens who affirm a comprehensive orientation or, in his term, a "comprehensive doctrine."[1] In this respect, several discussions of Rawls's solution have effectively made the point (see Wolterstorff, Eberle), and I find especially convincing the internal criticism of Rawls included in Jeffrey Stout's recent *Democracy and Tradition*. Stout's work is the more important for our present discussion because of the alternative he develops, and I will approach the metaphysics of democracy through a conversation with that proposal.

In a way Rawls does not, Stout seeks to credit within the democratic process the comprehensive orientations provided by religious convictions. For this reason, he formulates a third alternative to Rawls, on the one hand, and, on the other, to the indictment of democratic politics advanced by what Stout calls "the new traditionalism" in Christian theology. With Rawls, however, Stout defends an account of democracy that purports to be independent of all metaphysics, and thus he provides a challenge to the position the present work seeks to commend. *Democracy and Tradition*, we may say, pursues political thought consistent not only with Kant's deconstruction of metaphysics in the strict sense but also with the critique of universal reason, discussed in chapter 1 and chapter 2, and thus of political thought independent of metaphysics in the broad sense. To be sure, chapter 2 sought to show, through its discussion with Heidegger, why the critique of universal reason is unconvincing. But the conversation with Stout will test that conclusion by asking whether and, if so, how metaphysical necessity is consistent with democratic politics.

Democracy without Metaphysics

"Stated in Rawlsian terms," Stout says, "my topic . . . is the role of free public reason in a political culture that includes conflicting religious conceptions of the good" (Stout 2004a, 2).[2] Seeking "a satisfactory account of the role of religious traditions in modern democracy" (183), he defends democratic politics against "the new traditionalism," a Christian theological understanding that threatens "to deprive us of the actual and potential benefits of exchanging reasons across the boundaries of enclaves" (183) and is represented by thinkers such as Alasdair MacIntyre, John Milbank, and Stanley Hauerwas. On their view, liberal democracy as such is hostile to religion generally and Christianity specifically, and thus they counsel withdrawal from liberal political participation. Liberal politics, their indictment reads, is essentially secularistic or antireligious and, as a consequence, destructive of communal tradition and the cultivation of virtue.

But this attack, Stout argues, is aimed in fact at "contractarian" liberalism (84), which new traditionalists falsely take to be an accurate representation of the modern democratic ideal. Preeminently formulated by the later Rawls, such liberalism founds democracy on "freestanding" principles, commonly affirmed by citizens with diverse religious and philosophical views or what Rawls calls "reasonable comprehensive doctrines" (Rawls 2005, 12, 144–45). As new traditionalists assert, contractarian liberalism is indeed antireligious and thus secularistic because, on its account, politics by way of public reason is, at least in the end, independent of any comprehensive doctrine and, thereby, prescribes constraint on political appeal to one's religious belief.[3] That all citizens can and should understand justice to be freestanding, religious convictions notwithstanding, is precisely what new traditionalists rightly deny. Hence, Stout's response to the new traditionalists must also discredit Rawlsian liberalism and must make "an affirmative case for seeing modern democracy" in contrast to both (2). So central to his project is the dialogue with these two views that "a successful philosophical account of democratic political culture" is said to "overcome the weaknesses . . . in these approaches while simultaneously inheriting their strengths" (183).

Stout subjects the two antagonist views to extended internal critiques I find admirably thorough, judicious, and, excepting the few occasions when his own philosophical position is implied, convincing. He rightly concludes that both "thrive on exposing one another's weaknesses" (183), and the consequence is destructive confusion. Vindicating a third alternative, he argues, depends, against the claims of both, on seeing democracy itself as a tradition. Here "tradition" means "a discursive practice considered in the dimension of history" (135) or "viewed diachronically" (136) and is distinguished from the kind of "*traditionalist* practice" affirmed by the new traditionalists, which includes deference to "authoritative texts and authoritative interpreters of texts" and requires "institutions . . . capable of securing agreement on a doctrine of the good" (136). Summarily stated, the democratic tradition is a discursive practice "of giving and asking for ethical reasons" (6) and is marked by "ideals of equal voice and equal consideration of all citizens" (3), so that "all have some share in electing rulers and are free to speak their minds in a wide-ranging discussion that rulers are bound to take seriously" (4). As such, the practice is also marked, contrary to what new traditionalists assert, by its own set of virtues important to "guiding a citizen through the process of discursive exchange and political decision making" (85; for examples of the relevant virtues, see 84–85, 207).

Appreciating this third alternative requires recognition that "the ethical discourse of most modern democracies is *secularized*" but is not, as new traditionalists charge and Rawlsian liberals imply, "a reflection of commitment to *secularism*" (93). The latter "entails the denial of theological assumptions" and expels "theological expression from the public sphere" (93). In contrast, a secularized discourse means only "that participants in a given discursive practice are not in a position to take for granted that their interlocutors are making the same religious assumptions they are" (97); participants cannot assume a shared conviction about "what is most important" (327, n. 20) or shared conception of the comprehensive good. To the contrary, the discourse includes many "comprehensive visions" (2); "modern democratic culture . . . does not have a single view of the grand scheme of things; it opens up space in which many such views can be held and acted upon" (199). Accordingly, "what becomes secularized . . . is a set of discursive presuppositions, not necessarily the worldview . . . of participants" (175), and resentment of secularized discourse "is indistinguishable from resentment of religious diversity" (99). The third alternative, then, does not depend on the secularism of contractarian liberalism, even while affirming the exchange of reasons, or the traditionalist refusal of secularized discourse, even while insisting on the "full participation in public life" of "citizens with strong religious commitments" (296).

Still, Stout is aware that his third alternative cannot be convincing unless itself immune to the kind of internal criticism he directs toward the others—or, what comes to the same thing, unless the distinction between secularized discourse and secularism can be theoretically sustained. Were the third alternative equally problematic, it would only compound the confusion. The book's final part, then, "aims to make explicit what a *democratic tradition* involves" (213) and, specifically, to clarify its secularized discourse through an explication variously called "pragmatic expressivism" (184), "modest pragmatism" (255), and "a pragmatic version of *deliberative democracy*" (339, n. 11).[4] With respect to moral theory, the explication centers on an account of norms as "creatures of discursive social practices" (246) and thus of "the ethical life of a people" (197). In brief, the material practical inferences of individuals and groups, that is, inferences from a given understanding of factual circumstances to a moral conclusion (as well as "noninferential" or "perceptual" judgments [217]), include implied normative affirmations that can be made explicit or expressed as "statement[s] of rules" (273), whereby they are opened to the demand for reasons and thus to criticism and self-criticism.

Thus, norms are "instituted by a form of ethical life (which shapes the subjectivity and rationality of the individuals who participate in it)" (273)—and, having been made explicit, norms can be transformed through "expressive freedom" (80). Novel performances can be implicit critics of established rules, and, further, "it . . . becomes possible . . . to inject into the discussion a novel normative claim that is not yet implicitly accepted into anybody's material practical reasoning" (Stout 2005, 722). Like all others, specifically political norms are instituted in this way (see 273). Although Stout does not develop systematically a set of democratic rights, it seems apparent that explicit affirmations in which "ideals of equal voice and equal consideration of all citizens" (3) are expressed in a democratic constitution as the familiar rights of democratic citizenship should themselves be seen as "creatures of the practices of accountability in which we exchange reasons with one another" (185; see also 12). These rights, the practice they constitute, and the correlative democratic virtues define the tradition of secularized discourse that, on Stout's proposal, is hospitable to diverse secularistic and religious worldviews or comprehensive visions.

The distinction between secularized discourse and secularism, in the sense that constitutive norms of the former properly allow debate about the latter (and, thereby, also properly allow debate about theistic affirmations) is, I think, incisive.[5] Moreover, I find more to accept than to question in Stout's explication of democratic discourse as a practice in which normative affirmations implicit in the life of a people are made explicit and thus subjected to contestation and the demand for reasons by citizens who rightly have equal voice—and, accordingly, one is well advised to appropriate Stout's effective account of democracy as a tradition having its own characteristic virtues. But whether Stout provides an adequate explication of secularized discourse is another matter, and there is cause for doubt when his presentation of pragmatic expressivism leads him to endorse "ethics without metaphysics" (246).

Stout means, he tells us, "metaphysics in the pejorative sense" (331, n. 1). In his book, he does not explain that sense, but the discussion as a whole makes his intent sufficiently clear. He does not mean to deny all moral claims based on beliefs about the nature of human beings or the nature of reality, that is, moral claims related to what Rawls calls comprehensive doctrines. Many such doctrines are, on Stout's accounting, metaphysical in a nonpejorative sense and thus fully consistent with democracy; indeed, were this not the case, it would be obviously inconsistent to say that secularized discourse is hospitable to diverse secularistic and religious worldviews. Still, there is a kind of metaphysics of which ethics, Stout holds, has no need, and metaphysics in this pejorative sense at least includes any account on which rationality or human activity is bound by principles or conditions necessary to all subjects, such that those principles or conditions are independent of any specific practices and insofar define all moral and immoral human activities or practices. To affirm principles or conditions as metaphysical in this sense is to purport that every denial of what one thereby affirms is pragmatically self-contradictory, the act of denial implying what it denies.[6]

Notwithstanding this restriction on the sense in which ethics is without metaphysics, what Stout excludes is nonetheless metaphysics in the broad sense, that is, reflection on the conditions or character of subjectivity as such or existence with understanding as such. If we assume that metaphysics in the strict sense is possible, then necessary conditions of subjectivity include but are not exhausted by necessary conditions of reality. But when he rejects "metaphysics in the pejorative sense," Stout means that ethics is or can be without any necessary conditions of subjectivity, whether or not these conditions are said to include metaphysical conditions in the strict sense. On his view, ethics no more requires a Kantian than a Platonic metaphysics of morals—and in this chapter, I will, unless otherwise noted, henceforth also use "metaphysics" in this way. Exclusion of any such metaphysical principles is how Stout should be understood when he refuses all notions of "pure practical reason" or "practical reason operating independently of the ethical life of a people" (197).[7] No moral principles are logically independent of specific historical context, so moral norms are entirely creatures of historically located social practices, and thus Stout's account of moral meaning and validity implicates the critique of universal reason. For want of another term, I will call his theoretical account an instance of *specific pragmatism*.

On this analysis, then, Stout's third alternative to contractarian liberalism and the new traditionalism depends on his specific pragmatism and thus cannot be sustained unless ethics is independent of metaphysics. But if we are led to this accounting, some might object, Stout has been misread. Although himself a specific pragmatist, he intends his claim for this theory to occur *within* the secularized discourse he proposes as the third alternative. His conception of discourse, in other words, does not require that all democratic citizens agree to be specific pragmatists. To the contrary, his discussion of ethics without metaphysics belongs to the exchange of reasons into which democracy also welcomes those who affirm the transcendental or metaphysical enterprise.

Indeed, Stout himself clarifies his intention in just this way when he responds to critical discussions of his book: the chapter entitled "Ethics without Metaphysics" did not mean "to ban metaphysical commitments from democratic deliberation." That he here refers to metaphysical views in what he calls the pejorative sense becomes apparent when he continues: "Nor did I mean to imply that full-fledged participation in the democratic tradition involves being committed to nonmetaphysical pragmatism." To the contrary, "the broader democratic tradition includes people with various sorts of metaphysical commitments and some people who are suspicious of metaphysics. In my view, there is ample room in the discussion for all of these people" (2004b, 370). The chapter in question, Stout summarizes, describes "the relationship between metaphysical commitments and normative discourse from my point of view" but is "not saying . . . that my view of this relationship is itself a presupposition of democratic normative discourse" (2004b, 371) any more than a metaphysical view is such a "presupposition."

Democracy without Metaphysics: A Critique

In taking account of this clarification, we should note how Stout intends the term "presupposition" when he designates presuppositions of normative discourse. As he explains in differentiating "two senses of the term 'presupposition' " (97), he does *not* mean commitments or affirmations that may be *implicit* in one's assertions or one's participation in a certain practice—as, for instance, a certain comprehensive vision may be implicit when a given citizen endorses a given political proposal. Rather, he speaks of discursive presuppositions in a second sense, namely, commitments to which all participants must explicitly adhere in order for a given discourse to occur. Such presuppositions are, in other words, *explicit* conditions of the practice, in the sense that each participant can take certain norms or assumptions to be explicitly shared by all others (see 97–98)—and we might also say, with respect to political discourse, that these presuppositions define the ethics of citizenship. Hence, the participation of any given citizen is properly rejected if she or he does not act in accord with those presuppositions and, thereby, violates the ethics of citizenship.

Consider, for instance, a political community in which some given religion or conception of the comprehensive good is established, that is, constitutionally stipulated as official in the sense that requires all citizens to be adherents thereof. Affirmation of this religion or conception is then included within the ethics of citizenship, and deliberation within the discourse is legitimate only when it seeks to specify that conception to other political decisions. Accordingly, when Stout says of secularized discourse "that participants . . . are not in a position to take for granted that their interlocutors are making the same religious assumptions they are" (97), he means that such assumptions are not presuppositions of the discourse in the sense of explicit conditions. Similarly, when he denies that his view of "the relationship between metaphysical commitments and normative discourse . . . is itself a presupposition of democratic normative discourse" (2004b, 371), he means that affirmation of specific pragmatism is not itself part of the ethics of citizenship.

Still, any account of politics as rule by way of discussion and debate requires a conception of public reason, precisely because one does not explicate what democratic discourse is without articulating in what discourse consists. Indeed, the problem Stout has with contractarian liberalism is precisely the conception of public reason on which the ethics of citizenship is itself secularistic because committed to freestanding principles of justice, and his "topic . . . is the role of free public reason in a political culture that includes conflicting religious conceptions of the good" (2). Hence, we can pursue whether specific pragmatism is an explicit condition of Stout's secularized discourse by asking about his conception of democracy's exchange of reasons.

When Stout discusses ethical discourse and, thereby, the kind of reasoning to be expected in democratic discussion and debate, he emphasizes, just as his critiques of Rawlsian liberalism and the new traditionalism exemplify, "Socratic questioning" (73) and "immanent criticism" (85). On some occasions, "straightforward argument on the basis of commonly held standards" can occur, but that possibility "carries us only so far" (90–91). When disagreements do not admit of such argument, immanent criticism is what allows conversation to continue. If I understand rightly, Stout here means reasoning within the terms of one's interlocutor in order to disclose inconsistencies between two or more affirmations she or he makes or can be presumed to accept. In other words, one seeks to show how a discourse partner's set of affirmations is internally problematic and why one's own position, inclusive perhaps of some important beliefs also held by the other, is free of similar inconsistency.

With respect to the ethics of citizenship, then, I take Stout's intention to be something like the following: although developed by a specific pragmatist and thus consistent with specific pragmatism, his conception of public reason does not make nonmetaphysical ethics a discursive presupposition because both specific pragmatists and those with metaphysical views can be equal partners in an exchange of immanent criticism. If some citizens persist in the metaphysical quest, they are welcome to do so and are invited to present a critique of specific pragmatism, showing why the refusal of necessary moral principles, that is, principles of practical reason as such, is internally problematic. Stout believes that no such metaphysical argument has been convincing, and thus all attempts so far offered to show nonmetaphysical ethics problematic are failures. Nonetheless, he insists, holding each other accountable through Socratic questioning does not require nonmetaphysical ethics as a discursive presupposition because his assessment of some metaphysical proposal may be wrong, and, in any event, new metaphysical proposals or new arguments for old ones are not excluded from the discourse. "There is ample room in the discussion for all of these people" (2004b, 370). At the same time, this conception of public reason is also consistent with moral and political norms that have no metaphysical backing and thus are entirely creatures of specific social practices, and Stout himself honors the ethics of citizenship by refusing a metaphysical backing until the need for it is demonstrated.

If the point expressed in Stout's clarification is captured by something like this reading, it provides the setting in which he defends specific pragmatism against what he takes to be the main immanent criticism presented by all metaphysical views. I propose now to take up that defense because asking whether it succeeds is one way to determine whether he can consistently affirm specific pragmatism and also exclude his refusal of metaphysics from the explicit conditions of democratic discourse. In the response to critical discussions of his book, Stout says that metaphysicians have asserted a realism with respect to truth, such that no statement or proposition can be true unless it is somehow "absolute" in the sense of corresponding to or being authorized by reality independent of any specific human practice. Metaphysical realism is "the doctrine that 'correspondence to reality' explains what it is for a true proposition to be true" (2004b, 372). On Stout's review, "attempting to *define* truth as a 'substantial something' has proven to be a fruitless enterprise" (250, citing Arthur Fine); as we noted, the history of metaphysics in the pejorative sense is, he believes, littered with failure.[8] But his principal concern is not to document these failures. Rather, he seeks to defend a refusal of metaphysics against the internal criticism metaphysical realism implies, namely, that nonmetaphysical pragmatism precludes a conception of truth as the object of discourse—or, to reformulate the same critique, a refusal of metaphysics is required "in the end to view truth as a matter of communal agreement" (276) and thus implies a "relativistic conception of truth" (238).

Throughout his discussion of expressive pragmatism, this is the challenge Stout seems most concerned to meet (see 14). He returns to it in several contexts and seeks continually to respond by asserting a distinction between justification and truth. "Being justified in believing something is a contextual affair" (234), dependent on the understandings a given believer has available, and justifying a belief, in the sense of arguing for it, is also contextual, delivered to a specific audience capable of understanding the reasons offered and addressed to relevant doubts about the given belief. In contrast, "truth pertains to the conceptual content of a claim, not the epistemic responsibility of the person who accepts or asserts it. Truth or accuracy is an objective status as well as a normative one, . . . and whether our beliefs and claims actually enjoy this status is not up to us" (255).

This distinction serves to turn aside the objection, Stout holds, because the contextual character of justification and justifying does not entail the contextual character of truth. Accordingly, the most important use of "true," at least with respect to the objection, is *"cautionary . . . ,* as in the sentence, 'We may be justified nowadays in believing P, but P might not be true' " (249). Absent this distinction, he continues, we cannot be "suitably humble in what we claim to know" (234), even justifiably claim to know, that is, cannot acknowledge our ever present fallibility, and thus Stout says that he wants "in particular . . . to preserve the cautionary use" of "true" (253). But if, with the distinction, we have "figured out how the term 'true' behaves in all of the relevant contexts, what remains to be explained? We should content ourselves with accounting for its characteristic nonphilosophical uses—the ones that do not presuppose a metaphysical picture" (251).

In prescribing this avoidance of metaphysics, Stout presumably repeats that metaphysical realism has proven to be "a fruitless enterprise," so that we are better advised to refuse the project until the need for it is demonstrated. We should note, in any event, that affirming the difference between justification and truth does not commit one to specific pragmatism. That justification is or can be relative to the given believer or context is one thing; that all reasoning is nonmetaphysical is something else. What Stout's refusal excludes are beliefs in metaphysical principles or conditions that might be justified by metaphysical arguments, which show that these principles are necessary to or implied by human practices as such. Nothing in the distinction between justification and truth implies this exclusion.

Because Stout mentions being "suitably humble in what we claim to know," we should also avoid another possible misunderstanding: as with the difference between justification and truth, affirmation of our ever-present fallibility does not entail specific pragmatism. The metaphysical project has sometimes been charged with implying that its supposedly true conclusions are infallible. But this indictment confuses the logical status of something believed with the epistemic status of believing. Whether the content of a belief is transcendental, in the sense that it explicates a condition implied by every specific subjective context, is one thing; whether the believing is certain, in the sense that the subject cannot be wrong, is another. To be sure, if the content is indeed transcendental, the subject cannot be wrong, but this coincidence is trivial because no subject whose belief has a true content (whether transcendental or not) can in that respect be wrong. A belief is fallible because, whether its content is true or false, a subject's having the belief does not guarantee the truth of its content, so that neither the subject nor any others can properly rule out the possibility that it is wrong. Metaphysical beliefs, in the sense pertinent here, are fallible. That certain conditions define subjectivity as such does not entail that a subject's assent to any given explication of those conditions cannot be wrong, and being suitably humble requires only the recognition that no claim to validity for some metaphysical explication is immune to contestation and, when contested, requires validation by argument. In sum, the realm of what we might explicitly "claim to know" may include a difference between necessary and historically specific conditions without compromising the possibility that any such claim is wrong.[9]

But these last two paragraphs are aimed against possible readings Stout himself would, I believe, take to be misunderstandings. He does not distinguish between justification and truth in order thereby to invalidate metaphysics as such. Rather, he seeks to sustain his refusal of metaphysics by defending his position against the charge of relativism with respect to truth—and his success in this regard is what we need to assess. Toward doing so, we may ask the following question: once the difference between justification and truth is formulated within specific pragmatism, what is the status of the distinction? Do we have reason to call the distinction itself true, whereby we attribute to it an objective status independent of epistemic context, or is the formulated difference itself a contextual affair, justified for some given discursive practice? At one point, Stout addresses this question: "There is indeed a sense in which our use of the term 'true' rests on agreement within a social practice," namely, "a practical agreement that we exhibit when we use the terms 'true' and 'justified' differently. What we have agreed to do, in effect, is to treat truth in practice as something that cannot be settled simply by communal agreement. It is this underlying social agreement on the use of certain words in the process of self-criticism that gives the term 'true' its nonrelative status" (276–77). This is puzzling. If the distinction between justification and truth depends on a specific communal agreement regarding the use of certain words, then we have at least one instance in which we do *not* "treat truth in practice as something that cannot be settled by communal agreement"—namely, with respect to the use of "truth" in this distinction. If this is so, then perhaps the very distinction can be justifiably believed within the community that so agrees, but the conception of truth is relative to that community.[10]

It does not help to add, as Stout does, "the agreement at issue here operates on a different, more basic level" (277)—unless, against specific pragmatism, this basic level is the level common to all discourse about ethical life, and the distinction is, at least by implication, metaphysical. In fact, Stout says some things wherein precisely this status seems to be implied. For instance, "we cannot get by without taking a specific point of view, and when we do this, we are *bound* to draw a distinction between 'what is correct and what is merely taken to be correct' " (279; emphasis added; the internal citation is from Robert B. Brandom). Or, again: "What does an ethical community share that makes it an ethical community? My answer thus far has been: a way of thinking and talking about ethical topics, or more precisely, a discursive social practice. . . . [We can add to this] initial answer a claim about what makes a discursive social practice social. It is not the indefeasible authority of the community, its conventions, or a social contract that makes such a practice social. It is rather the need for each participant in the practice to keep track of other participants' commitments and to assess those commitments from her or his own point of view" (279–80). But if we ask about what makes a discursive social practice social ("the fundamental social structure," as Stout also calls it [279]), the answer, it would seem, cannot itself be the creature of a specific social practice. To all appearances, this answer designates an inescapable condition of all discursive social practices and thus expresses something about their metaphysical features. It is, therefore, no surprise when Stout immediately says that "*no* ethical community could sustain a discursive practice" (280; emphasis added) without this structure.

But however the distinction between justification and truth is itself commended, the central issue is whether, as Stout holds, "truth" needs no authorization other than its cautionary use in discourse. "Truth-talk is not an implicitly metaphysical affair. . . . It is an aspect of ordinary language use, to be made sense of in terms of an empirically orientated linguistic theory" (255). So far as I can see, this means that "truth" is a concept whose content can be designated only by way of what it is not, only by negation: true belief is *not* equivalent to justified belief.[11] Stout appears to confirm this reading when, having said that "truth as correspondence has no explanatory value," he adds: "Furthermore, I have no other definition of truth to offer" (248).

I question whether a solely negative designation explicates what "truth-talk" typically implies. In our ordinary pursuit of critical reflection, we typically intend that some belief or claim, even a justified belief, may be false because it fails to meet or conform to some standard other than justified belief—and the implication is that this standard can be designated in positive terms, even if there may be considerable difficulty in doing so clearly and even if every attempt to do so is itself fallible.[12] To be told that truth cannot be conceived except by negation is, I suspect, a counter-intuitive explication of ordinary language use itself—and if there is a standard to which all true beliefs conform, it cannot itself be in all respects specific to a given form of ethical life without violating the distinction between justification and truth. For that reason, I expect, some of Stout's critics believe that he does not adequately interpret the "objectivity" of truth.

But so formulating the doubt about Stout's account is inconclusive because whether ordinary "truth-talk" is said implicitly to affirm a standard conceivable in positive terms will depend on the philosophical commitments of the interpreter. At the same time, this recognition counsels that appeal to our ordinary language use does not, as Stout appears to think, settle the philosophical issue. "By engaging in 'truth-talk,' we implicitly view our subject matter as something we might get wrong, despite our best cognitive efforts. . . . 'Realism' in the metaphysical sense combines this praiseworthy attitude with a dubious doctrine that is meant to legitimate it. Fortunately, the attitude needs no legitimation" (255). This last sentence simply asserts Stout's philosophical commitments and thus begs the question. Contrary to what he says, making explicit our cautionary use of 'true' does not itself show that specific pragmatism can sustain the difference between justification and truth. Stout also needs to show that a solely negative designation of "truth" is sufficient.

This philosophical question is, then, precisely what the present work addressed in its argument for metaphysical necessity: concepts that purport to designate solely by negation cannot be distinguished from putative concepts that do not designate at all—for instance, putative concepts that are self-contradictory. Both are supposed conceptions of something completely negative, and thus there can be no difference between them.[13] If Stout's account of "true belief" as different from "justified belief" cannot be explicated in positive terms, it makes no sense because "truth" cannot be distinguished from merely putative concepts. We might also make the point this way: unless all completely negative designations are meaningless, the only way to distinguish between those that are and those that are not is by mere stipulation. It then follows that no characterization of human rationality and activity, specific pragmatism included, can be sustained as anything other than the view of its proposer and those who happen to accept it, because no reasons can be given against supposing that the real character of human rationality and activity can be designated only by negation.[14] Hence, ordinary truth-talk does indeed imply a positive standard that "operates on a different, more basic level" than any communal agreement because it belongs to the conditions of subjectivity as such, and by refusing any such standard, specific pragmatism leaves itself with the relativism Stout intends to avoid.

We turned to Stout's account of truth, let us recall, in order to assess the clarification of "ethics without metaphysics" he has offered, namely, that his nonmetaphysical pragmatism is presented *within* the secularized democratic debate whose explicit conditions leave ample room also for metaphysical views. If the analysis we have pursued is sound, this clarification is unconvincing. Stout's proposal for secularized discourse requires (or *is*) a conception of public reason and, because he is a specific pragmatist, must at least be consistent with his own nonmetaphysical ethics. At the same time, his refusal of metaphysics entails a relativistic view of truth or must "in the end . . . view truth as a matter of communal agreement" (276). But a practice of discourse could not be so much as consistent with a communally determined meaning of truth unless that meaning is stipulated as a discursive presupposition. That ethics is independent of metaphysics—or, to say the same, that norms are entirely creatures of our specific social practices—must be, therefore, a condition of the discourse analogous to an established religion. Religious establishment means that political deliberation and debate properly pursues the specification of those religious beliefs to political decisions, and analogously, a definition of moral truth dependent on some given communal agreement must be explicitly accepted by all citizens in order to have politics by way of public reason. There is, in sum, every reason to think that Stout's third alternative cannot be separated from his chapter on ethics without metaphysics.

We may confirm this conclusion by reformulating the argument for it, beginning with the following recognition: if ethics so much as *can* be without metaphysics, then it *must* be. Metaphysical views affirm a necessary principle or principles of practical reason, such that no social practice, including the practice of discourse itself, can be independent of metaphysical conditions. A principle or principles of this kind could be absent only if they must be absent. By the very meaning of necessary, in other words, the presence or absence of metaphysical conditions cannot be a contingent matter—and if absent in any circumstances, such principles must be absent in all circumstances or necessarily absent. Hence, secularized discourse could not be so defined that its explicit conditions are consistent with but do not include ethics without metaphysics unless those discursive presuppositions at least *imply* specific pragmatism.

That Stout's position must pay this price seems apparent in his discussions of immanent criticism as the manner in which discourse continues when commonly held standards are not present. On his account, so far as I can see, the inconsistencies such criticism seeks to disclose obtain solely between *contingent* affirmations one's interlocutor makes or can be presumed to accept. Stout nowhere states or suggests that one might successfully criticize another's affirmations as inconsistent with a principle *all* discourse partners implicitly accept or accept necessarily, that is, a principle implied by the ethical life of *every* people because implied by practical reason as such. Since a principle of that kind would be metaphysical, such internal criticism would be a metaphysical argument. But if there *could* be a successful metaphysical argument, then there *must* be a metaphysical backing to morality—and the conception of public reason would then be inconsistent with norms as entirely the creatures of specific social practices. Hence, specific pragmatism must be at least implied by democratic discourse because immanent criticism must involve entirely contingent affirmations.

Nonetheless, some might say, this does not make commitment to nonmetaphysical ethics an *explicit* condition of discourse. What is implied by discourse is not necessarily a discursive presupposition; although metaphysical views are implicitly denied by the ethics of citizenship, they are still welcomed into the democratic process because the discussion and debate includes an argument about what the discursive presuppositions themselves imply. But Stout would not, I judge, endorse this account because, in fact, it is not coherent. Since metaphysical principles can never be absent unless they are necessarily absent, public reason cannot be independent of metaphysical conditions unless that fact is a condition of practical reason everywhere and always, that is, of practical reason as such. If this absence is implied by discourse, the implication is, in its own way and against the proposal, itself a metaphysical condition. Moreover, the condition thereby affirmed is, in its own way, a moral principle because it defines or helps to define the kind of reasoning proper to ethical discourse wherever and whenever it occurs, namely, that it concerns norms in all respects specific to context or to the community having the discourse. In other words, the assertion that discursive presuppositions imply specific pragmatism is pragmatically self-contradictory, since one thereby claims validity for a necessary principle. Argument about what the presuppositions of discourse imply cannot be about *whether* practical reason has any metaphysical principles but only about *what* its necessary principle or principles are. Hence, those presuppositions could not be consistent with specific pragmatism unless metaphysical arguments are excluded from the discourse by stipulation, whereby affirmation of ethics without metaphysics is included within the ethics of citizenship.

If these considerations confirm that Stout's third alternative depends on his specific pragmatism, they also require the conclusion that his proposal, like the Rawlsian liberalism and the new traditionalism he rejects, is internally problematic. Even if stipulated as an explicit condition of secularized discourse, ethics without metaphysics asserts the absence of any metaphysical condition for the political discussion and debate—and, as the previous paragraph argued, that statement is self-refuting. To assert the absence of metaphysical conditions anywhere is itself to imply a metaphysical assertion, namely, that everywhere norms are in all respects specific to the context or the community having the discourse. The claim, to be repetitious, is for the metaphysical assertion that no metaphysical assertions are true, and thereby the account implies, against itself as a metaphysical assertion, a relativistic conception of truth in ethical discourse. As a third alternative to the antagonists Stout rejects, his proposal only continues our confusion about democracy.

We are, then, advised to look elsewhere for "a satisfactory account of the role of religious traditions in modern democracy" (183). Stout's book is at pains to show how religious convictions and, specifically, Christian theism are full participants in the democratic exchange of reasons. But success is foreclosed if one assumes that religions or, at least, some of them make or imply claims to metaphysical truth about human life when they affirm a comprehensive vision. Indeed, one might say that metaphysical affirmations are implicit in any religious conception of the comprehensive good, so that substantively different conceptions disagree about what inescapable moral conditions human life as such implies. The point would not require that adherents of any given religion explicitly acknowledge its implied metaphysical claims. What is of moment, rather, is the logic of "comprehensive" with respect to a conception of the good, namely, that it designates a good to which strictly all human activity ought to be directed, so that every comprehensive vision is committed by implication to a metaphysical principle or principles.

Be that as it may, Stout's pragmatism requires that *no* religion includes this commitment. Because the explicit conditions of discourse must include adherence to nonmetaphysical ethics, the democratic discussion and debate cannot include "religious conceptions of the good" unless religions have another character. In keeping with this implication, Stout seems also to deny that religions make or imply metaphysical claims in what he calls the pejorative sense. Each comprehensive vision, he appears to say, is or involves a "final vocabulary" whose "user has no noncircular argumentative recourse" (89; see also 116). No religious adherent, in other words, can provide convincing argument for her or his religious affirmations and their implications without at some point merely assuming as premises the very affirmations or implications in question.

At least in this respect, it turns out, Stout, with Rawls, proposes an overlapping consensus on freestanding norms. Religious believers can participate in the exchange of reasons only if all agree that the proper character of democratic discourse is explicitly and implicitly independent of any given comprehensive vision. To be sure, Stout does not, to the best of my knowledge, call the presuppositions of discourse freestanding, and he rightly denies a freestanding conception of justice democratic discussion should apply to substantive laws and policies. Still, he does endorse an overlapping consensus on constitutional democracy (see 184 and 2004b, 379)—and so far as I can see, his account of democracy requires that constitutional norms be independent of any comprehensive vision. We can make the point in terms of public reason: just as Rawls stipulates that public reason, at least in the last analysis, does not appeal to comprehensive doctrines but, rather, to the specific public political culture of one's democratic society (see Rawls 2005, 440-90), so Stout implies a conception of public reason in which the defining commitments of specific pragmatism belong to the ethics of citizenship.

But some religious adherents may disagree with this account because they hold that no norms can stand free from the comprehensive good. One might well expect the new traditionalists, quite apart from their authoritarian commitment, to find in Stout's proposal a denial of their belief in a God on whom everything depends and thus to find Stout's democracy no less secularistic than Rawls's.[15] Far more clearly will the proposal be unacceptable to any religious adherent or thinker sensible of making or implying metaphysical claims. Democracy can then be, as Stout holds, neither friendly nor unfriendly to religion only if such adherents or thinkers are confused about the character of religion. But that is precisely what Stout cannot show because doing so would require a metaphysical argument for specific pragmatism. In his own terms, then, Stout's account of democracy has every appearance of being or depending on his own "final vocabulary,"[16] and this simply repeats its internal problem: secularized discourse cannot be relevantly neutral to all final vocabularies if commitment to it is commitment to one of them.

To the best of my reasoning, then, democracy as the kind of discursive social practice both Stout and I wish to affirm cannot be coherently explicated within the critique of universal reason and thus independently of metaphysics. That critique is itself pragmatically self-contradictory because it exemplifies an exercise of universal reason, and every attempt to defend democratic norms without metaphysics in truth refutes itself by implying metaphysical conditions of politics. If there are democratic rights, they depend, as do all principles and norms, on a principle or principles necessary to practical reason and thus to human existence as such. If there is a sound account of secularized discourse, to make the same point, it must be a *metaphysical pragmatism*, that is, a democratic theory insisting that the practice of democratic discourse itself, as all human practices, implies the necessary principle or principles of morality.

Such a theory might still be a pragmatic expressivism because it affirms that discourse begins with specific issues in the life of a political community and makes explicit the norms implicit in material inferences, thereby allowing moral criticism and the introduction of novel moral claims—and the exchange of reasons properly turns to the most fundamental principles only when discourse yields relevant disagreement incapable of resolution by considerations of lesser scope. Nonetheless, practical reason can operate "independently of the ethical life of a people" (197) in the sense that necessary principles are independent of any given location and thus of the criteria of meaning and truth peculiar to any given tradition or lifeworld, and no proposed norm can be valid unless consistent with these necessary principles. In the end, making explicit what is implicit in any material practical inference remains incomplete without a statement of its necessary conditions.

But whether metaphysical pragmatism can be a successful democratic theory, that is, can affirm principles implied by all human practices while nonetheless showing how the ethics of citizenship is properly neutral to debate about both secularistic and religious convictions, has not yet been addressed. Can a theory insist that secularized discourse implies metaphysics without making some metaphysical principle or set of principles an explicit condition of the discourse—and thereby provide beyond the three positions Stout discusses a fourth alternative that ends confusion about our democratic life? The next chapter defends a positive answer to this question.

Chapter 6

The Metaphysics of Democracy, Part 2

The Principle of Communicative Respect

The argument in chapter 5 was negative, that is, argued against democratic theory without metaphysics. But this is insufficient to conclude that democracy can be given convincing statement *with* metaphysics. No more than for Stout or his two antagonists does it suffice here to expose the weaknesses of one's opponents; if one affirms democracy, one must also give it a coherent account. Toward this end, this chapter argues that a backing for secularized discourse and thus government by the people is given by the metaphysics of human purpose previously developed.

As an approach to that discussion, it will be useful to mention the political objection most often leveled against metaphysical moral theories. Whether the theories in question include metaphysics in the strict sense or affirm a metaphysics of subjectivity or morality without implications about existence as such, this objection is, for those who advance it, decisive. Far more obviously than Stout's specific pragmatism, the indictment goes, a metaphysical pragmatism is inconsistent with democratic neutrality toward diverse secularistic and religious convictions—and if secularized discourse cannot be coherently explicated without metaphysics, then democratic discourse cannot be coherently explicated. Precisely because a metaphysical ethic asserts a principle or set of principles for morality and politics as such, the objection reasons, any political theory thereby included is bound to affirm the constitutional establishment of a particular fundamental conviction, that is, affirm a prescription of some supposedly necessary principle or principles within the ethics of citizenship. Since metaphysical conditions are implied by all human practice, they must be stipulated as discursive presuppositions. Hence, discourse as conceived by metaphysical pragmatism cannot be truly secularized, and metaphysical pragmatism implies "resentment of religious diversity" (Stout 2004a, 99). For Rawls, this is why political principles in a modern democracy must be freestanding; the only alternative is the coercive imposition of a comprehensive doctrine.

The challenge this reasoning presents requires an extended response, the burden of which might first be summarily stated: the objection has not considered all of the options because, to formulate the point in terms of Stout's "two senses of the term 'presupposition' " (see 2004a, 97), the supreme moral principle presupposed as an *implicit* condition of democratic discourse is not required as a discursive presupposition or *explicit* condition of the practice. That practical reason is inseparable from necessary moral and political conditions does not entail that a democratic constitution should establish a view of the comprehensive good. To the contrary, the task of a constitution is to stipulate no more and no less than a discourse about the terms of political assessment and their application to particular political decisions. Thereby, the constitution is *explicitly* neutral to all fundamental convictions—that is, all convictions about the ultimate terms of political assessment, whether these are religious or philosophical, secularistic or theistic—whose differences are to be clarified and assessed in the discourse. Constitutional stipulations will indeed *imply* the metaphysical terms by which all human decisions are properly assessed, but what those implications are is precisely what the discourse should determine.

This summary statement, I recognize, makes for metaphysical pragmatism precisely the claim that, according to the previous chapter, cannot be validly made for specific pragmatism. On Stout's conception, I argued, the explicit conditions of democratic discourse cannot merely imply his pragmatism, and thus the independence of ethics from metaphysics must be stipulated as what he calls a discursive presupposition; that is, its acceptance must be included within the ethics of citizenship. In contrast, I now propose, a democratic constitution may imply a metaphysics of human purpose without making it a constitutional provision. The difference obtains, I hold, because the ethical principles implied by discourse are, in truth, metaphysical in character. For this reason, as the previous chapter argued, Stout's pragmatism itself implies, against itself, a metaphysical condition of moral discourse, namely, that norms everywhere and always are specific to communal context. Thus, specific pragmatism cannot be implied by democratic discourse, and its express denial of all metaphysical conditions can only mean a stipulation of that denial as something to be explicitly accepted by all discourse participants. In contrast, true metaphysical understandings can be implied without being explicitly accepted by those who engage in discourse about what they are, and democracy may be so constituted that the ultimate terms of political assessment implied by the constitution, along with their application to particular decisions, are the objects of discussion and debate. The remainder of this work will outline a democratic theory of this kind.

Success in doing so requires a defense of the distinction just mentioned, namely, between a constituted discourse explicitly neutral to all convictions about the ultimate terms of political assessment, on the one hand, and, on the other, the ultimate terms of political assessment implied by and thus authorizing that constitution itself. Unless this distinction can be clarified and sustained, one cannot show that practical reason as such is bound by necessary conditions even while those very conditions prescribe a democratic political community, one in which citizens are free to hold and to advocate whatever fundamental beliefs they find convincing. But defense of this distinction and thus of democracy with metaphysical conditions may be more demanding than first appears, as becomes evident, I think, if we reformulate the challenge presented or implied by Rawls and others and summarized above.

Commitment to government by way of discourse—or, in that sense, by way of reason—must have grounds common to all citizens notwithstanding their differences about the ultimate terms of political assessment. This simply underscores that a democratic constitution does indeed constitute the political community and thus defines the ethics of citizenship; proper democratic participation includes explicit adherence to constitutional stipulations—roughly analogous to how proper participation in a meeting is typically defined by adherence to Robert's Rules of Order. If explicit adherence to the democratic way has no common grounds other than explicit belief in the valid terms of all political assessment, the ethics of citizenship must include acceptance of a particular fundamental conviction, and a political community cannot legitimate all such convictions citizens find convincing. To the contrary, then, democracy with a metaphysical backing requires grounds for proper political participation consistent with such legitimation and, thereby, common to citizens who disagree about the ultimate terms of political assessment. But how can there be any such grounds other than the valid terms of all political assessment, given that these are said to authorize a democratic constitution itself?

This question may be answered, I propose, through recurring to the universal social practice of communicative respect, presented during the defense in chapter 4 of a deontological principle or principles of human rights consistent with neoclassical metaphysics. That universal social practice allows a distinction between, as I will call them, the metaethical form and the normative content of any claim to moral validity and thus any political claim[1]—and this distinction authorizes, as I will try to show, the relevant difference between an ethics of citizenship and diverse convictions about the ultimate terms of political assessment. In making this case, it will be useful to restate the argument for communicative respect.

"Claim to moral validity," here means the claim made or implied by any human activity to be at least morally permissible and thus in accord with the moral law—and, by extension, any claim to validity made or implied for any rule, norm, or principle in conformity with which some activity or activities are said to be morally proper. To be sure, one might contest whether every human activity makes a claim to moral validity and, if it does, whether it claims to be in accord with *the* moral law. But this work has previously argued for a principle or set of principles by which practical reason as such is bound, and we are here asking whether metaphysical pragmatism can consistently authorize democratic discourse, so that such objections are not pertinent. "Metaethical" designates the common character of all claims to moral validity, in the sense that any statement of this common feature is explicitly neutral to the validity or invalidity of any given claim. The metaethical form of a moral claim, in other words, defines it in distinction from nonmoral claims and is insofar neutral to all normative understandings. In contrast, the normative content of a moral claim defines it in distinction from what are thereby said to be immoral claims. Considered metaethically, for instance, a moral claim is defined by its claim to validity for some or other evaluation of possible purposes as obligatory or as permitted and thus for some choice or prescription as consistent with what ought to be done or what reason requires—and this definition is explicitly neutral to all statements about what evaluations *are* obligatory or what reason requires.

Notwithstanding this explicit neutrality, however, the normative content of some moral claims is in fact metaethically senseless. A claim to validity for a prescription[2] cannot be valid, for instance, whenever an individual to whom the prescription is said to apply cannot choose as it requires; her or his possible activities must include the required one, and if they do not, the prescription is metaethically senseless. Ought implies can; no human can be obligated to do what she or he cannot do. In addition, as mentioned earlier in a different context, the dictum "ought implies can" has another meaning; namely, an agent cannot be obligated to act in a certain way unless she or he can do so because the prescription is valid, that is, with understanding that she or he is so obligated. This dictum also means that relevant agents must be able to take the prescribed decision because they ought to do so, and if they cannot, the prescription is metaethically senseless. It then follows that a prescription is also metaethically senseless whenever an individual to whom it is said to apply cannot contest its validity, that is, choose in a manner that expresses dissent. Absent the latter alternative, the prescription's validity would be irrelevant to the agent's decision, and the activity could not be chosen because it is moral.

Let us now focus on activity that affects another individual or individuals and call it social action. In claiming to be morally valid, any social action includes or implies a prescription applicable to recipients of the action, namely, that they should respond to the effects in accord with the same understanding of the moral law expressed in the action. This is because a claim to moral validity is a claim to obey the moral law by which all subjects and thus the action's recipients are bound. But "ought implies can"; recipients cannot decide in accord with the implied prescription if they cannot also decide in a manner that expresses dissent. Hence, a social action is metaethically senseless if it seeks to prevent recipients from contesting its claim to moral validity. By extension, then, the same is true of social practices, that is, patterns of interaction constituted or defined by norms prescribing reciprocal rights and duties or roles to be played. Social practices are metaethically senseless if some affected individual cannot participate by way of decision, that is, if she or he is unable to contest the practice and thus cannot participate as an exercise of practical reason alone.[3] Hence, the metaethical form of social actions or social practices implies a common decision about the validity of relevant moral claims.

All social action, we can now see, implies commitment to a certain social practice, given only that engagement in the practice is possible, and one has learned whatever is needed to understand the requirement—namely, the specific practice designed to pursue a common decision when the validity of social prescriptions is contested. In the face of dissent, common decision making is itself an associational practice and requires its own norms of interaction. Those norms, moreover, must constitute a practice in which contested moral claims are validated and invalidated by the giving or exchanging of reasons because its specific purpose is to determine what social prescriptions persons should commonly accept by practical reason alone. I will call this the practice of moral discourse, giving to "discourse" a designation appropriated from Jürgen Habermas, namely, the specific social practice that suspends other purposes in order to assess through argumentation or common critical reflection the validity of contested claims (see Habermas 1984, 17, 18, 25, 42; 1990, 158–60). Commitment to this practice, I recognize, remains vague until its meaning is clarified in terms of articulated patterns or institutions, and the attempt to pursue that matter will turn directly to political community. Before taking that turn, however, it is important to fill out the broader metaethical commitment implied by social action.

The metaethical form of moral claims implies commitment to a principle for social action universally: in all human relationships, each individual who has learned whatever is needed to understand the requirement ought to treat all others as *potential participants in moral discourse*. The specific practice of moral discourse, in other words, is inseparable from the universal practice in which no individual treats another in a manner that denies her or him the possibility of contesting claims to moral validity, which is simply to repeat that all social prescriptions imply common decisions about the validity of relevant moral claims. This universal practice, we can also say, is constituted by the rights that define all individuals as potential participants in moral discourse, one of which is the right to be or become an actual participant in such discourse. Such rights cannot be overridden by any other prescription for which validity is claimed, precisely because they are implied by the metaethical form of any moral claim, whatever its normative content.

While the principle constituting this universal social practice has normative content, we should underscore its distinctive character, namely, that its denial is metaethically senseless. As a consequence, the principle is also explicitly neutral to all normative content in the following sense: the social action prescribed is not explicitly partisan in any possible moral disagreement. On its face, one might object, this is implausible. A normative principle cannot be neutral to all normative content, and specifically, a prescription of universal rights cannot be explicitly neutral to disagreement about the principle itself. But we should distinguish between a statement of the principle, on the one hand, and, on the other, the action prescribed. The statement is indeed explicitly partisan in a disagreement with any denial of such rights. But this is not the case with the action prescribed, namely, to treat all recipients as potential participants in moral discourse. That action is explicitly neutral even to disagreement about the statement, since that disagreement defines a question for discourse. The one commitment explicitly neutral to all moral and political disagreements, we can say, is the commitment to assess contested claims by argument or by the exchange of reasons, and this alone is prescribed as constituting this universal social practice.

In order to mark this singular character, I will call the principle a "formative" one, in distinction from all "substantive" prescriptions. Among moral principles or norms, in other words, a difference is marked between those whose prescribed action is explicitly neutral to all possible moral disagreements, on the one hand, and, on the other, those whose prescribed action is explicitly partisan in some or other moral disagreement. Unlike the formative prescription to treat all others as potential participants in moral discourse, for instance, a prescription of charity toward the poor is substantive, since action in accord with this norm is explicitly partisan in a disagreement with any who believe, say, that poverty is a condition for which a person is responsible, and charity is inimical to her or his moral character. Again, the prescription to provide public education for all is substantive, since action in accord with this prescription (for instance, political advocacy of public education) is partisan in a disagreement with any who assert that education should be left entirely to private associations. On this distinction, then, the action prescribed by a formative principle is explicitly neutral even to disagreement about the principle; were this not the case, the prescription would be substantive.

The explication here of this universal social practice is especially indebted to Karl-Otto Apel. "All beings," he writes, "who are capable of linguistic communication must be recognized as persons since in all their actions and utterances they are potential participants in a discussion" (1980, 59). Use of the terms "communicative respect" and "communicative rights" to name the universal formative principle also betrays a debt to Apel, for whom they articulate the valid meaning one can give to the second formulation of Kant's categorical imperative: "So act as to treat humanity, whether in thine own person or in that of any other, in every case as an end withal, never as means only" (Kant 1949, 46; emphasis deleted). Because implied or presupposed[4] by practical reason as such, the principle of communicative respect is metaphysical.

As mentioned in chapter 4, however, communicative respect as a metaphysical prescription is not equivalent to respect for all *human* individuals or persons, because existence with understanding and thus with the capacity for making and contesting moral claims is not necessarily human existence. That subjectivity has emerged in our world in human beings (and, in a more rudimentary respect, perhaps also in some other higher animals) is contingent with respect to subjectivity as such and thus is a specification of existence with understanding. In that sense, Kant rightly says that the moral law "must be valid not merely for men, but for all *rational creatures generally*" (1949, 26). Strictly speaking, then, the content of communicative rights articulated in terms of human existence is not entirely metaphysical. To the contrary, at least some of these rights depend, as we will see, on the fact that human subjectivity occurs within a human body.

Given that human beings are creatures of practical reason, however, the metaphysical principle of communicative respect entails its application in a formative principle or principles of human rights. Moreover, human beings are, I will here assume, the only individuals of whom we are aware that exist with understanding. Perhaps there is now sufficient evidence that some other higher animals exist with understanding and, at least in rudimentary measure, with language. If so, then an extended discussion is needed to clarify the consequences for the rights of such animals. I am not in a position to pursue this discussion and, therefore, will proceed on the stated assumption—recognizing that conclusions reached may well need to be qualified once adequate account is taken of whether understanding occurs within animals other than humans. Given the assumption, the distinction between metaphysical principles and their application in universal principles for human association, including substantive principles to be discussed later, is not relevant to the account of democracy I will propose, and in what follows I will not call attention to the difference.

The formative rights belonging to all humans, we have said, define every individual as a potential participant in moral discourse. Hence, their content can be derived from the necessary conditions of discourse as a specific social practice. Since the defining purpose of discourse is to validate and invalidate contested moral claims, the success of discourse depends solely on the soundness of arguments, the opportunity for criticism, and the common pursuit of the truth. Accordingly, the necessary conditions of this practice include the equal freedom of all participants to advance and contest any claim and the arguments for it; the absence of internal coercion in the form of strategic activity or, stated positively, the uncompromised commitment on the part of all participants to aim at truth; and the absence of external coercion by which the acceptance or contestation of claims might be affected (see Habermas 1984, 25; 1993, 31).

We may call coercion external in the relevant sense when its character is not peculiar to the practice of discourse. Any specific social practice occurs in the context of social relationships generally and thus specifies more general norms or principles of social action. Thereby, the latter are external normative conditions of the specific practice. For instance, valid norms of criminal law are external normative conditions of, say, the specific practice of economic bargaining. In the nature of the case, the more general normative conditions cannot be suspended by the internal norms of the specific practice. A legal prohibition of assault, for instance, entails that assault is impermissible in economic bargaining. Thus, if some or all participants in the specific practice of discourse were permitted to coerce others in relationships generally, the coercion could invade the discourse and corrupt its pursuit of truth. Suppose, for instance, that males are permitted to assault females, and a given man and woman are to have a discourse about some matter. Under these conditions, the general norms of gender relations are external conditions, and it would be morally permissible for the man to control the supposed discourse by assault—or, if assault in fact ends the discussion, by threat that assault will occur once the discussion has ceased. Reaching agreement by the power of argument alone would not be morally required. Thus, the specific practice of discourse requires a general normative prohibition on external coercion by which the contestation or acceptance of claims might be affected.

To be sure, coercion can occur in many forms. Generally defined as "dominating, restraining, or controlling another forcibly" (American Heritage Dictionary), coercion involves interference with freedom, whereby the freedom in question is lessened in comparison with what it would have been had the interfering individual or group not acted at all. Clearly, this broad definition leaves open to dispute what kinds of such interference are immoral. But the relevant meaning of coercion is determined by the formative character of communicative respect, that is, the proscription of external interference must be explicitly neutral to all substantive social prescriptions. Since every such prescription is subject to dissent, the relevant freedom cannot be so defined as to answer explicitly any substantive question about good human association. If we abstract from the practice of discourse itself, then, the communicative rights protect only those freedoms whose definition does not explicitly refer to human association. Insofar as freedom cannot be so defined, a proscription on external coercion requires a substantive principle or norm of social action.

There is, in other words, a strictly individualistic character to the freedoms in question, and they include freedom to affirm one's own future as an individual, freedom to control one's own body, freedom to use personal property, and freedom to choose one's own understanding of the good. We can speak of corresponding rights to life, to bodily integrity, to the use of personal property, and to conscience—where having the right means that all others have the duty not to interfere[5] I will call these formative rights the rights to "private liberties," where the term "private" means here that these freedoms can be defined without explicit reference to human association. Clearly, the private liberties to which any given individual has a right are not unlimited. The principle of communicative respect prescribes the same rights for all, so that each person's freedom is morally constrained by, and subject to interference in order to prevent her or his invasion of, the rightful freedom of others. Moreover, each has a right to equal freedom because equal freedom is a necessary condition of discourse. But it remains that this community of rights cannot be overridden by any other moral prescription.[6]

Constitutional Principles of Justice

It is now important to show that private liberties cannot exhaust the freedoms protected by communicative rights. The right to be treated as a potential participant in discourse implies the right sometimes to be an *actual* participant in discourse. Consideration of the latter right turns attention to actual patterns or institutions in or through which contested moral claims may be validated or invalidated. In one sense, moral discourse can occur at any time and any place. This specific practice requires only that two or more individuals agree to suspend other purposes in order to assess the validity of contested moral claims. Still, an individual cannot be morally bound to engage in discourse whenever a recipient of her or his action contests its moral validity. On that prescription, participants in an economic transaction would be bound to halt their activity whenever any affected individual objects to it, or a criminal court judge would be bound to halt trial proceedings if the accused dissents from a particular rule of the judicial system. Social action would or, at least, could be constantly disrupted. Moreover, the decision to halt other social action in order to engage in discourse is itself a social action, and the principle prescribing that decision whenever social action is contested should itself be subject to dissent and common decision. But this is not possible without a particular discourse in which common decisions are taken about when and where actual discourse is required or permitted.

What the formative principle of communicative respect prescribes, then, is a particular discourse in which the widest possible common decisions are taken. Indeed, ad hoc engagements in discourse always imply this widest possible exchange of reasons in the sense that argument about the validity of any social prescription is potentially an argument about the most general moral principles and thus about social action generally. Whatever else is involved, in other words, the right to engage in moral discourse must mean freedom to participate in a particular association constituted as the widest possible moral discourse, in or through which common decisions may determine the character of social action generally. Given this association, it is not necessary that all other social action be halted whenever any participant contests its moral claims. Whether and, if so, when more local engagement in discourse is required or permitted (for instance, between lawyers in a civil or criminal trial) can itself be a common decision of the wider exchange of reasons, because every individual's right to discourse is fulfilled by her or his opportunity to express dissent in the particular association whose common decisions are about the moral permissibility of all specific projects or practices.

The right to engage in moral discourse is or includes, more precisely, the right to participate in political discourse, that is, in a particular association or social practice having nonetheless a general character because its distinguishing purpose is to order or govern all action and association in a society. The formative principle of communicative respect prescribes a democratic political association, a government for which "we the people," together as equals, are the final ruling power.[7] Moral grounds for the distinctively legal character of political decisions are, I believe, included in this prescription. Because the communicative right to participate in democratic politics cancels the right to halt at any time any social action whose moral validity one contests, the principle of communicative respect includes the right to have democratic decisions coercively enforced. An association making common decisions governing all social action does not honor each individual's right to dissent from the moral claim of any social action unless the association prevents other individuals from violating its governing decisions. It now follows that constitutive principles of this political association must also be legal in character; that is, an institutional process through which governing activities are properly determined must itself be coercively enforced.

As the last comment may suggest, I have pursued the formative character of social action because, on my proposal, the task of a democratic constitution is to institutionalize politically the principle of communicative respect. If we use "justice" to designate the norms and activities of proper governance, the task of a democratic constitution is to stipulate no more and no less than formative principles of justice. In sum, the political association should be constituted as a full and free political discourse. It should be free in the sense that all individuals subject to the common decisions in question have equal rights to participation, and the discourse should be full in the sense that no principle or norm is immune from dissent. Calling this association a discourse means that every principle or norm, if questioned, can be redeemed only by argument. "Full and free discourse" is, then, a summary expression of the *internal* conditions of discourse noted earlier: equal freedom of all participants to advance and contest any claim and the arguments for it, and uncompromised commitment on the part of all participants to the aim at truth. "Full and free *political* discourse" means that these internal conditions characterize the process by which governance is determined.

For this reason, a democratic constitution should institutionalize the state and stipulate the decision-making procedures through which officials of the state are selected and legislation is enacted, interpreted, and enforced. Also, the constitution should stipulate the procedure by which the constitution itself can be changed, because whether any actual constitution is or should be democratic is itself subject to debate. These general requirements need not imply any specific set of political institutions, whereby the constitutions of all democracies should be identical in detail; differences may be commended by differing settings. Whatever the detailed provisions, however, they are not fully democratic unless they allow the political association to maximize the measure in which the taking, interpreting, and enforcing of governing decisions is effected through full and free discourse.

Thus, the constitution must also stipulate the right of all citizens to be participants in the democratic discourse. Observing duties correlative with these rights must be explicitly neutral to all social prescriptions precisely because the discourse is about those prescriptions in their pertinence to legal norms. A democratic constitution, properly speaking, provides the one set of legal prescriptions to which all citizens should adhere as participants in the political discourse, even if they contest whether this very constitution is in fact democratic and, indeed, whether democracy itself is the proper form of political association. The constitutional rights of citizens, we might say, are those all political participants must respect in order to have a full and free political discourse about what all political participants must respect in order to have a full and free political discourse—and it is this character that makes the rights formative. Communicative rights, then, are not exhausted by the private liberties previously discussed (for instance, rights to life, bodily integrity, personal property, and conscience), and a democratic constitution must also stipulate a set of rights to "public liberties," which include the familiar rights to freedom of speech, freedom of the press, freedom to assemble and petition, due process, and equal protection of the laws.

The rights to public liberties also include the right to religious freedom. To be sure, attempts to define religion are immensely controversial, and this is one reason why the religion clauses in the First Amendment to the United States Constitution evoke persistent and varied disagreements. Still, some understanding of the term is required if the relation of politics to religion is to be discussed. A religion, I proposed on turning attention to democracy, is a cultural formation or set of concepts and symbols and associated communal practices in terms of which or through which its adherents explicitly affirm as decisive an understanding of their relation to existence as such, seeking thereby to mediate a comprehensive orientation in their lives. Most who discuss the relation of politics to religion, I expect, use "religion" in a sense roughly equivalent to this description, although often the designation is further limited such that comprehensive visions, to use Stout's term, are religious only when they implicate a transcendent reality, that is, a reality other than the world of spatially and temporally located things and individuals.

In any event, the important point is this: religions are politically relevant because each includes or implies a conviction about the ultimate terms of political assessment. But once this point is recognized, it follows that religious freedom concerns a wider class of convictions than religious convictions in the sense or senses we have just formulated. As stipulating a formative right, this democratic principle protects or legitimates *any* explicit conviction about the ultimate terms of political assessment, whether that conviction does or does not include affirmation of a transcendent reality and whether or not it is represented by a communal system of symbols and associated practices designed to mediate adherence throughout one's life. This wider class is the relevant one because the freedom to decide one's own belief about the ultimate terms of political assessment is required if all political claims can be contested and, when contested, be objects of discourse. For constitutional purposes, we may say, "religious" in "religious freedom" has an extended meaning designating any explicit belief about the grounds for all political assessment and thus any explicit belief about reality and human purpose as such.

Indeed, we may call religious freedom the inclusive constitutional right of democratic citizens, in the sense that all other constitutional rights may be seen as conditions of it. The right to free participation in political discourse, whereby all may participate as equals, is required when all fundamental convictions are legitimated. Any constitutional limitation on which members of the political community belong to "we the people" (for instance, a stipulation of racial or aristocratic restrictions on political participation) is also a denial of religious freedom, because no citizen may then legitimately decide for ultimate terms of political assessment inconsistent with the stated limitation. In contrast, the right to free participation does not deny religious freedom to nondemocratic convictions (for instance, those that affirm racial or aristocratic restrictions on political participation), because democratic discourse includes the right to make claims for those beliefs and to advocate them by argument. Moreover, the right to participation in a full discourse—one in which no political claim is immune to criticism, and any such claim, if contested, needs argumentative redemption—is also required by religious freedom, precisely because the latter legitimates every decision about the ultimate terms of political assessment.

All implications considered, in other words, religious freedom explicates "the sovereignty of the people." Each member of the political community is sovereign over her or his assessment of all political claims, meaning that the state may not legitimately stipulate or dictate that assessment, because she or he has the right to choose her or his explicit belief about the ultimate terms of political assessment. Hence, the principle of religious freedom also implies that constitutional stipulations cannot properly require of any citizen as a political participant adherence to any substantive prescription for social actions because doing so would stipulate the assessment of some political claim or claims. The constitution should do nothing more than institutionalize politically the formative principle of communicative respect. Precisely because the constitution is formative, moreover, the rights it protects cannot be overridden by any other moral prescription, including any religious one, by which activities of the state ought to be controlled.

As may be apparent, then, the constitution's formative character insures that democratic discourse is, in Stout's term, secularized, explicitly neutral to all beliefs about "what is most important" (Stout 2004a, 327, n. 20) or all conceptions of the comprehensive good. Thus, citizens cannot take for granted that they share with their interlocutors the same ultimate terms of political assessment. For the same reason, all citizens have grounds to accept a democratic constitution, or government by way of reason, notwithstanding their fundamental disagreements legitimated by the principle of religious freedom. The ethics of democratic citizenship can be derived from the formative character of every social action and, thereby, from the claim to validity all citizens make or imply when they assert or imply their diverse convictions about the ultimate terms of political assessment. In this respect, making or implying a political claim is analogous to making or implying a promise: the latter commits one to keeping the promise, whatever the content promised may be, and making or implying a political claim pledges that it can be redeemed by the giving of reasons, whatever the content for which validity is claimed. All citizens commit themselves to the ethics of democratic citizenship even if they claim that democracy itself is immoral or unjust, because they pledge that this assessment can be validated by argument.

But commitment to discourse, some will object, is not in fact explicitly neutral to all fundamental convictions; rather, it takes sides against authoritarian religious beliefs, which are also legitimated by the principle of religious freedom. To all appearances, the new traditionalists, for whom Stout's proposal must be counted among secularistic views of political life, would also renounce the present proposal because, on their assertion, the true understanding of reality and human purpose as such cannot be argumentatively redeemed. We are bound to concede, so far as I can see, that democracy as government by way of discourse is indeed impossible if differing convictions about the ultimate terms of political assessment are not open to reasoned adjudication—or, as we may also say, if the question about those terms is not a rational question. "We the people" as inclusive of many fundamental convictions about human purpose have no principled possibility of political union except common commitment to decision through discourse. If differing beliefs about the most basic principles of political life are beyond the reach of argumentative assessment, a political community inclusive of this plurality can avoid sheer coercion by the stronger only so long as adherents of each find some other form of decision making strategically acceptable—and thus only so long as no conflict arises wherein, for one or more parties to it, the position defended is more important than civil peace. A substantive diversity of authoritarian convictions at the most basic level is then a civil war waiting to happen.

For the new traditionalists, I expect, this only confirms that democracy as a secularized discourse is impossible. But those for whom the ultimate terms of political assessment do not answer a rational question rarely argue for this view. Typically, that account itself is—and, so far as I can see, must be—asserted on authoritarian grounds. No assertion that valid moral and political principles cannot be established by argument could itself appeal to argument without being self-defeating, for the following reasons: The appeal could not be successful unless proper access to such principles (that is, whatever authoritarian expression is said to be properly accepted) is also identified and defended—because, absent that defense, one could conclude that, in truth, there are no valid moral and political principles. Against itself, however, a successful argument for supposedly authoritarian access to such principles would simultaneously show that our question about them is rational. For instance, if one could defend by argument that appeal to the New Testament alone is the proper access to moral and political principles, then one would thereby establish by argument whatever principles appeal to the New Testament provides, and the principles would no longer be asserted on authoritarian grounds. Hence, the supposed need for an authoritarian appeal can itself be defended only by an authoritarian appeal.

As a consequence, disagreement about whether ultimate principles answer a rational question has the following form: Those for whom the question is not rational cannot argue for their denial and thus can only assert it. But those for whom the question is rational can argue for their affirmation, namely, by arguing for the truth of some fundamental conviction and, thereby, arguing against authoritarians. In other words, disagreement about whether fundamental convictions are open to discourse is itself open to discourse if and only if, in truth, they are. Given that the question *is* rational, moreover, even those who assert ultimate political terms on authoritarian grounds pledge that their political claim can be redeemed by argument, notwithstanding that this pledge is contradicted by their authoritarian assertion. In that event, they are relevantly similar to someone who promises to do something she or he has no power to do. The act of promising is a commitment to keep the promise, notwithstanding that this commitment is contradicted by the content promised. If the question about ultimate political terms is rational, then the act of making a political claim pledges that it can be redeemed by argument, even if what one asserts includes a denial that it can be rationally validated.[8] In other words, making political claims is, like promising, participation in a social practice and thus a commitment to the norms or principles by which the practice is constituted, in this case, the principle prescribing argumentative assessment of contested claims. Accordingly, a formative constitution imposes nothing on adherents of authoritarian religions they do not impose on themselves in making or implying political claims and legitimates every religion in the only sense it can legitimate any; namely, each is invited to argue for its terms of assessment within the political discourse.

Some who insist on the authoritarian basis of religious commitment also insist that religious convictions cannot properly be objects of discourse because each is, in the nature of the case, total in a sense that excludes being surrendered. As defining the ultimate context of human life, a religious belief is one with which all other beliefs, including belief about the nature and capacities of reason, must be consistent. Accordingly, a religious commitment cannot consistently entertain a fundamental challenge. Adherence to a religion includes, to appropriate a term from our discussion of Stout, acceptance of a "final vocabulary," such that speaking of full and free discourse about religious beliefs involves a kind of category mistake. But this view simply reasserts that diverse religions do not, in their differing beliefs about human purpose as such, answer a rational question. If, to the contrary, such beliefs define a rational order of reflection, then religions are not properly understood as incapable of being surrendered. What follows instead is that religious beliefs, at least in their political relevance, are differing attempts to represent explicitly what is presupposed in all human practice and, in that sense, something commonly experienced or implicitly believed by all humans, whatever else they experience or believe.

To be sure, a religious believer takes her or his religion to explicate in its own way the belief with which all other beliefs ought to be consistent. But this fundamental belief is now the implicit belief of all humans. What is then incapable of surrender is commitment to life or practice consistent with the *valid* understanding of being human at all, and one adheres to a given religion because one now takes it to be a valid representation of authentic humanity as such. Accordingly, every religious adherent may recognize that her or his religion is or involves a *claim to validity* whose validity can be assessed by argument appealing to common human experience—an assessment in which, moreover, she or he can have a vital interest by virtue of her or his interest in being authentically human. That there is such an appeal to common human experience is precisely what the earlier explication of our original beliefs, about both existence as such and subjectivity as such, sought to clarify. It is, in other words, just this appeal that metaphysical pragmatism may affirm. The ultimate terms of political assessment can indeed be the object of discourse because they are necessary to human existence as such and thus implied or presupposed by any moral or political belief—or any belief at all. In any event, it is democracy with a metaphysical backing the present chapter seeks to explicate, and the assertion that religious commitment cannot accept government by way of reason is not an objection within but, rather, simply a withdrawal from the discussion.

Democracy and Substantive Justice

Because the formative principles of justice are derived from the meta-ethical form of every claim to moral validity, the metaphysical (in the broad sense) basis of a democratic constitution is apparent. Still, we have not yet shown that all substantive principles of justice, by which activities of the state ought to be controlled, also depend on a metaphysical principle or principles. Indeed, Karl-Otto Apel, to whom the previous argument is indebted, denies any such dependence, restricting the metaphysical conditions of practical reason to the principle of communicative respect. On his account, that principle is "a meta-norm for communicatively generating material norms" (Apel 1979, 335), where this means that the meta-norm does not imply a metaphysical principle all other material norms ought to specify. Clearly, the meta-norm is not, for Apel, the only valid social prescription because the principle implies that claims for material norms can be contested and thus their validity and invalidity assessed by argument. Apel's position would be senseless if the only prescription from which one could dissent were the prescription of a right to dissent. For the same reason, democratic politics makes no sense in the absence of something about which citizens might engage in full and free discourse. Government by way of reason cannot be solely a discourse about constitutional norms. To the contrary, democratic politics is also about the activities of the state or the substantive norms and principles by which all social action will be governed, and were valid claims for substantive prescriptions impossible, governance by discourse could not govern.

For Apel, we can say, communicative respect presupposes *that* there are valid substantive norms but implies no supreme principle for *what* they are. So far as I can see, however, this position is self-contradictory. The presupposition that substantive prescriptions can be valid is also senseless unless the formative principle implies the meaning of "valid substantive prescription," that is, implies the criterion in terms of which substantive prescriptions can be distinguished as valid or invalid. But a criterion for this distinction is itself a substantive moral principle. It is, moreover, a metaphysical principle, since the implications of anything characterizing practical reason as such also characterize practical reason as such. For Apel, I recognize, the criterion of all valid substantive prescriptions is simply their openness to redemption by argument. But the formative character of moral discourse cannot itself be the criterion in terms of which sound and unsound arguments can be distinguished through discourse. To the contrary, this distinction presupposes a principle of substantive moral validity, such that a sound argument shows the conformity of a given prescription to that principle. Hence, a democratic constitution implies not only the possibility of valid substantive prescriptions but also a metaphysical principle to which all activities of the state or legislated norms governing social action ought to conform.

As relevant to politics, the point can be captured by saying that justice has a compound character. Justice, properly speaking, requires an internal distinction between the formative principle or principles that should be explicitly articulated in a democratic constitution and the substantive principle or principles that should control decisions taken in or through the full and free political discourse. Because this distinction is internal to it, the character of justice must be logically complex, and the nature of this complexity may be stated as follows: the substantive principle or set of principles consistently implies as an aspect of itself the formative principles of a democratic constitution, and thus the formative or constitutional principles imply as their own moral ground the substantive principle or principles of justice, even if it is no business of the constitution to stipulate what is substantively required. So far as I can see, all attempts to formulate nonmetaphysical accounts of public reason or democratic discourse, including Rawls's affirmation of principles independent of comprehensive doctrines and Stout's formulation of specific pragmatism independent of final vocabularies, seek to do the work that only the compound character of justice can do.

Some, I recognize, will object to this conception of justice because, for them, it is itself finally nondemocratic. On this objection, a strictly formative constitution is at odds with the very democratic politics it seeks to establish and thus at odds with itself because the right to participate in democratic discourse is hollow without access to other conditions the community ought to provide. At the least, severe ignorance or illness or poverty effectively prevents such participation—and, in addition, those enjoying unjust economic and social advantages are, in effect, given privileged entry into the political process, having more resources relevant to bending it in directions they advocate. Accordingly, a constitution cannot consistently establish a full and free discourse without stipulating, along with rights to public and private liberties, substantive rights to certain conditions, such as the right to an education or to work or to health care or to a certain measure of economic resources. Moreover, the objection might continue, such substantive stipulations are not inconsistent with full and free discourse, given only a constitutional provision for constitutional amendment, so that all constitutional provisions are subject to contestation and change.

In response to this objection, let us consider first its concluding defense of substantive constitutional principles. To assert their consistency with full and free discourse if only the constitution is open to amendment is to ignore the difference between constitutional provisions and statutory laws. Precisely because the constitution constitutes the political process, its provisions, as mentioned above, define the ethics of citizenship; that is, they stipulate prescriptions to which all citizens as political participants should explicitly adhere. But such adherence to some substantive prescription can only mean that one advocates politically nothing inconsistent with that prescription. The situation is then relevantly similar to stipulating a decision about some item of business within the rules of order to which all should adhere as they participate in the meeting. If certain social and economic rights are constitutionally stipulated, for instance, the ethics of citizenship require that all political participants take these as givens, with which all of their political claims should be in accord. Simultaneously to legitimate pursuit of constitutional change in this respect is to define an absurd kind of political participation, namely, political activity in which one contests a substantive prescription one is required as a citizen explicitly to accept. Perhaps the point might be underscored in this way: Were substantive constitutional provisions consistent with full and free political discourse, they could also include an established religion or, at least, a constitutional stipulation of the ultimate terms of political assessment in view of which all citizens ought to deliberate—since that provision, too, could be altered by constitutional amendment. Hence, citizens could legitimately decide whether change is needed only if change were consistent with the very terms of assessment they are supposedly assessing.

It is true that statutory laws are or can be substantive prescriptions to which members of the political community are bound to adhere; that is, these laws, if enacted in accord with a democratic constitution, ought to be obeyed, and the state has both the right and the duty to teach them. Prominent among such laws are those regulating in greater or lesser measure the distribution of social and economic resources—for instance, access to safety and security, education, health care, work and income, and so forth. But the state's substantive prescriptions differ from constitutional provisions in this all-important respect: the former are not properly prescriptions to which citizens as political participants are taught to adhere. To the contrary, substantive laws are always open to contestation by democratic citizens. Every enactment that is partisan in some or other possible disagreement is open to change through the full and free political discourse and its decision-making procedures. Hence, all prescriptions of the state should honor the distinction between citizens as ruled by the governing order and citizens as the final ruling power.

For this reason, statutory laws are properly confined to specific or noncomprehensive norms of human association—about such matters as, for instance, those mentioned above—that individuals can obey without contradicting their right to question the justice of those very laws. What statutory law may never do is to teach or support the teaching of, or in some other way to stipulate, principles in terms of which actual or proposed activities of the state should be assessed, that is, to stipulate the ultimate terms of political assessment. Were it allowed to teach a conception of those terms, the state would violate the derivative or nonconstitutional nature of its authority, acting as if it were "we the people." In a democratic political process, religious conceptions (in the extended sense of "religious") can be explicit only as objects of full and free discourse, and therefore religious freedom prohibits not only a constitutional provision but also any law by which ultimate terms of political assessment are established.

Turning, then, to the objection's main point: a democratic constitution explicitly neutral to all substantive prescriptions is, we are told, at odds with itself because one's right to participate in democratic discourse is hollow without access to other conditions the community ought to provide. The apparent force in this indictment depends on a prior premise, namely, that the constitution should guarantee, at least in some respects, substantive justice. But affirming that all citizens have a substantive right or set of rights the state should secure is one thing, and stipulating those rights constitutionally is something else—and what justice as compound requires us to say is this: a democratic constitution *anticipates* that the full and free discourse will be successful and thus will, through statutory law, provide or promote for all in the community the substantive conditions necessary to full equality in the political process itself. Democratic politics is not a substantive possibility unless the government fulfills its moral obligation by pursuing substantive justice. To be sure, that obligation may not be fully met, so that we can speak of substantively successful democracy only in the compromised sense that justice is achieved in tolerable measure. Insofar as the anticipation is unfulfilled, however, the political community is at odds with its constitution, not the constitution with itself. A democratic constitution cannot stipulate success in the political process if its point is to found politics in which each citizen is sovereign over her or his assessment of every political claim, that is, if its point is rule through discourse in which all are together as equals.[9] So far as I can see, this simply restates the character of justice as indeed compound: formative justice *implies and is implied by* a substantive principle or set of principles—or, again, constitutional principles are a self-differentiation and thus an aspect of full democratic justice.

Perhaps some who resist this account do so because they assume one or both of the following correlations: first, permanent principles belong in the constitution, and the political process properly concerns itself with changing norms for the changing circumstances of the political community; second and what may finally come to the same thing, the most important matters should be constitutionally guaranteed, and statutory law should be concerned with lesser matters. Hence, a strictly formative constitution implies that substantive justice has no permanent character and/or is less important. But there is no reason to accept either correlation. Because a democratic constitution implies a substantive principle or set of principles, both the former and the latter are equally permanent, even if the constitution does not stipulate the content of substantive justice. For the same reason, the constitution does not imply that substantive justice is less important. To the contrary, the entire purpose of constituting a full and free discourse is that substantive norms of the political community might specify valid principles.

The essential point, then, is that neither correlation is consistent with full and free political discourse. If substantive provisions are included in the constitution, acceptance of them belongs to the ethics of citizenship, and dissent from them is not legitimate. However unintentionally, those who urge constitutional stipulation of economic and social conditions in fact seek to remove some understanding of substantive justice from contestation and thus from the sovereignty of the people. In truth, substantive rights are *too important* to be constitutionally defined. No claim for any account of them should be exempt from criticism because it cannot be valid unless it can be redeemed by argument. Otherwise, democracy cannot be government by the exchange of reasons—and, in the end, this is simply to say that government by the people depends entirely on the people.

If government by way of reason depends on a compound character of justice implied by human practice as such and thus is explicated by metaphysical pragmatism, we should underscore that "metaphysical" has been, throughout the discussion of democracy, used in the broad sense, that is, to designate reflection on conditions of subjectivity or existence with understanding as such. Insofar, an alternative to Stout's specific pragmatism has been commended. But nothing has been said to show that democratic justice depends as well on conditions of all possible existence or reality as such. As a departure from the Platonic tradition of metaphysics in the strict sense, the critique of universal reason was preceded by Kant's deconstruction of that tradition. Taking a step back from that critique, we are still left with Kantian theories of human rights as an alternative to a metaphysical pragmatism on which human existence implies or relates to conditions of reality as such.

To be sure, we have already criticized Apel's Kantian account, wherein the principle of communicative respect is said to be formal or independent of any metaphysical principle defining all valid substantive norms, and I expect that a similar criticism is successful against Kant's own formulation of the categorical imperative.[10] But others in the Kantian tradition, most especially Alan Gewirth, agree that principles implied by human practice as such cannot be exhausted by, in my terms, formative rights yet also hold that supreme substantive principles of morality and politics are independent of metaphysics in the strict sense.

On Gewirth's account, for instance, all humans have generic rights to freedom and well-being, where well-being includes several substantive aspects, and thus all agents are bound in all they do to "act in accord with the generic rights of your recipients as well as of yourself." This "Principle of Generic Consistency" (1996, 19; emphasis deleted; see also 1978) provides the basis for principles of substantive justice (see especially 1996). Still, justice does not depend on the character of reality as such because, as in all Kantian theories, the metaphysical conditions of democracy do not depend on an inclusive good. Human rights are said to be implied by practice as such—or, as Gewirth formulates the point, affirmed by dialectical necessity whenever an agent decides for any purpose at all—but they do not require a good to which all human purposes in their entirety ought to be directed. Conceptions of an inclusive good, then, are morally permissible when they are consistent with the human rights defined independently of any particular one, so that such conceptions are themselves in all respects specific to traditions or communities or individuals.

I will not here pursue the engagement deserved by particular Kantian accounts of substantive justice.[11] In effect, the entire argument for metaphysical necessity offered in chapters 1 to 4 above, designed to show that and how subjectivity as such is a specification of the possible as such and thus to defend a neoclassical revision of the metaphysical tradition behind Kant, is also designed, by implication, to discredit all Kantian accounts. Still, a summary critique addressed explicitly to their metaphysics of justice may be useful. Theories of this kind face a fundamental problem in seeking coherence between a person's conception of an inclusive good and the duties prescribed by human rights. Whatever one's conception of the good, Brian Barry remarks, "I take it as unproblematic that it has motivational force. The problem is . . . to explain why people might do anything else" (Barry, 112). Barry is, in fact, among those who seek to give that explanation.[12] But the nature of this problem, so far as I can see, prevents a solution. A conception of inclusive good sets terms for one's *inclusive* evaluation of the open alternatives and thus provides the inclusive basis for one's motivation to act. Accordingly, motivation to accept prescribed duties depends on this good—or, what comes to the same thing, practical principles or norms contradict one's motivation to act unless they are aspects of or derived from the inclusive assessment of alternatives. If the metaphysics of morals does not define an inclusive good, then a given actor's decision cannot imply any obligation except that she or he be directed by the purpose she or he has chosen—and if all humans are bound to act in accord with human rights, there must be an inclusive good all humans are bound to pursue.

Another way to make the same point is this: the asserted independence of metaphysical principles from an inclusive good must itself be implied by human practice as such. Necessary rights that are anywhere so separated must be everywhere so separated. Just as Stout's pragmatism implies a necessary absence of any metaphysical principle, so Kantian ethics implies the necessary absence of any inclusive purpose defining humanity as such. Hence, the statement that no conception of an inclusive good can be universal must itself formulate a metaphysical principle and, thereby, an evaluation of all goods humans do or might pursue—namely, that these goods, beyond their conformity with human rights, can be properly assessed only in nonmoral terms entirely specific to traditions or communities or individuals. But an evaluation of goods to which purposes are or might be directed requires a criterion of the good, and since *all* goods are here evaluated, the criterion can only be an inclusive good. Against itself, in other words, a Kantian metaphysics of morals implies an inclusive good.

These summary reflections, it will be recognized, simply repeat in somewhat differing terms the case against nonteleological ethics presented at the conclusion of chapter 4: all such moral theories commit the partialist fallacy. By defining moral and immoral in terms of some aspect of human purposes, they imply that differences among human purposes in other respects are morally indifferent. But the latter conclusion is itself a moral evaluation and thus implies a principle in terms of which purposes are evaluated in all respects. A Kantian metaphysics of morals, then, implies an inclusive purpose defining humanity as such.

Democracy and the Comprehensive Good

It remains to underscore that Kantian accounts typically separate the moral law from an inclusive good because, they recognize, a valid definition of the latter could only be, as we have argued in chapter 4, metaphysical in the strict sense and, in that sense, a comprehensive good. Kant himself was lucid on this point. An a priori evaluation of ends to be pursued could only be defined by the necessary character of things-in-themselves, and precisely because he thought such metaphysical knowledge impossible, he insisted on a moral law independent of purposes. Thus, success in turning aside both political thought within the critique of universal reason and political thought based on nonteleological principles gives one good reason to agree with a summary dictum of Alfred North Whitehead: democracy loses "its security of intellectual justification" if its principles are separated from humanity's relation to "the rest of things" (Whitehead 1961, 36, 38). Still, we cannot confirm that democracy *gains* security of intellectual justification from our relation to the rest of things without substantive clarification of justice as compound. Recall the condition this character sets for a substantive principle of justice: it must be internally complex, whereby it consistently implies as an aspect of itself the formative principles of a democracy constitution. My concluding effort, therefore, is to review how neoclassical metaphysics can provide this clarification.[13]

Summarily restated, neoclassical metaphysics understands the final real things or actualities to be exemplifications of "creativity," defined as "the many become one, and are increased by one." As designating actualities, then, "creativity" is both descriptive and evaluative. On the one hand, all final real things are equally described by that term, each being nothing other than an exemplification of creativity. On the other hand, "the many become one, and are increased by one" defines a metaphysical variable because actualities may be greater or lesser by virtue of unifying reenactments of a greater or lesser diversity. Hence, creativity defines the good in its metaphysical sense. An actuality realizes greater good because it realizes greater creativity, and the greater good of all realizations together is the greater realization of unity-in-diversity. With Whitehead, we can say that concrete good is defined aesthetically.

Given this metaphysical definition, the good requires an actuality in which all that has become actual is completely reenacted. The very idea that creativity is a variable and can be realized by differing exemplifications in greater or lesser measure makes no sense without a comparison of those exemplifications. Since the exemplifications or realizations are concrete, the same is required of the comparison—that is, the comparison requires an actuality fully inclusive of all exemplifications. Hence, the necessary conditions of all things include a metaphysical or divine individual in whose successive actualities all that has become is again and again unified. The same metaphysical individual is required in order to speak consistently of pursuing maximal good overall, which implies the actual togetherness of good that will be or might be realized in the multiple actualizations of the worldly future. Existence as such, in other words, implies the difference between God and the world, and the comprehensive purpose is maximal creativity or unity-in-diversity realized in the world and, therefore, in the divine individual.

For each worldly actuality, creative possibilities depend on the aesthetic order in the relevant past, that is, on the measure in which the past as contributing to the present is a greater diversity because greater past creativities are so ordered as to permit simultaneous reenactment. "The Universe," Whitehead writes, "achieves its values by reason of its coördination into societies of societies, and into societies of societies of societies" (1961, 206), where a society within the world is an aggregate of diverse actualities with genetic order; that is, some distinguishing feature is exemplified throughout the aggregate because later members reenact earlier ones. The point is illustrated empirically by the human condition. Because of the aesthetic context provided by our natural habitat, the human body, and human associations, our actualities or activities enjoy, in comparison with nonhuman worldly existence of which we are aware, opportunities for good that are vastly extended. The difference is finally a difference of degree, but the degree of difference is so dramatic that Whitehead can say "the Rubicon has been crossed" (1938, 38), and the far side is marked by the human capacity for understanding or, at least, for understanding facilitated by participation in a rich and complex language.

I will assume this reading of our dramatically higher possibilities. It then follows, at least in a summary sense, that our effects on nonhuman societies in the world maximize value when they maximize the possibilities of human creativity. This is emphatically not to say that good is identical with human achievement. To the contrary, unity-in-diversity is intrinsically good wherever it occurs because good is defined metaphysically or, to say the same, every realization of it makes a difference to the divine individual. The conclusion here concerns the teleological order within the world as a principle for practical deliberation and, in that sense, asserts a coincidence between maximizing creativity in the world as such and maximizing future human good.[14] On this conclusion, the comprehensive purpose as a principle for moral decisions may be formulated: maximize human creativity—and, since the good realized somewhere cannot for that reason be more important than the good realized elsewhere, in the long run. The categorical imperative is: maximize creativity in the human future as such.

Given the summary coincidence between maximizing creativity in the future and maximizing creativity in the human future, pursuit of the comprehensive good also means maximizing the measure in which each moment of human life inherits other human achievements. If the Rubicon has been crossed with the emergence of subjectivity (or, at least, subjectivity in extensive measure), then higher possibilities for a given human activity are a gift from a favorably ordered human past, where the human past includes both the previous activities of the individual in question and the communities of individuals to whom she or he relates. Because humans enjoy dramatically greater potential for creativity, in other words, human achievements can also add most to the possibilities of other human activities. To be sure, a person's relations to the nonhuman world also affect her or his present possibilities. But given the world's teleological order, that is, the achievement of value through societies of societies of societies, maximizing the inheritance by humans of human creativity will include relating humans to their larger worldly habitat in ways that maximize the nonhuman creativity to be subsequently inherited. The comprehensive purpose, we can say, prescribes pursuit of our maximal common humanity and, by implication, in the long run, although this formulation intends "common humanity" in a distinctive sense. If this term is sometimes used to mean descriptively the characteristics or normatively the rights universally human, I use it, in contrast to both, to designate thereby the common world insofar as it is constituted by communication of distinctively human achievement.

What should be maximized, in other words, is the creativity shared between or among human individuals—in the long run. On my reading, this is Whitehead's point when he speaks of "the hope of the statesman," namely, that "variously coordinated groups should contribute to the complex pattern of community life, each in virtue of its own peculiarity. In this way individuality gains the effectiveness which issues from coördination, and freedom obtains power necessary to its perfection" (1961, 67). As something to be maximized, our common humanity in this sense has a certain self-surpassing character: relativity to a greater common humanity offers individuals the possibility for a greater contribution to it, and the possibility realized amplifies opportunity further. To be sure, the possibility may not be realized; individuals may compromise the achievement they might otherwise contribute or debase the human order of which they are the beneficiaries. Hence, the self-surpassing character of our common humanity is a teleological feature in the normative sense; it marks what is meant to be the case.

Naturally, each individual must decide what to make of the possibilities she or he is given. As a moral and political principle, therefore, our maximal common humanity may be restated in terms of conditions by which humans are emancipated or empowered. On this suggestion, emancipation means the human opportunity to be creative, the measure of power that "issues from coördination," and individuals are more or less empowered depending on the natural and human context in which their lives are set. Since the order created by human achievements is greater insofar as each individual benefits from and contributes to it, our comprehensive purpose prescribes pursuit of everyone's emancipation. The relevant conditions for any given individual are always in part distinctively hers or his, but they also extend through those specific to her or his intimate and local associations to those shared within increasingly wider communities. We may call those of the widest kind general conditions of emancipation, conditions important or potentially important to the creativity of any individual in the political community. I have in mind conditions such as physical and psychological well-being, including good habits; economic provision and opportunity; educational attainment and opportunity; cultural richness; beauty and integrity in the nonhuman world, both natural and artificial; and, implicated in all of these as well as for its own sake, favorable patterns of associations, including freedom of association.

Insofar as they can be affected by human decisions, such general conditions of empowerment are, on this accounting, the subject matter of justice, the conditions with which activities of the state are properly concerned. Because governing norms and policies, as all purposes, ought to serve our maximal common humanity, the substantive principle of justice may then be formulated as follows: maximize the measure of general conditions of emancipation that is equally available to all. Or, more concisely: maximize the general conditions of emancipation to which there is equal access. I will call the character of justice so defined "justice as general emancipation," using the term "general" to express not only the kind of empowering conditions with which justice is properly concerned but also the prescription to maximize the measure of those conditions generally available or equally available to all.

Much more needs to be said in order adequately to clarify this account of justice in a manner that is internally coherent and practically consequential. Among other things, one must explicate how pursuit of our maximal common humanity relates the several differing general conditions of emancipation, many of which are at some point in their enhancement competitive with others. Within limits set by our maximal common humanity, I expect, there is no precise organization of these general conditions prescriptive for all political communities. That some communities sacrifice some measure of economic provision in order to enhance participation in the natural world or emphasize local associations more than wider ones, while other communities take a contrary course, may well be indifferent so far as justice is concerned and thus, recurring to Stout's term, be specific to "the ethical life of a people." But I will not seek here a more complete theory of justice, hoping that enough has been said to outline how a metaphysical definition of the good may be articulated in relation to politics. If we assume that a more or less complete theory can be successfully developed from this outline, we are also in a position to formulate a substantive human right that I will call the "right to general emancipation": human individuals as such have a right to the greatest measure of general emancipatory conditions a legal order can provide or promote equally for all. The order legislated by a political association has as its specific purpose nothing other than securing for all in the political community this universal right.

The reasoning to a substantive principle of justice, we should emphasize, includes an important empirical premise, namely, that nonhuman possibilities in the world we know are—or, at least, may be so considered in political deliberation—teleologically ordered to the human future as such. For this reason alone, justice as general emancipation cannot itself be called metaphysical, notwithstanding its dependence on the good defined by reality as such, and the principle may be rejected by some who pursue moral and political theory backed by neoclassical metaphysics. The assumption, it may be said, fails adequately to represent responsibilities to our natural habitat, especially to the diversity of species in the nonhuman world and to other individual animals, at least within species whose members exhibit the capacity to suffer—and this failure is the more apparent if the nonhuman world includes other higher animals who exist with understanding and even rudimentary forms of language. Those who respond in this way will seek to formulate a differing substantive principle of justice, in which pursuit of our common humanity is somehow constrained by duties to nonhuman existence.

This issue requires a discussion I am not in a position to engage. For present purposes, therefore, I will recur to a weaker premise, mentioned earlier, that is not, I expect, controversial—namely, the capacity for creativity emergent with human subjectivity is sufficiently distinctive that human subjects as a community are not teleologically subservient to creativity realized in any other creature or community of creatures of which we are aware. Given solely this premise, the pursuit of human good in whatever measure the comprehensive good may authorize is pursuit of our common humanity, that is, our maximal common humanity consistent with whatever constraints our duties to the nonhuman world may impose. With or without such constraints, politics properly seeks the greatest possible measure of general emancipatory conditions to which all have equal access. That conclusion is important because, with it, the character of justice is compound; that is, substantive justice is self-differentiating, consistently implying the formative justice of a democratic constitution as an aspect of itself. This is because the principle of communicative respect defines a noncompetitive contribution to the empowerment of all.

The public and private liberties, in other words, are themselves emancipating and, moreover, do not conflict with whatever measure of general substantive emancipation is possible and prescribed. Equal rights to these liberties always enhance and never diminish the extent of general creative opportunity equally available to all. We can assume a political order providing or promoting equal access for all to any measure we please of physical and psychological well-being, economic provision and opportunity, education, and so forth. General emancipation can only be greater if citizens also enjoy the right to formative equality in the discourse through which justice is pursued. Hence, the right to general emancipation is itself fully honored only if the greatest possible measure of empowerment is promoted or provided through a legal order determined by the way of reason.

In sum, government by the people is prescribed by the pursuit of maximal creativity in the future as such. Wherever democracy is possible, the constitutional mutuality of a democratic community is essential to whatever substantive mutuality can be achieved. Or, again: a democratic constitution stipulates a formative condition of our common humanity, without which the human community is impoverished and with which the human good is only enhanced. Nor can this formative condition conflict with constraints, if there are such, imposed by duties to the nonhuman world—because general emancipation consistent with such constraints will be greater if political decisions are taken democratically. Hence, constitutive democratic rights cannot be overridden by any substantive prescription, and the substantive principle of justice as general emancipation, with or without environmental constraints, implies as an aspect of itself the formative principle of justice as government by the people.

On this accounting, to rephrase the conclusion, government by way of secularized discourse is prescribed by the relation of human existence to reality as such and thus to the comprehensive good, and general emancipation is the substantive character of justice implied by and authorizing a democratic constitution. But it is no business of the constitution to stipulate its own substantive backing. Rather, the principle of justice as general emancipation—with or without environmental constraints—is the principle that ought to be convincing in a full and free political discourse, so that all activities of the state are consistent with it, and what the constitution anticipates for the political community is realized. The present work, therefore, can only be a voice within the democratic debate, and the account of politics presented here cannot command assent unless the neoclassical metaphysics it articulates can be redeemed. But if it can, then democracy itself and the justice to which it is directed are authorized solely by the ultimate nature of things and thus by the God who alone gives ultimate worth to human purpose.

Notes

Chapter 1

1. For the text from which citations from Aristotle are taken, see works cited.

2. S.T. abbreviates *Summa Theologicae*. For the text from which citations are taken, see works cited, Aquinas 1973.

3. I have sought critically to assess Aquinas's account of theistic analogies in Gamwell 2001.

4. S. C. G. abbreviates *Summa Contra Gentiles*. For the text from which the citation is taken, see works cited, Aquinas 1975. On some readings of Aquinas, I recognize, he affirms positive predication of God that is literal, that is, neither analogical nor metaphorical. So far as I can see, these are misreadings—or, at least, Aquinas cannot consistently so affirm—and I have argued the point in Gamwell 2001.

5. Speaking of "exists" as the predicate of "x exists," it might be objected, begs the question against Kant because he famously asserts that "existence" is not a predicate. But this objection is not pertinent. Kant means that "existence" is not a predicate belonging to or contained in the concept of a thing (see Kant 1929, 500–07; A592–A602=B620–30), so that there is no instance of "x exists" whose denial is self-contradictory. One need not explicitly disagree with Kant in order sensibly to say of some object conceived that it exists, so that, grammatically, "exists" is the predicate of this statement whether or not this predicate is contained in the concept of the thing in question. Were this not the case, Kant could not write the following: "By whatever and by however many predicates we may think a thing . . . we do not make the least addition to the thing when we further declare that this thing *is*. Otherwise . . . we could not . . . say that the exact object of my concept exists" (1929, 505; A600=B628). Obviously, Kant can make his point only because we can "say that the exact object of my concept exists" and, in that sense, predicate "exists" of a grammatical subject.

6. "Common content" here means any statement implied by both "something exists" and "nothing exists"—just as, mutatis mutandis, "something lives" and "nothing lives" both imply, on their typical usage, "something exists." The

question, then, is whether "something exists" and "nothing exists" commonly imply anything at all whereby "nothing exists" can be distinguished from a putative statement of the form "x exists" that, by virtue of its grammatical subject, is meaningless.

7. At the same time, Oppy rightly continues, no such failure occurs if the relevant premise or premises are those that "any reasonable person . . . must accept on *a priori* grounds," such that an atheist or agnostic who does not accept them does not have, all implications considered, a consistent set of beliefs (Oppy, 57).

8. In the present paragraph, other references to this book will occur by page number alone.

9. On my understanding, "warrant" here is not, at least in the first instance, applied to belief in the scheme, such that the believer would be justified in taking it to be universal throughout all experience. To be sure, a person who understood why the scheme is necessary would, in this sense, be warranted in so believing. But the presence of warrant in that sense varies, depending on the epistemic context of the person in question. Instead, Whitehead speaks of the scheme itself having its own warrant, just as he also defines the scheme as coherent, logical, applicable, and adequate (see the next paragraph in the text).

10. In a footnote on "the unknowable is unknown," Whitehead adds: "This doctrine is a paradox. Indulging in a species of false modesty, 'cautious' philosophers undertake its definition" (1978, 4). On my understanding, the doctrine is a paradox if taken to be an assertion about something called "the unknowable." Those who so take it are cautious philosophers because they limit what can be known and thus seek to define the unknowable by defining that limit. Thus, for instance, Kant defines the unknowable as "not-phenomenal." But this is false modesty because no such definition can be self-consistent. The paradoxical character of the "doctrine" cancels its meaning. There can be no something called "the unknowable" because this putative grammatical subject is meaningless.

11. For this reason, Whitehead also writes: "There are no definitions" of "ultimate notions," that is, of metaphysical ideas in a true metaphysical scheme. Precisely because each such idea is maximally general, the meaning of a given one cannot be fixed in the traditional form of genus and specific differentia—as in, say, the definition of "human" as "rational animal." Ultimate notions are "incapable of analysis in terms of factors more far-reaching than themselves," and thus "each must be displayed as necessary to the various meanings of groups of notions, of equal depth with itself" (1938, 1). Given that true metaphysical statements in the strict sense are coherent, the meaning of a given one can be explicated only through other statements that are implied by and imply it.

We may recognize that the linguistic terms with which metaphysical features or characteristics are designated may also have more specific meanings in the given language community—as with, for instance, "relative," "concrete," "self and other," and so forth. Indeed, some or all metaphysical terms may be generalizations of more specific terms for the purposes of metaphysical thought and communication, and, in some instances, this is one way in which to ensure applicability. As with all discourse, what understanding is marked by a given term is a matter of convention among participants. Still, the designation of a term used metaphysically remains distinctive in this: it cannot be explicated except as "necessary to the various meanings of groups of notions, of equal depth with itself."

12. Some have objected that pursuit of metaphysical universality is simply inconsistent with fallible understanding because the former implies the quest for certainty. But this indictment confuses logical certainty, that is, necessary truth, with epistemic certainty, that is, beliefs immune to contestation. Claims to necessary truth may be epistemically fallible, so that the realm of fallible claims includes both metaphysical and nonmetaphysical assertions. Indeed, the criticism, by implication, makes its own claim to logical certainty, asserting that human fallibility implies the impossibility of metaphysical necessity.

13. The criteria for these judgments, I believe, are those of coherence and adequacy. But these criteria, it might be objected, imply the metaphysical statement that something must exist, and if they provide terms in which relative success in metaphysical formulation is assessed, *this* metaphysical statement now seems immune from the incompleteness of metaphysical schemes these very criteria are said to imply. This objection, I believe, is misguided. That no *scheme* can be complete does not entail that everything asserted in such a scheme is explicitly only a partial truth. Indeed, were that the case, we could not define what a metaphysical scheme is and, having that definition, affirm the incompleteness of any given one. To the contrary, then, some metaphysical assertions may be simply true, even if all of their implications cannot be explicated, and in that sense, the assertions cannot be fully validated. As the next paragraph in the text also says, the present metaphysical account asserts the following: "something exists" is necessarily true, and the ideal of a complete metaphysical scheme as an explication of what must, therefore, be the case is precisely what allows us also to recognize that each attempt to actualize this ideal is inescapably incomplete, and thus its success is relative to proposed others.

14. Because it has this character, Richard Rorty has argued, such validation cannot be successful (see Rorty 1979). On my analysis, his argument depends on the assumption that "nothing exists" is possibly true, and I have explicated and assessed his critique in Gamwell 1990, 104–14.

15. The basic point here is this: given that (1) some x designated by complete negation may be the grammatical subject of a possibly true statement of the form "x exists," and (2) there is no way to distinguish among statements having both that form and grammatical subjects of that kind those that are and are not possibly true, then (3) there is no way except by stipulation to exclude the possible truth of a statement having the form "a kind of y, which can be designated only by negation, exists"—for instance, "a kind of sense experience, which can be designated only by complete negation, exists" or "a kind

of human being, which can be designated only by complete negation, exists." The conclusion follows because, in each case, the grammatical subject is also completely negative, for instance "an unknowable kind of sense experience" or "an unknowable kind of human being." Once something unknowable is said to be possible, all instances of any given y can be knowable only if the designation of y is merely stipulated.

16. It follows, naturally, that we can speak of *this* sentence about truth as true only in the same sense. I have offered a critical assessment of Rorty's proposal in Gamwell 1990, 114–22.

Chapter 2

1. Subsequent references in this section to "What Is Metaphysics?" will be by page number alone.

2. Translations of Heidegger sometimes do and sometimes do not capitalize the first letter of "Nothing" in "the Nothing." I will henceforth do so, except when citing a translated text that does not, in order to keep clear Heidegger's distinctive meaning.

3. For this last formulation of the question, I am indebted to Polt; see chapter 1.

4. The metaphysical tradition has included this difference in distinguishing *metaphysica generalis* from *metaphysica specialis*, given that the latter has included psychology along with theology and cosmology as distinct disciplines. For neoclassical metaphysics, as I will subsequently argue, theology and cosmology cannot be disciplines distinct from *metaphysica generalis* because reality as such is self-differentiating and implies the distinction between God and the world. But the remaining distinction between *metaphysica generalis* and psychology is the distinction between metaphysics in its strict and broad senses (see Ogden 1975).

5. Understandings that are true by virtue of pragmatic necessity might for that reason also be called necessarily true—and, correspondingly, an understanding that is pragmatically self-contradictory might for that reason also be called not possibly true. But these pragmatic senses of "necessarily true" and "not possibly true" are different than the logical senses in which I have heretofore used these terms, because the propositional content of a pragmatically self-contradictory understanding is not necessarily self-contradictory. For instance, "no subject exists" is, while not possibly true in the pragmatic sense, not nonsense. I will continue to use "necessarily true" and "not possibly true" only in their logical senses. Even then, so far as I can see, pragmatically necessary understandings might be so formulated as to be necessarily true, namely, if the formulation predicates something of existence with understanding. If, for instance, subjects as such are bound by the moral law, then "a subject is bound by the moral law" is necessarily true. In other words, a denial of this understanding is self-contradictory in the same way that a denial of "a triangle has three sides" is so. It remains, however, that

pragmatically necessary understandings cannot be necessarily true if they are formulated as existential statements; "nothing bound by the moral law exists" is not nonsense.

6. This view may include the dependence of any given understanding on the meaning of totality (or, in Heidegger's sense, of Being as the difference it makes that there are beings rather than nothing)—even if that understanding of totality or Being has not itself been learned by a given subject. The point then is this: the lifeworld interpretations this subject does have through learning are inseparable from an understanding of totality that itself somehow emerged and has been given expression within the specific historical background.

Chapter 3

1. It will not help to say that y and z entirely cause x because their effects are unified in accord with some natural law. If we assume that the notion of "natural law" can be plausibly explicated without a prior conception of multiple effects unified, what is called a natural law becomes another cause and thus simply adds to the plurality—which now consists of y, z, and the natural law—and the unification of the effects of this plurality is more than any one.

2. This formulation, as any equivalent description, clearly implies priority and posteriority in some sense, that is, the priority of an actuality's reenactment of the past and the posteriority of its completion for the future. An actuality cannot complete what was not previously begun. That circumstance calls for an accounting because the priority and posteriority in question cannot be temporal; to the contrary, unification of relations to the past as a condition of the future defines the present. Indeed, neoclassical metaphysics may seem here caught in a dilemma. It will not help, the criticism continues, if the priority/posteriority succession internal to an actuality is said to be logical rather than temporal. As such, the succession would not be extensive, and a sequence of actualities each characterized by this kind of beginning and ending would not be temporal. But this supposed dilemma obtains only on the assumption that temporal and logical priority and posteriority exhaust the relevant kinds—and, moreover, this assumption leaves the question of how the two kinds are related. Because actualities as becomings are, for neoclassical metaphysics, the final real things, the priority/posteriority succession internal to a concrete singular is thereby said to be the metaphysically concrete kind, such that the other two kinds are abstractions from it. As we have discussed, temporal priority and posteriority abstract from the decision through which actualization occurs the difference between others that help to determine the given actualization, the actualization itself, and others it helps to determine. Logical priority and posteriority, we might say, abstract from the unification that occurs the difference between certain features exemplified. For instance, an actuality that exemplifies the feature yellow also exemplifies the feature

color, and because yellow implies but is not implied by color, the former is, in that sense, logically prior to the latter. On this account, the priority/posteriority succession is metaphysical and, moreover, is self-differentiating, its metaphysically concrete kind both implying and being implied by both temporal and logical priority and posteriority.

3. It might be proposed that two all-inclusive actualities could be contemporaries and still have differing pasts because the past for each is defined relative to standpoint or perspective. But this proposal, as it were, assumes something not in evidence, namely, the possibility of differing contemporary standpoints. In other words, the possibility of differing spatial locations itself requires a metaphysical explication, in the way that "the many become one, and are increased by one" is shown to imply temporal location. So far as I can see, the concept of an all-inclusive actuality—the many in all respects become one, and are increased by one—does not imply the possibility of spatial location. To the contrary, as the next paragraph in the text will discuss, what implies and is implied by spatial location is fragmentariness; that is, spatial location limits a becoming's reenactments by virtue of other copresent fragmentary becomings.

4. Indeed, fragmentariness would then violate the necessity of "something exists," specifically, the implication that something being absent implies something else being present, such that what is present excludes what is absent. If nothing prevents an actuality relating all-inclusively to the past, fragmentariness would mean that something is absent without anything exclusive of it being present. What is present that excludes all-inclusiveness, then, is relation to other space as being constituted by contemporaries.

5. There is also another problem in Post's position worthy of note, especially given our later focus on human purpose. His view implies that human freedom, in the sense of decision that determines what is objectively true at a given temporal-spatial locus, is an illusion in the same sense as becoming or change, since decision in this sense entails change. In addition to being profoundly counterintuitive, that implication is, I will subsequently argue, inconsistent with the capacity of human existence to understand itself, that is, the capacity for self-understanding, a reality Post affirms.

6. For this reason, Charles Hartshorne is, I think, right to insist that all abstracts other than metaphysical ones are emergent and thus is right to reject Whitehead's apparent conviction that some nonmetaphysical abstracts are also "eternal objects." See Hartshorne 1972.

7. Typically (but, perhaps, not necessarily), to say that a given feature exists is to say that it is presently exemplified in the actualities of one or more societies. For instance, courage exists because it is a virtue of one or more present individuals. Thus, the feature in question need not be an aspect of the identifying characteristic of those societies but, rather, may characterize some subsequence of the society or societies in question. Courage, for instance, may not belong to the identifying characteristic of any human individual but be, rather, an acquired disposition.

8. I recognize that the formulations I have offered allow the odd statements "existence as such exists" and "the possible as such exists," since, in each case, the most general features are said to be presently exemplified in actualities. I take these statements to be reassertions that a complete absence of existence is impossible and their odd nature to reflect the distinctive necessity of true metaphysical statements in the strict sense.

9. Metaphysical necessity as here understood clearly means an infinite past and future, and some object that an infinite past is impossible because, were the past infinite, there would be an actual infinite. This is a demanding discussion to which I am not fully competent. So far as I understand the matter, however, the objection is not convincing. Bede Rundle also affirms an infinite past, although, if I understand correctly, he sets aside the objection because past and future are "symmetrical" ontologically. On his account, "only current events *are* real"; only "present events are actual." Thus, "the only way I can see to favour past rather than future events with talk of actuality or reality relates to the greater liklihood of knowledge with respect to the former," and "epistemological considerations aside, past and future appear to be on a par in terms of their contrast to the present" (Rundle, 172, 173). Given this recognition, he continues, we can suppose that any given day (or time, or event) in the past had a predecessor, just as we can suppose that any given day in the future will have a successor.

Neoclassical metaphysics cannot agree that past and future are ontologically symmetrical, even if we need not deny that present actuality is, in one sense, all that there is. For any given actuality, the past consists of fully determinate objects of present relations, while the future consists of indeterminate objects of present relations. Given the affirmation of divine relativity, strictly all that ever occurred in the past is the object of present divine relations (although this does not mean an infinity of present relations because some or all of the past is reenacted in the divine present by virtue of relation to the immediately preceding divine actuality), and all indeterminates of the future are likewise the objects of present divine relations. Thus, both the past and the future in their entirety *are* in the divine, even while there is an ontological asymmetry between past and future. Still, we may, I think, affirm a formulation analogous to Rundle's: whatever day in the past is designated, we not only may but also must suppose that it had a predecessor, because final real things relate to what is fully determinate. This formulation may seem to leave us with an infinite past that becomes actual. But there is no given day in the past infinitely distant from the present. The time to any such day is finite. The impossibility of an infinite that becomes actual seems to depend, in other words, on a series that has a beginning, and the point is that the past had no beginning. I am indebted to Alex Vishio for help in reaching this understanding.

10. The only alternative is that a divine actuality is nowhere and thus temporally but not spatially extended. Since complete negations are nonsensical, solely temporal extension would mean that something must be present

that prevents a divine actuality being spatially extended. So far as I can see, the only candidate for this something is the collection of contemporary actualities in the world. But they can exclude the divine spatiality only if worldly extensions cannot be cooccupied by an all-inclusive actuality, and I will subsequently argue that such cooccupation is coherent.

11. This argument might be restated: Existential absence implies existence presence, such that what is present excludes what is absent. If an individual exists contingently, there are possible states of affairs exclusive of this individual and thus states of affairs to which it cannot be relative. Hence, a greater individual is possible, namely, one capable of relativity to all possible states of affairs. Because it must be capable of the greatest possible relativity, the greatest possible individual must have necessary existence.

12. Quite apart from an explicit defense of transcendental metaphysics, I doubt that any treatment of ontological arguments can remain neutral to various ontological positions. These arguments concern the greatest possible being—or, in Anselm's formulation, "that-than-which-nothing-greater-can-be-conceived." At the least, it is difficult to see how arguments for a being so designated can be endorsed or criticized without implying some account of whether—and, if so, according to what variable or variables—beings can be greater or lesser *beings*, in distinction from greater or lesser with respect to a kind of being, for instance, a greater or lesser island or human being. But any implication about comparison of beings as beings is ontological.

13. I am not completely clear whether Rundle takes "particular being" to mean something completely determinate, so that he here rightly faults any argument on which an abstract or indeterminate implies a given actuality. This may be his thought when he reformulates the point as follows: "To say that it is logically impossible that God should not have existed is to say that it is logically impossible that nothing should have been divine. This is not a proposition about an individual, God, but about whatever 'nothing' ranges over, that is, about whatever exists. Reality had to include a deity. It is thus inappropriate to speak of necessary existence as a perfection attributable to an individual" (Rundle, 107-08; see also 144). But this argument involves a non sequitur if "deity" designates the individual actualized again and again as all-inclusive relativity. On that assumption, "reality had to include a deity" implies "reality had to include the one and only possible deity," as the neoclassical project here outlined argues.

14. This statement, some may object, ignores the role of the previous world, that is, the worldly contemporaries of the previous divine actuality. What they became may seem also to be effective in determining the present divine extension. But I intend to show, in the next section of the text, how a divine becoming, in contrast to any worldly becoming, relates to worldly contemporaries upon their completion. On that accounting, any worldly decisions prior to a given divine becoming will be included within the previous divine actuality.

15. On this accounting, some worldly contemporaries of a divine actuality must become complete during the extension of that actuality, in order

that the divine becoming's reenactment of its divine predecessor may be integrated with other actualities.

16. Some have criticized the idea that divine omnipresence involves real relations to contemporaries because "double determination" of a worldly locus or region is said to be implied. On this reading, the locus is determined once by worldly decision and a second time by the divine, and a locus cannot be determinate in two differing ways. Any force this objection may seem to have derives, I judge, from assuming that God reenacts each worldly actuality as it becomes, that is, reenacts the very process of becoming as it occurs. But omnipresence should not be so understood. To the contrary, divine reenactment occurs only on completion of each occurrence in the world. One may call this reenactment essential to determination of a worldly locus, but "double determination" in this sense is not problematic. Precisely because each concrete singular is both a "decision to" and a "decision for," is "the many become one, and are increased by one," determination of what it is includes God's relation to it. Thus, we might distinguish between *full* determination of a worldly locus, effected by the actualizing decision, and *final* determination of the locus, which includes full determination as an object of divine reenactment. Specified to human life, this metaphysical condition means that what we are is determined not only by our world and our decisions but also by the everlasting difference we make to God. To be sure, the divine reenactment in question belongs to a divine becoming, so that any given contemporary is not *finally* determinate until the given divine actuality is unified. But this, too, is not problematic. That a worldly locus is fully determinate (or has become one) is sufficient for it to be an object for all subsequent worldly becomings, since the divine reenactment does not alter the particularity to which those subsequent actualities relate.

17. I do not mean to imply that internal relations to indeterminates are exhausted by exemplifying relations. To the contrary, some of the former are relations to future possibilities the actuality in question does not exemplify; they remain for it features that will be or might be exemplified by subsequent becomings. But I here focus on exemplifying relations because we are concerned with metaphysical abstracts, in the respect that every actuality exemplifies them.

18. This is why, as noted earlier, genetic inheritance cannot be the only reason that member actualities of the metaphysical individual exhibit the same identifying characteristic.

19. I am not convinced by those neoclassical thinkers for whom worldly becoming itself occurs only through reenactment. On that account, if I understand it correctly, relations to a worldly past, with which any given actuality begins, require the metaphysical feature of final causation, that is, the aim at unification (or the "subjective aim," as Whitehead called it [1978, 27]), and the presence of final causation occurs only through reenactment of a divine actuality. God is the metaphysical individual, in whose becomings all of the world is again and again included, so that each divine actuality is defined by a metaphysical telos or, as we may say, an all-inclusive purpose.

Only reenactment of this telos as present in a divine actuality accounts for the presence of final causation in worldly actualities as such. But this explication is, so far as I can see, unconvincing because reenactments themselves, including the reenactment of a divine actuality, presuppose a present process of becoming and thus the exemplification of final causation in its metaphysical sense.

20. This is true even if the worldly actuality is contemporary with two or more divine actualities.

Chapter 4

1. In speaking of a consciousness of nonconscious relations, I include consciousness of the integration of those relations as the activity in question unifies, and this integration may itself be the integration of conscious relations—as, for instance, when an activity unifies its own thoughts. The point is simply that relations in which objects are discriminated presuppose nonconscious relations with which the activity originates.

2. This does not deny that creatures who are conscious without understanding may pursue ends and manifest a kind of learning and memory in doing so. The point is only that such ends and associated learning are nonconscious. If not conscious of themselves, moreover, creatures who are conscious of actualities and aggregates in the immediate past cannot be conscious of these *as other than themselves*, because such awareness requires a distinction between self and other and thus a discrimination of self. This is not to deny that such creatures *relate* to actualities and aggregates of the past as other than themselves. So far as consciousness is concerned, however, there is no such distinction.

3. In fact, *t* as a chosen telos may be a very complicated one, such that a series of tele' are involved, with the more proximate understood as contributions to the more remote. One may, for instance, decide to vote in order to help elect a certain candidate in order to help effect a certain political agenda in order to help realize insofar as possible a longer-term structure of justice.

4. Philosophers on both sides of the so-called free will debate have typically acknowledged the internal sense of decision that seems to be an aspect of our experience. Those who defend free will typically appeal to this apparent experience, and it is something for which those who defend complete other-determination typically seek to account. On the present proposal, this sense of decision is transcendental to subjectivity because every subject understands itself as a chosen relation to the future.

5. I say "at best" because, on my understanding, neither the ideal speech situation nor the indefinite argumentation community can, in fact, ever be realized or become actual.

6. I take this to be an implication of Whitehead's statement: "The truth is nothing else than how the composite natures of the organic actualities of the world obtain adequate representation in the divine nature" (1978, 12). If

Whitehead there equates truth with whatever is the case, he implies a definition of true understandings in terms of their affects on God. I have discussed this pragmatic account of truth more extensively in Gamwell 2000, 151–75.

7. Hume concludes that "the great difference between a . . . [matter] of *fact* and one of *right*" means that "after every circumstance, every relation is known, the understanding has no further room to operate, nor any object on which it could employ itself. The approbation . . . which then ensues cannot be the work of judgment, but of the heart; and is not a speculative proposition or affirmation, but an active feeling or sentiment" (1975, 290). On my understanding of Hume, he could so conclude because he was an empiricist for whom understanding can have no existential object other than factual states of affairs, and he therefore denied the possibility of a metaphysical principle of the good, such as the one for which this work will presently argue.

8. For earlier discussion of the partialist fallacy, see Gamwell 1984, 34, 56–57, 68–91.

9. See n. 7. Having denied any factual character of better and worse, Hume drew exactly the conclusion his empiricism required, namely, "after every circumstance, every relation is known, the understanding has no further room to operate" (1975, 290).

10. Indeed, the objection, to reformulate the point, is self-refuting. Were it correct, "alternatives cannot be evaluatively compared" would always be a true understanding of the alternatives and thus of oneself. One would always misunderstand oneself if one believed that alternatives can be compared in terms of a principle of value. But assertion of this supposedly true self-understanding is assertion of the understanding for which everyone ought to decide in every occasion of decision and, thereby, assertion of how alternatives are always properly compared with respect to choosing. In other words, the belief that alternatives cannot be evaluatively compared is, by implication, a comparison of them as morally indifferent and, thereby, all equally good. Hence, any subject who asserts the objection engages in a pragmatic self-contradiction. Denying that she or he understands a principle in terms of which alternatives for purpose ought to be compared with respect to choosing, she or he simultaneously asserts one.

11. Even if one prescribes decision for some balance between one's own present realization of creativity and the pursuit of future creativity, it remains that this decision might not maximize present creativity—and, in this sense, the good for which one should decide (in the present and the future) would not be creativity but, rather, pursuit of creativity. Each decision ought to compromise the present realization of creativity in whatever measure the proper balance with the future requires. In any event, the notion of deciding about the creativity realized in one's present action, where this is considered independently of a future telos, is I think, not a meaningful one. Conscious decision requires alternatives that are understood and evaluated, and there are no such alternatives for present action independently of alternative future states of affairs to be pursued. But this is simply to repeat that self-understanding is prospective; what the subject takes as object is its own self-expression, and

a self-expression is an actuality's contribution to the future. What we choose when we choose a self-understanding is the difference we decide to make.

12. Perhaps some thinkers in the Western tradition of moral thought, especially some for whom, with Aristotle, the supreme good to be pursued is happiness, have equated pursuit of *the* good with pursuit of *my* good (see MacIntyre 1967). I will not seek to assess whether that characterization of them is correct. In contrast to that assertion, the present account implies that moral sacrifice of one's own future good is a real possibility and, sometimes, a moral demand. I have discussed the relation between virtue and happiness in Gamwell 2000, chapter 3.

13. I do not contest that a subjective individual may be morally culpable for ignorance in her or his present activity. If this is so, however, the present activity is not morally culpable in this respect, since the culpability depends on some previous decision or decisions of the individual in question. Accordingly, the previous decision or decisions making the individual morally culpable for present ignorance cannot have been taken in ignorance of the relevant moral obligation.

14. For some, this argument may seem tendentious. A subject, the objection holds, might believe some norm or prescription more or less specific to her or his situation even while lacking an understanding of the moral law and, thereby, may be moral or immoral in obeying or disobeying this specific prescription. For instance, a given norm for relations to one's family might be believed without an understanding of the comprehensive good this norm does, let us allow, specify to certain situations, and that belief is sufficient to call the subject's decision "morally responsible." But this objection is untenable. As she or he acts in accord with or violation of the norm, the subject evaluates alternatives for purpose and, thereby, decides for a belief in one or another alternative as good. Since belief that good is defined by the given norm of family relations is not necessary to subjectivity as such, the decision between alternative beliefs becomes, in effect, an arbitrary positing of what is good, and the subject acts in ignorance of her or his moral obligation. To be sure, the objection might assert that belief in the specific norm is dispositional, so that the present activity cannot simply give it up. In that case, current belief in, say, the given norm of family relations is the unavoidable consequence of contingent conditions in the individual's past; for instance, she or he was taught this norm by her or his parents. Accordingly, violating the norm is a decision for an evaluative belief contrary to a belief one simultaneously affirms. Absent a belief in the moral law necessary to subjectivity as such, however, we can still say that the subject acts in ignorance of her or his moral obligation. Because one's belief in the specific norm is fated by contingent conditions in one's past, a decision against this belief is the assertion that those contingent conditions should have been different, and the subject has no reason to believe that this assertion is false. It makes no difference, let us underscore, if the object of dispositional belief is a valid specification of the moral law, since it remains that the subject in question is, by hypothesis, ignorant of this fact. So far as I can see, understanding one's obligation as one's obligation in the sense required for moral and immoral decision requires a belief in the good

that is necessary to being a subject and thus presupposed in every choice to the contrary, that is, an original belief in the moral law.

15. To ask how this duplicity may be explicated is, in my judgment, to pose one of the most vexing questions about existence with understanding. In traditional theological terms, the problem is why such an individual would be tempted to sin if she or he is aware of God as the ground of all good. Kant posed a similar question in asking why a rational being might choose a fundamental maxim other than the moral law and said that the answer is "inscrutable to us" (Kant 1934, 38). I have sought to provide an account in Gamwell 2000, chapter 2.

16. These reflections counsel caution in judging the specific activities of other people to be immoral. The specific alternatives among which someone at a given time and place is free to choose depend on the particular past she or he then inherits, and the decision for maximal creativity in the future as such can be expressed only in an activity included within her or his understanding of the possibilities presented by the past. To be sure, there is a range of activities we have good reason to believe are typically open to most adult people in a given group in given circumstances, so that the judgment of moral fault when such people fail to act in accord with certain rules is generally secure. Moreover, assignments of legal responsibility typically and rightly assume that certain activities fall within the specific possible purposes of the people held accountable for them. Still, no one can know all of the circumstances within which another individual decides, and there are clearly cases in which a person in certain circumstances may indeed decide for the comprehensive purpose but not express it in a specific purpose generally taken to be moral in that kind of situation—because, in fact, that specific purpose was not within her or his possibilities as understood.

17. The preceding discussion of social practices is especially indebted to Brian Barry's work, although he may not agree with all I say.

18. Here, again, an appeal to our fragmentary understanding is unconvincing. If the difference between direct and indirect applications is erased in principle, then to insist that, say, democracy is required in certain contexts because all relevant individuals do not or cannot sufficiently understand all of the pertinent circumstances is to imply that democratic principles do not, in fact, constitute a social practice but are, rather, guiding rules. Presumably, then, they can be overridden when, but only when, it is sufficiently clear that direct pursuit of the maximal good so prescribes or permits. But this higher-order principle with respect to democratic principles is a universal deontological principle and, moreover, one that is hopelessly vague.

19. This further assumption, I also expect, often betrays the view that modern utilitarianism, prescribing action directed to maximizing the pleasure or utility of all humans or all sentient creatures, is the only plausible candidate for a teleological ethic. Although I will not pursue the point here, I am inclined to think that no universal social practice implies and is implied by typical formulations of this comprehensive purpose, betraying the fact that pursuit of maximal pleasure or utility is not a purpose implied by subjectivity as such.

20. I borrow the term "communicative rights" from Karl-Otto Apel. See Apel 1995.

21. I here continue to assume that subjective activities depend on being member actualities of subjective individuals, and thus I intend the transcendental principle to prescribe relations among subjects as individuals. But if subjectivity can occur without actualizing an individual, the transcendental obligation of respect for all subsequent activities remains, and this is sufficient for deriving a deontological principle from the claim to moral validity of every subjective activity.

22. In order to prevent misunderstanding, I should note that communicative rights define a community of rights, so duties implied by them may sometimes be canceled when others in the community do not participate in the practice. Perhaps the most obvious example concerns the proscription against taking the life of another subjective individual, which duty, I hold, may be canceled in certain circumstances where another subjective individual violates the practice. In this respect, there is, I believe, a right to self-defense or to the defense of others. Fully explicating the principle of communicate respect would require clarifying insofar as possible when violation of the practice by some releases others from the otherwise applicable duties. In calling the principle deontological, however, I mean to signal that one cannot be released from its obligations by appeal to one's pursuit of maximally good consequences. Moreover, this social practice is universal, so that its requirements cannot be overridden by those of any other social practice or any specific circumstances, and release from its duties cannot occur unless the universal practice is not honored by others.

Chapter 5

1. Also, I have discussed Rawls's political thought in Gamwell 1995, chapter 3, and Gamwell 2000, chapter 4.

2. In this chapter, subsequent citations from this book will be by page number alone.

3. To the best of my reading, Stout is not especially concerned to distinguish between Rawls's earlier proposal in *a Theory of Justice* and his later formulation in *Political Liberalism*, because Stout takes both to be versions of contractarian liberalism and thus antireligious.

4. Nicholas Wolterstorff comments that Stout's *Democracy and Tradition* does not provide a theory of liberal democracy, and thus the "luster of what he has accomplished" consists in his internal critique of the new traditionalists. But just because those thinkers view democracy as inherently secularistic, Wolterstorff continues, Stout's "defense of democracy against its contemporary Christian critics is incomplete and precarious until he tells us in a systematic way what . . . [democratic] norms are and shows that there is no inherent conflict between those norms and the norms of Christian existence" (Wolterstorff, 639). In response, Stout acknowledges that he did "not offer a

systematic account and defense of democracy" but he also says, "I felt that I would not have succeeded in responding fully to this [new traditionalist] challenge unless I could give an alternative account" of the discourse characteristic of modern democracies (2005, 716).

5. For a similar distinction in another context, see Ogden 1966, 6–12.

6. On my intention, to repeat the explication given earlier, a denial of *p* is pragmatically self-contradictory when every act of denying *p* implies what *p* asserts, and thus *p* is pragmatically necessary. For instance, "some subject exists" or "subjectivity is exemplified" cannot, I hold, be denied without pragmatic self-contradiction. This explication, I also argued above, is equivalent to the following: a belief is pragmatically self-contradictory when it denies an understanding every act of believing believes, at least implicitly, and thus denies a belief necessary to believing or to subjectivity as such.

7. The latter phrase is, I think, ambiguous. On the one hand, it might designate the "operation" of practical reasoning, whereby participation in practical discourse is said to be at fault unless it explicitly derives norms from necessary principles, the view some might call foundationalism. On the other hand, the phrase might designate the "operation" of practical reason's principles, whereby they are *logically* independent of norms specific to a given form of ethical life. To the best of my reading, Stout rejects "practical reason operating independently" in both senses. Thus, "ethics without metaphysics" means, whatever else it means, the following: practical reasoning makes explicit and reflects on the specific ethical life of a given people (or, perhaps, given set of peoples), and in no respect are practical norms or principles logically independent of such specificities.

8. It is not clear that all metaphysics in the pejorative sense asserts metaphysical realism in the sense just defined, at least if the latter holds that correspondence to reality explains what it is for any and thus every true proposition to be true. On that definition, Kant's metaphysics is not metaphysical realism because, for him, the truth of propositions of theoretical reason is not explained by such correspondence. Because this account of theoretical reason leads Kant to affirm "pure practical reason" (Stout 2004a, 197), his metaphysics as a whole is, if I understand correctly, metaphysics in the pejorative sense. Thereby, Kant seems also to exemplify another definition of metaphysics Stout gives in response to critical discussions of his book, namely, "the project of legitimating our practices from a vantage point outside those practices" (2004b, 374), that is, of authorizing our practices, as Kant does, by conditions or principles independent of any specific practice. Perhaps, then, metaphysics in the pejorative sense includes but is not exhausted by metaphysical realism. Still, we might say that, for Kant, *moral* truth is metaphysically realistic, because the moral law corresponds to the necessary conditions of rational being, and thus Kant insofar defines moral truth as a "substantial something."

9. As may be apparent, this discussion of fallible beliefs abstracts from the character of what I previously called original beliefs, which are necessary to subjectivity as such and thus are true beliefs. On the metaphysical proposal pursued in this work, subjects as such implicitly assent to the true

understanding of subjectivity as such as a specification of existence as such. But it remains that all metaphysical proposals are fallible because they seek to explicate this original belief or set of beliefs.

10. For instance, a given community may agree to the cautionary use of "true," but if this meaning is settled by that agreement, another community may without pragmatic self-contradiction use "true" to mean whatever commands consensus in that community. Hence, the conception of truth is, in each case, relativistic.

11. Naturally, true belief is also not equivalent to many other things. But "not equivalent to justified belief" is the immediately relevant negation.

12. This reading seems the more proper if one thinks, as I do, that "truth-talk" without such a standard does not permit a distinction between the kind of argument by which the truth of a belief can be redeemed and the kind of argument by which someone's or some group's entitlement to that belief can be confirmed. But making this case requires a considerably more extended discussion.

13. The extended argument occurs in chapter 1; see the section entitled "The Necessity of Existence."

14. This may seem only to confirm Stout's position, namely, that discourse has no other appeal except, in his sense, "immanent criticism." But the point is far more radical: that one may argue by showing inconsistencies in one's interlocutor's position and freedom therefrom in one's own is itself a conception of discourse that can be nothing other than the view of its proposer and those who happen to accept it. One's interlocutor is on equal grounds if she or he simply rejects the appeal to consistency, since the relevance of consistency cannot be determined if the real character of human rationality can be designated only by negation and thus cannot be distinguished from conceptions that are self-contradictory. Accordingly, any common commitment as to what "the exchange of reasons" involves is sheerly fortuitous.

15. To all appearances, any religious adherents for whom a divine reality is the source and end of all things would contradict themselves were they to allow any explication of ethical life that does not imply reference to God. Stout recognizes this issue, as becomes evident when he concedes that, for some theists, "it makes little sense to insist that excellence [and, by implication, any norm] . . . is a creature of *human* practices" (2004a, 268)—a point, he notes, Timothy Jackson urged him to include (2004a, 336, n. 44). Stout responds, if I understand correctly, that his ethical theory is independent of whether God does or does not exist. "If the God of the philosophers is dead, not everything is permitted. . . . Pragmatism comes into conflict with theology in ethical theory mainly at those points where someone asserts that the truth-claiming function of ethics depends, for its objectivity, on positing a transcendent and perfect being. Metaphysics asserts the need and then posits the divine explainer to satisfy it. Pragmatism questions the need and then doubts the coherence of the explanation" (2004a, 268). But this response interprets the theism at issue in Stout's own terms and, on my reading, misses Jackson's point: the dependence of ethics on "a perfect being" is precisely

what theism asserts, so that Stout's pragmatism, claiming to be independent of whether God does or does not exist, is a denial of theism.

16. For this reason, Stout's response is unconvincing when he asks whether "pragmatism, pursued as a general antimetaphysical strategy within philosophy, is inherently antitheological" (2004a, 256) and argues for a negative answer. He first notes "the fact that there are numerous theologians and theologically committed philosophers who hope to free themselves and the culture as a whole from the compulsion of pursuing metaphysics in the pejorative sense" (2004a, 256). But this appeal to congenial religious thinkers begs the question, since it depends on whether they are right. He then argues that neither of two theologians (Timothy Jackson and Robert Merrihew Adams) who assert the need for metaphysics has successfully defended his position (see 2004a, 256–69). But Stout's critique, if sound, only shows that their arguments are inadequate, not that their conclusion is wrong.

Chapter 6

1. Here, "political claim" means a claim for the justice of any actual or proposed activity of the state or government or for the validity of any norm or principle of justice.

2. Here and throughout this discussion, I use "prescription" to mean "moral prescription."

3. Consider in this context the social practice of slavery as institutionalized in antebellum America and defined, for present purposes, as an order of interaction whose norms prescribe for some individuals exclusive disposal over the lives and activities of others. If slavery is in force, in the sense that slave owners adhere to its norms and the political community enforces them, then slaves cannot choose in a manner that expresses dissent from the putative validity of the practice. Having no standing in the community that creates the practice, they cannot politically or socially contest it. To be sure, slaves might seek to escape or rebel. But these ways of expressing dissent are not themselves recognized by the rules of slavery. To the contrary, the intended practice is meant to be so designed that such possibilities are coercively precluded, and they only betray that the practice cannot be fully instituted. A slave might indeed protest her or his condition by committing suicide. But suicide is withdrawal from all social practices. Hence, the possibility of protest in this form cannot mean that a slave's failure to commit suicide expresses her or his assent to the validity of slavery and, thereby, her or his participation in this particular practice by way of decision. That this practice is metaethically senseless is confirmed by the fact that individuals whose service to another depends on their own decision are not slaves.

4. Here and henceforth, I use "presupposed" to mean what is implied by or is a necessary condition for the truth of an understanding or belief, a usage at least similar to the first sense Stout explicates for "presupposition" (see 2004a, 97).

5. Each of these freedoms can be increased by favorable participation in human association. For instance, freedom to affirm one's own future or to control one's own body can be enhanced by resources with which to meet biological needs or by available medical treatment, and these depend in greatest measure on social context. But insofar as freedoms might be enhanced by human association, they cannot be defined without explicit reference to it and thus cannot be protected by the formative rights of communicative respect. In one sense, we may also note, the freedom so protected is not possible in abstraction from human association. To all appearances, at least, individuals do not develop the capacity to understand and, therefore, do not become free in the human sense at all without the kind of learning that requires communication. But the discussion here is about proscribed coercion. Hence, the relevant rights assume that individuals have the freedoms or capacities in question, in the sense that they can be exercised in the absence of interference. Once having been acquired, in other words, the learning is one's own, and some of the choices it makes possible can be defined without explicit reference to human association.

6. I do not mean to deny that rights of differing individuals to private liberties may in certain circumstances conflict, and that such cases may be especially vexing for those in positions of political leadership who are charged with protecting such rights. I will not try to address such issues of possible conflict. In some circumstances, perhaps, a genuine conflict is properly resolved by appeal to the maximal overall good. But if so, this appeal to the maximal good does not override the community of rights because the appeal occurs when the principle of communicative rights itself cannot determine a prescribed decision.

7. In saying that democracy is prescribed by the formative principle of communicative respect, one implies that the prescription is universal. To this, some may object that democracy is not in fact possible in the absence of certain material and social preconditions that cannot be secured in the presence of widespread ignorance and severe poverty. There is, I expect, some truth in this judgment, although it is a sound maxim in such situations that the possibilities of approaching democracy are considerably greater than those who exercise nondemocratic power would have one believe. In any event, here, as in all cases, "ought implies can," and, when democracy is not possible, the universality of the prescription means that political decision making of some other form should honor the principle of communicative respect in whatever ways or measure is possible and should pursue conditions in which democracy can occur.

8. Assuming that the question about ultimate terms of political assessment is a rational one, we can make the relevant point in the following technical terms: Formative principles of a democratic constitution derive solely from the *pragmatic* character of political claims to validity, in distinction from the *semantic* or propositional content for which validity is claimed. Hence, the semantic content of a claim may or may not be consistent with the principles to which the pragmatic character of making the claim commits a political

participant. To claim validity for a religious belief one also says is immune to argumentative assessment is to contradict the semantic content of one's claim in the act of making it.

9. It follows, I believe, that citizens have a moral right under certain conditions to alter the present regime by extralegal means. When the substantive barriers to full and free discourse are sufficiently acute, the formative nature of a democratic constitution implies that people subject to the regime are morally permitted to violate statutory law with a view to making the political process substantively democratic. I would not be inclined to say that the constitution stipulates such permission, because the right in question is a substantive one. Still, this moral right is implied by that to which both constitutional and statutory law are morally responsible, namely, the compound character of justice. I will not seek here to identify the circumstances that might warrant civil disobedience or even rebellion or to specify the moral restraints on those forms of action.

10. I have so criticized Kant's metaphysics of morals in Gamwell 1990, chapter 2.

11. I have pursued that engagement in Gamwell 2000, chapter 5.

12. So far as I can see, Barry's own explanation begs the question because he simply posits "the agreement motive," that is, the willingness of all to abide by principles or rules for our life together that are independent of anyone's conception of the good (see Barry, 164–69).

13. I will here abstract from questions about relations between a democratic political community and the larger community of political communities involved in what we call international relations. Those questions are, the more so in the twenty-first century, transparently important. But they require another extended discussion. Seeking first to make sense of justice internal to a given democratic community will, I hope, provide terms with which the larger context may be considered, recognizing that those terms will also be tested in that subsequent discussion.

14. For this reason, the good is not *defined* as human creativity or human happiness, as in some forms of utilitarianism and in many solely humanistic accounts of the good.

Works Cited

Apel, Karl Otto. 1979. "Types of Rationality Today: The Continuum of Reason between Science and Ethics." In *Rationality Today*, ed. Theodore Gereats. Ottawa: University Press, 307–40.
———. 1980. "C. S. Pierce and the Post-Tarskian Problem of an Adequate Explication of the Meaning of Truth: Towards a Transcendental-Pragmatic Theory of Truth, Part I." *The Monist* 63: 386–407.
———. 1996. *Selected Essays, Volume Two: Ethics and the Theory of Rationality*. New Jersey: Humanities.
———. 1998. *From a Transcendental-semiotic Point of View*. Manchester and New York: Manchester University Press.
Aquinas, St. Thomas. 1973. *Basic Writings of Saint Thomas Aquinas*. Ed. Anton C. Pegis. Indianapolis: Hackett.
———. 1975. *Summa Contra Gentiles, Book One: God*. Trans. Anton C. Pegis. Notre Dame: University of Notre Dame Press.
Aristotle. 1941. *The Basic Works of Aristotle*. Ed. Richard McKeon. New York: Random House.
Ayer, Alfred Jules. 1936. *Language, Truth, and Logic*. London: Gollancz.
Barry, Brian. 1995. *Justice as Impartiality*. Oxford, UK: Clarendon.
Dewey, John. 1957. *Reconstruction in Philosophy*. Boston: Beacon.
———. 1958. *Experience and Nature*. New York: Dover.
Donagan, Alan. 1977. *The Theory of Morality*. Chicago: University of Chicago Press.
Eberle, Christopher J. 2002. *Religious Convictions in Liberal Politics*. New York: Cambridge University Press.
Gale, Richard M. 1991. *On the Nature and Existence of God*. New York: Cambridge University Press.
Gamwell, Franklin I. 1984. *Beyond Preference: Liberal Theories of Independent Associations*. Chicago: University of Chicago Press.
———. 1990. *The Divine Good: Modern Moral Theory and the Necessity of God*. San Francisco: HarperCollins.
———. 2000. *Democracy on Purpose: Justice and the Reality of God*. Washington, DC: Georgetown University Press.
———. 2001. "Speaking of God after Aquinas." *The Journal of Religion* 81: 185–210.

Gewirth, Alan. 1978. *Reason and Morality*. Chicago: University of Chicago Press.
———. 1996. *The Community of Rights*. Chicago: University of Chicago Press.
Griffin, David Ray. 2004. *God, Power, and Evil*. Louisville, KY: Westminster John Knox.
———. 2007. *Whitehead's Radically Different Postmodern Philosophy: An Argument for Its Contemporary Relevance*. Albany: State University of New York Press.
Habermas, Jürgen. 1984. *The Theory of Communicative Action, Volume I: Reason and the Rationalization of Society*. Trans. Thomas McCarthy. Boston: Beacon.
———. 1987. *The Theory of Communicative Action. Volume II: Lifeworld and System: A Critique of Functionalist Reason*. Trans. Thomas McCarthy. Boston: Beacon.
———. 1990. *Moral Consciousness and Communicative Action*. Trans. Christian Lenhardt and Shierry Weber Nicholson. Cambridge, MA: MIT Press.
———. 1992. *Postmetaphysical Thinking: Philosophical Essays*. Trans. William Mark Hohengarten. Cambridge, MA: MIT Press.
———. 1993. *Justification and Application: Remarks on Discourse Ethics*. Trans. Ciaran P. Cronin. Cambridge, MA: MIT Press.
Hartshorne, Charles. 1965. *Anselm's Discovery: A Re-examination of the Ontological Argument for God's Existence*. LaSalle, IL: Open Court.
———. 1966. "A New Look at the Problem of Evil." In *Current Philosophical Issues: Essays in Honor of Curt John Ducasse*, ed. F. C. Dommeyer. Springfield, IL: Thomas, 201–212.
———. 1967. *A Natural Theology for Our Time*. LaSalle, IL: Open Court.
———. 1970. *Creative Synthesis and Philosophic Method*. LaSalle, IL: Open Court.
———. 1972. *Whitehead's Philosophy: Selected Essay, 1935–70*. Lincoln: University of Nebraska Press.
Heidegger, Martin. 1949. *Existence and Being*. Chicago: Regnery.
———. 1959. *An Introduction to Metaphysics*. Trans. Ralph Manheim. New Haven: Yale University Press.
———. 1962. *Being and Time*. Trans. John Macquarrie and Edward Robinson. San Francisco: Harper San Francisco.
———. 1993. *Basic Writings*. Ed. David Farrell Krell. San Francisco: Harper San Francisco.
———. 1997. *Kant and the Problem of Metaphysics*. Trans. Richard Taft. Bloomington and Indianapolis: Indiana University Press.
———. 2002. *On Time and Being*. Chicago: University of Chicago Press.
Hobbes, Thomas. 1962. *Leviathan: Or the Matter, Forme and Power of a Commonwealth Civil and Ecclesiastical*. New York: Collier Macmillan.
Hick, John. 1971. *Arguments for the Existence of God*. New York: Herder and Herder.
Hume, David. 1955. *Dialogues Concerning Natural Religion*. New York: Hafner.
———. 1975. *Enquiries concerning Human Understanding and concerning the Principles of Morals*. Oxford, UK: Clarendon.
Kant, Immanuel. 1929. *Critique of Pure Reason*. Trans. Norman Kemp Smith. New York: St. Martin's.

———. 1934. *Religion within the Limits of Reason Alone*. Trans. Theodore M. Greene and Hoyt H. Hudson. New York: Harper & Row.

———. 1949. *Fundamental Principles of the Metaphysic of Morals*. Trans. Thomas K. Abbott. Indianapolis: Bobbs-Merrill.

———. 1977. *Prolegomena to Any Future Metaphysics*. Trans. Paul Curtis and revised by James W. Ellington. Indianapolis: Hackett.

MacIntyre, Alasdair. 1967. "Egoism and Altruism." In *The Encyclopedia of Philosophy*, II, ed. Paul Edwards. New York: Macmillan, 462–466.

Ogden, Schubert M. 1966. *The Reality of God and Other Essays*. New York: Harper & Row.

———. 1975. "The Criterion of Metaphysical Truth and the Senses of 'Metaphysics.'" *Process Studies* 5: 47–48.

Oppy, Graham. 1995. *Ontological Arguments and Belief in God*. New York: Cambridge University Press.

Pöggeler, Otto. 1987. *Martin Heidegger's Path of Thinking*. Trans. Daniel Magurshak and Sigmund Barber. Atlantic Highlands, NJ: Humanities Press International.

Polt, Richard. 1999. *Heidegger: An Introduction*. Ithaca, NY: Cornell University Press.

Post, John F. 1987. *The Many Faces of Existence: An Essay in Nonreductive Metaphysics*. Ithaca: Cornell University Press.

Rawls, John. 1955. "Two Concepts of Rules." *The Philosophical Review* 64: 3–32.

———. 1971. *A Theory of Justice*. Cambridge, MA: Belknap.

———. 2005. *Political Liberalism*, expanded edition. New York: Columbia University Press.

Rorty, Richard. "Transcendental Arguments, Self-Reference, and Pragmatism." *Transcendental Arguments and Science*. Ed. Peter Bieri, Rolf Horstman, and Lorenz Kreuger. Dortrect, Holland: Reidel, 77–103.

———. 1982. *Consequences of Pragmatism*. Minneapolis: University of Minnesota Press.

Rundle, Bede. 2004. *Why there is Something rather than Nothing*. Oxford, UK: Oxford University Press.

Sartre, Jean-Paul. 1977. *Existentialism and Humanism*. Brooklyn: Haskell House.

Searle, John R. 1983. *Intentionality: An Essay in the Philosophy of Mind*. New York: Cambridge University Press.

———. 1995. *The Construction of Social Reality*. New York: Free.

Stout, Jeffrey. 2004a. *Democracy and Tradition*. Princeton: Princeton University Press.

———. 2004b. "Responses to Five Critical Papers on *Democracy and Tradition*." *Soundings: An Interdisciplinary Journal* 87: 369–72.

———. 2005. "Comments on Six Responses to *Democracy and Tradition*." *Journal of Religious Ethics* 33: 709–44.

Wolterstorff, Nicholas. 1997. "The Role of Religion in Decision and Discussion of Political Issues." In *Religion in the Public Square: The Place of Religious Convictions in Political Debate*, ed. Robert Audi and Nicholas Wolterstorff. Landham, MD: Rowan and Littlefield, 67–120.

———. 2005. "Jeffrey Stout on Democracy and Its Contemporary Christian Critics." *Journal of Religious Ethics* 33: 633–47.
Whitehead, Alfred North. 1938. *Modes of Thought*. New York: Capricorn Books.
———. 1961. *Adventures of Ideas*. New York: Free.
———. 1963. *Science and the Modern World*. New York: New American Library.
———. 1978. *Process and Reality: And Essay in Cosmology*, corrected edition. Ed. David Ray Griffin and Donald W. Sherburne. New York: Free.

Index

Adams, Robert Merrihew, 195n16
amoralists, 103
animal(s), 60, 64, 69, 70, 71, 72, 154, 176, 180n11
Anselm, Saint, 29–30, 186n12
Apel, Karl-Otto, 10, 13, 42, 44, 45–46, 48, 98, 153, 164, 169, 192n20
Aquinas, St. Thomas, 20–21, 23–24, 30, 61, 74, 91, 179n4
argument against putative thoughts, 25
Aristotle, 3, 18, 19–22, 61, 111, 190n12
Augustine, Saint, 103
authenticity, 9–10, 112–113
Ayer, Alfred Jules, 104

Barry, Brian 115, 117, 119, 121, 170, 191n17, 197n12
Being and Time (Heidegger), 42, 44, 47
big bang, the, 88
Brandom, Robert B., 140

categorical imperative, the, 102–103, 153, 169, 173
Christianity, 130
citizenship
  conditions for, 14
  democratic, 14, 132
  ethics of, 135, 136, 137, 143–146, 148–150, 160–161, 166, 168
  obligations of, 116
civil disobedience, 197n9

civil war, 161
coercion, 154–155, 161, 196n5
comprehensive doctrine(s), 13, 14, 129, 130, 133, 145, 148, 165
comprehensive good, the, ix, 2, 7, 101–107
  democracy and, 148, 171–177
  human purpose and, 109–115
  human rights and, 116–126
  religion and, 144, 145
  Stout and, 131, 135, 160
  subjectivity and, 9–10, 190n14
  See also teleology
comprehensive purpose. *See* comprehensive good, the
consciousness
  fragmentary, 53, 54, 94
  human, 17, 56
  internality of, 94
  and nonconsciousness, 188n1
  prominence in, 92
  self-, 10, 32, 95
  and understanding, 55–56, 95, 96, 97, 101, 188n2
  Whitehead and, 32, 52, 55, 64
contractarian liberalism, 13, 130, 132, 134, 135, 144, 192n3. *See also* Rawlsian liberalism
creativity. *See* unity-in-diversity
criteria of adequacy, 33, 35
criterion of coherence, 33, 35, 60

Dasein, 5, 40–48, 50, 52, 53, 58, 98, 106

203

Index

democracy, 15, 127
  and the comprehensive good,
    171–177
  metaphysical authorization of, 2,
    14–15, 146, 147–164, 168–169,
    177, 191n18, 196n7
  and religion, 128, 144, 145, 159,
    163–164
  Stout and, 13–14, 129–146,
    192–193n4
  and substantive justice, 164–171
Democracy and Tradition (Stout), 13,
  129, 192n4
democratic constitution, 2, 14, 15,
  120, 121, 132, 148–149, 157–160,
  164–168, 176, 177, 196n8, 197n9
democratic discourse,
  conditions for, 135, 137, 145,
    146–150, 165
  neutrality of, 13–14, 158, 160, 167
  Stout's conception of, 133, 143,
    148, 149, 165
  substance of, 14–15
Dewey, John, 36–38
discursive presupposition, 131, 135,
  136, 142–143, 148
divine actuality, 74, 82, 85–88, 90–91,
  185n9, 185–186n10, 186n14,
  186n15, 187n16, 187–188n19
divine individual, the, 71–85. *See
  also* God
divine reenactment, 87–88, 187n16
divine relativity, 98, 185n9. *See also*
  divine individual, the
Donagan, Alan, 154

Eberle, Christopher, 129
empiricism, 37, 83, 189n9
equality, 167, 176
ethics
  Aristotle's conception of, 18
  of citizenship, 148–150, 160–161,
    166, 168
  deontological, 13, 102, 119, 120,
    121
  nonteleological, 170, 120

  Stout's conception of, 13–14, 133–
    137, 142–145, 193n7, 194–195n15
  teleological, 12, 116, 119–121, 123,
    191n19
experience
  everyday, 8
  freedom and, 11–12, 188n4
  of God, 92
  Hartshorne and, 64
  Heidegger and, 40, 41, 44, 46, 47,
    48, 52
  human, 163
  Kant and, 3–4, 22, 23, 37
  moral, 118
  religious, 89, 92, 113, 163
  richness of everyone's, 2
  sense-based, 22, 37, 181–182n15
  Whitehead and, 5, 6, 31–33, 55,
    64, 87–88, 94, 180n9

fallibility, 34, 57, 138–139, 181n12
fragmentariness, 67, 74, 86, 90, 119,
  184n3, 184n4
free will, 188n4
freedom
  and democratic rights, 125, 154,
    155–156, 157–159, 174, 196n5
  Kantian conception of, 101, 102, 169
  moral, 23, 108, 109, 111
  religious, 2, 15, 159–161, 167
  two senses of, 11–12, 108
foundationalism, 193n7
Frost, Robert, 86

Gale, Richard M., 27, 74–75
Gamwell, Franklin I., 179n3, 179n4,
  181n14, 182n16, 188–189n6,
  189n8, 190n12, 191n15, 192n1,
  197n10
Gewirth, Alan, 10, 13, 169
God
  dualistic conception of, 62
  monistic conception of, 62
  necessary belief in, 100–101, 106
  necessary existence of, 8, 24,
    29–30, 59–85, 106

neoclassical conception of, 8–9, 11, 59–92, 177, 182n4, 187–188n19
traditional conception of, 20–21, 23, 29, 79, 85, 91, 179n4
and the world, 85–92, 172, 187n16
good, the. *See* comprehensive good, the
government
　democratic, 2, 15, 115, 147, 157, 168, 177
　by way of discourse, 15, 149, 161
　by way of reason, 160, 164, 168

Habermas, Jürgen, 10, 56, 98, 128, 152, 154
habit, 114, 174
Hartshorne, Charles, 8, 9, 59, 64, 74, 77, 81, 85, 184n6
Hauerwas, Stanley, 130
Heidegger, Martin, 5–6, 38, 39–58, 66, 97, 105, 129, 183n6
hermeneutical turn, the, 22, 54, 55, 96
Hick, John, 29
Hobbes, Thomas, 104
human being(s),
　Heidegger's conception of, 40, 46, 49
　Kantian conception of, 153–54
　neoclassical conception of, 71, 93, 124, 153–154, 181–182n15
　and the ontological argument, 186n12
　premodern conception of, 60
　Stout's conception of, 133
human understanding
　explicit, 55–56, 96
　fragmentariness of, 119
　implicit, 55–56, 96
　lifeworld dependence of, 46
　transcendental principles of, 22
Hume, David, 22, 103, 189n7, 189n9

immanent criticism, 136–137, 143, 194n14
international relations, 197n13

Introduction to Metaphysics (Heidegger), 41

Jackson, Timothy, 194n15, 195n16
Jefferson, Thomas, ix, 2
justice
　compound character of, 165, 167, 168, 171, 197n9
　constitutional principles of, 156–164
　democratic principles of, ix, 2, 168
　formative principle(s) of, 14, 15, 153–157, 160, 162, 164–165, 168, 171, 176–177, 196n7, 196n8, 197n9
　as general emancipation, 15, 175–177
　independent of metaphysics, 1, 13, 14, 130, 145, 169
　in international relations, 197n13
　substantive principle(s) of, 15, 164, 171, 174–177

Kant, Immanuel
　and the Copernican revolution, 22
　and the critique of traditional metaphysics, 3, 5, 18–19, 21–22, 23–25, 27, 29, 30, 35–37, 49, 77–78, 171, 179n5, 180n10, 193n8
　and ethics, 170–171
　and Heidegger, 44–49
　and metaphysical dualism, 62
　and the moral law, 10, 23, 101–102, 104, 106, 110, 124, 153–154, 171, 191n15
　and Newtonian physics, 83
　and nonteleology, 13
Kant and the Problem of Metaphysics (Heidegger), 44

law(s)
　criminal, 155
　natural, 84, 87, 88, 90, 183n1
　of physics, 103
　statutory, 14, 166, 167, 168, 197n9

law(s) (continued)
  substantive, 145, 167
  See also moral law, the
"Letter on Humanism" (Heidegger), 40, 44
liberty
  private, 124–125, 156, 158, 165, 176, 196n6
  public, 129, 159
lifeworld, 54–57, 96, 146
  Heidegger's conception of, 6, 45–46, 54–55, 183n6
Lincoln, Abraham, 56
linguistic turn, the. *See* hermeneutical turn, the

MacIntyre, Alasdair, 130, 190n12
Marxism, 103, 127
maximal common humanity, 173–176
metaethical form, 123, 124, 150–151, 152, 164
metaphysica generalis, 182n4
metaphysica specialis, 182n4
metaphysical dualism, 71, 72
metaphysical individual, 73–74, 78–85, 92, 98, 172, 187n18, 187n19
metaphysical monism, 72
metaphysical pragmatism, 142, 146, 147–148, 150, 163, 168–169
metaphysical progress, 35
metaphysical realism, 137–138, 193n8
metaphysical self-differentiation, 83, 90, 98
metaphysical society, 73
Metaphysics (Aristotle), 18, 19
metaphysics
  Aquinas's, 20–21, 30, 61
  Aristotle's, 18, 19, 21, 22, 62
  broad sense of, ix, 6, 9, 49–58, 93–101
  of democracy, 13, 50, 127–130, 146, 148–164
  Dewey and, 36–38
  and God, 8, 71–85
  Hartshorne and, 8, 9, 59
  Heidegger and, 6, 38, 39–49, 52–58, 97, 106
  of human purpose, 10, 50, 93–115
  Kant and, 3, 5, 18–19, 21, 22–23, 30, 35–36, 38, 46, 49, 77, 129, 193n8
  neoclassical, ix, 3, 4, 5, 7, 8, 11, 34, 35, 38, 46, 51, 53, 55, 59, 61, 76–78, 79, 81, 98, 105, 106, 171, 177, 182n4, 183n2, 185n9
  post-Kantian dismissal of, 2, 128, 129
  Stout and, 13, 14, 130–146, 193n7, 193n8, 194n15, 195n16
  strict sense of, ix, 4, 6, 7, 22, 23–30, 48, 49, 50, 51, 52, 58, 59–85
  subjectivity and, 6, 49–50, 52, 93–101
  task of, 30–38
  teleology and, 12
  theistic, ix
  traditional, 3, 18, 19–22, 23, 45, 46, 58, 85
  transcendental, 7, 51, 54, 55, 56, 83, 186n12
  Western, 61, 62, 71
  Whitehead's, 3, 9, 11, 33, 35, 57, 59–71, 80–81, 84, 87–89, 94, 96, 99, 103, 105, 180n9–11, 187n19, 188n6
  and the world, 85–92
metaphysics of presence 48, 58
Milbank, John, 130
moral law, the
  Kantian conception of, 10, 102, 106, 110, 124, 154, 171, 191n15, 193n8
  in neoclassical metaphysics, 11, 101, 105, 107, 109, 110, 124, 150, 151, 154
  pragmatic necessity of, 50–51, 182–183n5, 190–191n14
moral learning, 13, 125

moral responsibility, 2, 7, 9, 11
moral validity, 12, 122, 123, 150–152, 156, 157, 164–165, 192n21
morality
  and democracy, 146
  metaphysics and, 18, 143, 147
  teleological nature of, 10
  two senses of, 110–111

The Nature and Existence of God (Gale), 74–75
necessity
  dialectical, 169
  of existence, 22–30
  of God, 73, 85–92
  logical, 29, 30, 76
  metaphysical, ix, 1, 8, 31, 39, 48, 56, 59–71, 79–80, 130, 141, 169, 181n12, 185n9. *See also* metaphysics
  ontological, 29, 30
  pragmatic, 50–51, 182n5
  and subjectivity, 50, 94–95
  of the world, 73, 85–92
New Testament, the, 162
new traditionalism, the, 13, 129, 130, 134, 136, 144
Nicomachean Ethics (Aristotle), 18
nominalism, 70, 75
Nothing, the. *See* Heidegger, Martin
nonteleology, 10

Ogden, Schubert M., 193n5
ontological argument, the, 8, 29, 74–75, 78–80, 186n12
Ontological Arguments and Belief in God (Oppy), 78
ontological asymmetry, 185n9
ontotheology, 45, 48, 58
Oppy, Graham, 26–27, 77–80, 180n7
original belief(s), 7, 9, 100–101, 105–107, 108, 109, 111–112, 123–126, 163, 191n14, 193–194n9
original decision, 9–10, 12, 111–113, 115, 125, 126, 128

paradox, 180n10
partialist fallacy, the, 10, 103, 117, 170, 189n8
Physics (Aristotle), 18
physics
  Aristotle's conception of, 20, 22
  contemporary conceptions of, 36, 82–84, 103
  Newtonian, 83
Plato, 21, 45, 134, 169
Pöggeler, Otto, 39
Political Liberalism (Rawls), 192n3
Polt, Richard, 42, 43, 44
poor, the, 153
Post, John F., 29, 68–69, 184n5
postmodern thought, 38
practical reason
  Apel on, 164
  and democracy, 148, 149, 154
  Kant's conception of, 5, 18, 23, 49, 83, 193n8
  necessary existence of, 142, 143, 146, 148, 150, 151, 153
  Stout on, 132, 134, 136, 143, 146, 193n7, 193n8
pragmatic expressivism, 132, 133, 146
pragmatic self-contradiction, 50–51, 52, 55, 56, 100, 123, 193n6, 194n10
principle of communicative respect, the, 13, 147–157
  Apel's conception of, 164, 169
  in democratic constitutions, 14, 156–157, 160, 176, 196n7
  deontological nature of, 123
  transcendental nature of, 123, 125
Process and Reality: An Essay in Cosmology (Whitehead), 3
process theologians, 74, 75
Prolegomena to Any Future Metaphysics (Kant), 18, 22
public education, 153
public reason
  metaphysical backing of, 143, 165
  Rawls and, 13, 130, 135–136, 145, 165

public reason *(continued)*
  and religious freedom, 145
  Stout's conception of, 13, 130, 135–136, 142, 143, 145, 165

Rawls, John, 13, 14, 115, 129, 130–131, 133, 136, 144, 145, 148, 149, 165, 192n3
Rawlsian liberalism, 130, 136, 144.
  See also contractarian liberalism
rebellion, 197n9
religion(s)
  and democracy, 128, 129, 135, 142, 144–145, 159, 162–163, 166
  as an expression of totality, 17
  function of, 126, 128
  and metaphysics, 1, 18
  true, 126
religious freedom. *See* freedom
right to general emancipation, the, 175–176
rights
  of animals, 154
  communicative, 12, 123, 153, 154, 155, 156, 158, 159, 192n22, 196n5
  conflicting, 196n6
  constitutional, 158
  democratic, 177
  formative, 124, 125, 154, 156, 158, 159, 169, 196n5
  human, 2, 12, 115–126, 150, 154, 170, 173
  reciprocal, 151
  substantive, 125, 165, 166, 168
Robert's Rules of Order, 149
Rorty, Richard, 38, 181n14, 182n16
Rubicon, the, 182, 183
Rundle, Bede, 31, 34, 42, 61, 80, 185n9, 186n13

Sartre, Jean-Paul, 104
Searle, John R., 56, 115
secularism, 13, 14, 131–133
self-understanding, ix
  and the comprehensive good, 101–107, 110–111

  decision for, 9, 11, 93–101, 110–111, 125, 189–190n11
  designating "immoral" and "moral," 110
  paradoxical character of, 9, 96
slavery, 195n3
social action, 151–152, 155, 156–157, 160, 164, 165
social practice(s), 13, 115–122, 124–125, 132, 134, 136, 140, 142–143, 150–152
  universal, 118, 120, 121–122, 124, 150, 152, 153, 192n19
societies of actualities, 70
specific pragmatism, 134–139, 141–145, 147–148, 165, 169
speculative philosophy, 31, 35, 57
Spinoza, Baruch, 2
Stout, Jeffrey, 13–14, 129–146, 147–148, 160–161, 163, 165, 169, 170, 175, 192n3, 192–193n4, 193n7–8, 194n14, 194–195n15, 195n16, 195n4
subjective activity, 10, 93–94, 97, 99, 101, 106, 107–112, 122, 192n21
subjective individual, 93, 94, 99, 107, 122, 124, 190n13, 192n21, 192n22
subjectivity. *See* metaphysics
Summa Contra Gentiles (Aquinas), 21
Summa Theologicae (Aquinas), 20, 21

teleology, ix, 10, 12, 118, 121
temporality
  of God, 73
  Heidegger's conception of, 5, 6, 43–44, 58, 66, 97
theism, 14
  Christian, 144
  Gale's conception of, 74–76
  metaphysical, 14
  neoclassical, 15, 74, 76, 80
  philosophical, 71
  Stout and, 194–195n15
theology
  Aristotle's conception of, 19–20
  Christian, 129

in neoclassical metaphysics, 182n4
philosophical, 21, 81
A Theory of Justice (Rawls), 192n3
transcendental reflection, 51. *See also* metaphysics
true metaphysical statements, 8, 32, 33, 34, 51, 52, 57, 59–60, 63, 100, 180n11, 185n8
true understanding, 98. *See also* self-understanding

unity-in-diversity
  as the comprehensive good, 11–12, 107–108, 123, 172–173
  and metaphysics, 105
universal reason
  defense of, 55–56, 129–30
  post-Kantian critique of, 5–6, 13, 37–38, 39, 46, 134, 146, 169, 171
universals, 95–96, 97, 99, 109

utilitarianism, 191n19, 197n14

Weber, Max, 104
"What is Metaphysics?" (Heidegger), 39, 41, 44, 45, 52, 106
Whitehead, Alfred North,
  and democracy, 171, 174
  and the good, 172
  and Heidegger, 52, 55
  metaphysics of, 3, 5, 6, 8–9, 11, 31–34, 49, 59–71, 80–81, 84, 87–89, 94, 96, 99, 103, 105, 180n9–11, 187n19, 188n6
  and speculative philosophy, 31, 35, 57
Why there is something rather than Nothing (Rundle), 31
Wittgenstein, Ludwig, 46
Wolterstorff, Nicholas, 129, 192n4